PALMERSTON STUDIES I

PALMERSTON STUDIES I

EDITED BY

DAVID BROWN AND MILES TAYLOR

HARTLEY INSTITUTE

UNIVERSITY OF SOUTHAMPTON

2007

ISBN 084532 851 3

Contents

Preface

Henry John Temple, third Viscount Palmerston (1784-1865), is the third of the trio of major British politicians whose papers are held in the Special Collections of the Hartley Library at the University of Southampton. Previous collections published by the Hartley Institute have been devoted to investigating the Duke of Wellington and Earl Mountbatten of Burma, but these two volumes are the first which take Palmerston as their subject. The volumes bring together a series of papers originally delivered at an international conference held at the University in July 2003. Sixty scholars from the UK, the USA, Canada, France, Japan and Germany attended the 'Palmerston congress', reflecting a renewal of serious historical interest — especially amongst younger scholars — in a Prime Minister who is often studied, and equally often misunderstood. From the conference 16 of the original papers have been selected for publication, and one new chapter (by David Brown) added for the sake of balance. The first of the two volumes covers aspects of Lord Palmerston's domestic career, whilst the second looks at his role in foreign policy.

The editors would like to take this opportunity to thank all those who helped to make the 2003 conference such a success, and who have also contributed to the assembling of these volumes: Muriel Chamberlain, Tom Power, Kim Reynolds and David Steele for delivering papers at the conference; Lord and Lady Romsey for their hospitality at Broadlands; Professor Bill Wakeham (Vice-Chancellor), the Hartley Institute and the Royal Historical Society for their financial support; Lee Clatworthy, Peter Gray, Shirley Matthews, and John Oldfield for their help with conference logistics; and above all, Chris Woolgar and Karen Robson, for all their indispensable advice before, during and after the event.

The editors and the authors would like to thank the Broadlands Archives Trust for permission to quote from the Broadlands papers in the Special Collections of the University Library, and the British Library and the National Archives for permission to cite materials in their possession. Other permissions are acknowledged in the notes to individual chapters.

Miles Taylor,
York, May 2005

Contributors

David Brown is a Lecturer in History at the University of Strathclyde. He is the author of *Palmerston and the politics of foreign policy, 1846-1855* (Manchester: Manchester University Press, 2002) and is currently completing a new study of Palmerston's life, to be published by Yale University Press.

James Gregory is currently Lecturer in History at the University of Bradford. He is the author of *Of Victorians and vegetarians: the vegetarian movement in nineteenth-century Britain* (London and New York: Tauris Academic Studies, forthcoming, 2007) and is currently working on a study of the Mount Temples.

Stephen M. Lee is Assistant Headteacher and Head of History and Politics at Torquay Boys' Grammar School. He is the author of *George Canning and Liberal Toryism, c.1801-1827* (Woodbridge: RHS Studies in History, forthcoming).

Joseph S. Meisel is programme officer for research universities and humanistic scholarship at the Andrew W. Mellon Foundation in New York. He is the author of *Public speech and the culture of public life in the age of Gladstone* (New York: Columbia University Press, 2001).

J.P. Parry is Reader in Modern British History at the University of Cambridge and a Fellow of Pembroke College. His works include *Democracy and religion: Gladstone and the Liberal party, 1867-75* (Cambridge: Cambridge University Press, 1986) and *The rise and fall of Liberal government in Victorian Britain* (London and New Haven: Yale University Press, 1993). His latest book is *The politics of patriotism: English Liberalism, national identity and Europe, 1830-86* (Cambridge: Cambridge University Press, 2006).

Miles Taylor is Professor of Modern History at the University of York. His recent books include the co-edited *The Victorians since 1901: histories, representations and revisions* (Manchester: Manchester University Press, 2004) and *Ernest Jones, Chartism and the romance of politics, 1819-69* (Oxford: Oxford University Press, 2003).

Karina Urbach is a Research Fellow at the German Historical Institute in London. She is the author of *Bismarck's favourite Englishman: Lord Odo Russell's mission to Berlin* (London: I.B. Tauris, 1999) and co-editor of *Der Zeitgeist und die Histoire* (Dettelbach: Röll, 2001) and *Birth or talent? A comparison of British-German elites* (Munich: Sauer, KG, 2005). Her edited book *Noble fascists? European aristocracies and the radical right* will be published by Oxford University Press in 2007.

Allen Warren is a member of the History Department at the University of York, of which he was Head of Department from 1996 to 2003. He is presently Colleges' Co-ordinator and Provost of Vanbrugh College. His books include (with Geoff Cubitt) *Heroic reputations and exemplary lives* (Manchester: Manchester University Press, 2000).

John Wolffe is Professor of Religious History at the Open University. He is the author of *Great deaths: grieving, religion and nationhood in Victorian and Edwardian Britain* (Oxford: Oxford University Press, 2000) and *The expansion of evangelicalism: the age of Wilberforce, More, Chalmers and Finney* (Nottingham: Apollos, 2006).

Abbreviations

BL   The British Library
BP   Broadlands Papers, University of Southampton
         Library, MS 62
TNA   The National Archives

CHAPTER 1

Palmerston and Canning
Stephen M. Lee

In the July 1840 edition of the *Edinburgh Review*, in the context of a review of a number of recent publications on British foreign policy, the anonymous author commented, with reference to Viscount Palmerston's arrival at the Foreign Office in 1830 as part of Earl Grey's reform ministry:

> Fortunately, there was placed in the direction of foreign affairs, a statesman whose abilities, discretion, and application, enabled him to meet and to surmount the difficulties of his position. Attached to the foreign policy of Canning, Lord Palmerston was well chosen to vindicate and to re-assert the enlarged and liberal principles on which that foreign policy had been founded.[1]

By 1840, therefore, the key elements of what might be called the Whig interpretation of George Canning's influence on Palmerston were in place. These elements consisted of an assertion that Palmerston was, at least in foreign policy terms, a disciple of Canning (that he was, as the article puts it, 'attached to the foreign policy of Canning'); that Canning's policy was one of 'enlarged and liberal principles'; and that Palmerston 're-assert[ed]' those principles following the hiatus caused by Canning's death in 1827. Like the commonplace contrasts that are still too easily made between the foreign policies of Canning and Castlereagh, the identification of Palmerston as a disciple of Canning's allegedly 'liberal' principles carries sufficient *prima facie* weight to convince the unwary that this is all there is to the matter. Nonetheless, despite their relatively early foundation and their superficial plausibility, all of these claims require serious qualification if they are to retain our assent. It will, therefore, be one of the purposes of this chapter to attempt a more nuanced account of the connections between Canning and Palmerston without rejecting out of hand the notion of a meaningful relationship between their respective policies and behaviour. For the sake of clarity of analysis it is convenient to do this under two separate headings, domestic politics and foreign policy, although, of course in practice it was impossible to unweave these two strands.

I

Let us begin our analysis in 1809. Due to his growing feeling of dissatisfaction with the Portland ministry's conduct of the war with Napoleon, Canning initiated a personally fateful series of events when he wrote to the Prime Minister, the Duke of Portland, in March 1809 requesting a reorganisation of ministerial responsibilities regarding the war.[2] In discussions with Portland this crystallised into a plan to remove Castlereagh from the War Department. The story of prevarication by Portland and by Castlereagh's relation Camden, which dragged out this affair through the summer of 1809, and the complicating factor of Castlereagh's role in the planning and execution of the disastrous Walcheren expedition, have been told often enough to require no re-iteration here. Suffice to say that in September 1809 the affair culminated in the resignations of Portland, Canning, and Castlereagh, the famous Canning-Castlereagh duel, and the succession of Spencer Perceval to the office of First Lord of the Treasury.[3] The events of 1809 would inaugurate what one might call the high period of Canning's career as a faction leader. The years 1809 to 1813 saw the foundation, development, and eventual dissolution of what Canning called his 'little Senate', a faction, at its height, of fifteen loyal supporters in the Commons.[4] Crucially, for our concerns here, these were events in which Palmerston did not figure to any degree of significance at all.

Although there are a few indications in the early years of

the century that Canning and Palmerston might have been moving closer together, they amount in fact to little more than a tenuous connection between people on the same side of the political divide. For the most part these connections were mediated via the figure of James Edward Fitzharris, second Earl of Malmesbury, and as the relationship between Malmesbury and Canning cooled, so did any chance of Palmerston becoming more closely attached to Canning.[5] Indeed, since one of the key defining characteristics of a Canningite in the years between 1809 and Canning's re-entry into government as part of the Liverpool ministry in 1816 (as President of the Board of Control) was a willingness to leave office with Canning in 1809 or, if not in office at the time, at least to remain out of office with him, Palmerston must be counted the very opposite of a Canningite, for it is in the shuffling of offices following Canning's departure in 1809 that Palmerston began his long occupation of the office of Secretary at War. (The Canningites expressed surprise at Palmerston's elevation to this office, Canning himself dismissing Palmerston as 'another younker'.[6]) In fact, as we shall see, it would be very late in the day that Palmerston would emerge as anything approximating to a Canningite.[7]

Palmerston, like many people, certainly had a high estimation of Canning's talents but also had worries about his character. For example, in the context of the political manoeuvrings that took place after the assassination of Spencer Perceval in 1812, Palmerston, commenting on Canning's chances of obtaining the premiership, stated to Malmesbury that 'Canning has a long and difficult lee way [sic] to make up before he can inspire as much confidence in his character as he extracts from his talents'.[8] This view persisted for some time: when Castlereagh committed suicide in 1822 and Canning's name was widely canvassed as his successor as Foreign Secretary, Palmerston wrote in the following vein to Laurence Sulivan:

I quite agree with you that there are many difficulties & objections to be overcome if Canning should be appointed. The King hates him, the Cabinet distrusts
him, the Hs. [of] Cns do not respect him & the public have little confidence in
him. In the otherside of the account are his *pre-eminent* talents as an orator which
in a constitution that is carried on by speaking in one room, the Hs. [of] Cns,
form a most important consideration. [9]

Nonetheless, Palmerston opposed Canning receiving the lead in the
House of Commons in addition to the Foreign Secretaryship[10] and
argued that Robert Peel, 'in discretion, in personal following, in
high mindedness … is superior to Canning'.[11] The key event in
shifting Palmerston to a more Canningite position, as it would be for
much of Palmerston's subsequent political development more
broadly, was to be the general election of 1826.

 Originally, the Liverpool ministry had been planning to go
to the country in 1825 but the rising tide of dissension among Tories
about the Catholic question had prompted Canning to argue successfully for a postponement of the election until the following year
in the hope that the tensions would relax somewhat.[12] The general
election of the summer of 1826 saw a net gain of 13 seats for the
anti-Catholic forces in Parliament,[13] and although the periodical
John Bull referred to its outcome as 'the triumph of Protestant
ascendancy',[14] it was hardly that. There were still signs of great
strains within the Tory party, however, most notably at Cambridge,
where Palmerston was opposed by two anti-Catholic governmental
colleagues, the Attorney-General, Sir John Copley, and the Chief
Secretary to Ireland, Henry Goulburn, and was returned only
through Whig support in virtue of his pro-Catholic views. Canning
himself was directly involved, albeit in a small way, in the campaign
for Palmerston's return. Palmerston had been outraged to find out
that Joseph Planta, Canning's under-secretary at the Foreign Office,
had been franking Copley's letters during the campaign and complained of this to Canning who responded by offering to frank the
same number of Palmerston's letters.[15]

 The events of the Cambridge election of 1826 seem to have

politicised Palmerston, turning him from a man of business, some-one who saw his role primarily as an administrator, into an active political animal. Not only can we detect a warmer feeling towards Canning but we can also see an increasing distance between Palmer-ston and the mainstream Tories. For, as Palmerston put it, 'the real opposition of the present day sit behind the Treasury Bench', and it was this 'stupid old Tory party' which impeded the ministry and the Whigs who supported it in its policies of 'improvement'.[16]

Palmerston's move towards a closer relationship with Canning was thus partly a response to domestic issues such as the Cambridge election and partly a response to Palmerston's inter-pretation of Canning's foreign policy, and partly a result of the long crisis which ensued in 1827 upon Lord Liverpool's incapacitating stroke and the battle for the succession to the premiership. The point worth re-iterating here is Palmerston's relatively late emergence as a friend of Canning: in a year Canning would be dead. Despite this late emergence, however, Palmerston quickly came to identify him-self closely with Canning and, just as importantly, came to be iden-tified with him by others.

When, in April 1827, Canning finally emerged victorious from the Tory power struggle, and Wellington, Peel and other lead-ing 'Protestants' declined to serve with him, he was forced into a large-scale reconstruction of the ministry, part of which involved offering Palmerston the Chancellorship of the Exchequer. Two months later, in circumstances which still remain rather unclear, this offer was withdrawn and eventually (after offers of Jamaica and India had been rejected) it was decided that Palmerston should remain Secretary at War but with a seat in the Cabinet.[17] Despite this false start Palmerston emerged as an important figure among the Canningites during Canning's short ministry and his feelings about Canning became almost hyperbolically loyal, reaching a peak when he wrote on 7 August 1827, anticipating Canning's imminent death: 'What a loss! Not merely to parties but to nations, not to friends only but to mankind.'[18] The following year, in a calmer state of mind, Palmerston was still willing to link the nation's welfare with adherence to Canning's policies:

> his principles and his policy were most excellently adapted for the benefit of this country; and … as the principles which emanated from him are followed, just in that proportion will those who adopt them conduce to its interest and advantage, and obtain for their government the confidence and approbation of the people.[19]

Quite quickly after Canning's death, Palmerston came to be seen by some as the one man who could fill the gap left by Canning. After a successful speech by Palmerston on the Catholic question in March 1829, Tierney called Palmerston 'an imitation of Canning, and not a bad one' and Sturges Bourne reportedly said 'that he thought eloquence in the House of Commons had expired with Canning, but that it had actually and positively revived in Palmerston'.[20] In Paris, even Talleyrand, among others, was reported by Mme Flahault to regard Palmerston as 'le seul qui pourra remplacer Canning'.[21] Such indeed, was the identification of Palmerston with the legacy of Canning that, during the debates on the Reform Bill, Palmerston felt the rhetorical necessity to explain how it was that the so-called Canningites were now in favour of reform when Canning was a notorious opponent of it.

> As to my own opinions, I have stated them: what the opinions of Mr Canning would have been in the present day, had he been spared to the country, I will not take upon me to say; but they are bad expounders of the opinions of Mr Canning, who look only to the particular sentiments which he may have expressed in particular times, without fathoming the depth of the great principle by which the whole course of his public life was guided. If ever there was a man who took great and enlarged views of human affairs, that man was Mr Canning, — if ever there was a man who, as it were, polarized his opinions by universal and all-pervading principles of action, that man was, undoubtedly, Mr Canning; and when our assailants on this question would endeavour to pin down his gigantic mind by the Lilliputian threads of verbal quotation, I repudiate in his name the conclusions which they would draw; and I feel convinced, that if he had been standing here now, his mighty genius would have embraced within its comprehensive grasp all the various necessities upon which our own conclusions have been founded, and that he would, in all probability, have stated to the House, with

powers, alas, how different from those of any now within these walls ! the same opinions which I venture humbly to submit. If any man wants a key to the opinions of Mr Canning, let him consult the concluding passage of his speech on the 24th of February, 1826, as applicable to the present occasion as to that upon which it was delivered; in which he says, that 'they who resist improvement because it is innovation, may find themselves compelled to accept innovation when it has ceased to be improvement.'[22]

These resounding words, however, conceal something that is frequently overlooked by those who unthinkingly apply the term 'Canningite' to Palmerston. That is, the fact that the claim to Canning's legacy was not uncontested: the decision by four of Canning's supporters, William Huskisson, Palmerston, Charles Grant, and Dudley, to enter Wellington's ministry in January 1828 had been bitterly criticized by other Canningites who clustered around Canning's widow, newly ennobled as Viscountess Canning.[23] In truth, partly for this reason and partly due to Huskisson's acknowledged leadership of the so-called Canningites in Wellington's ministry, in the years following Canning's death it is probably better to regard Palmerston as a 'Huskissonite', at least until Huskisson's own untimely death under the wheels of *The Rocket* in 1830. So, while Palmerston did in domestic politics, and albeit somewhat belatedly, emerge as a Canningite, even this ascription has to be used carefully. In the area of foreign policy this need for care will also become clear.

II

The details of Canning's foreign policy and also of Palmerston's lie well beyond the ambit of this paper but it is nevertheless possible to make some brief comments about the principles that Canning deployed when formulating his policy and to attempt some comparison with those adopted by Palmerston. Canning's principles have been concisely summarised by Temperley as

no Areopagus,[24] non-intervention; no European police system; every nation for itself, and God for us all; balance of power; respect for facts, not for abstract theories; respect for treaty rights, but caution in extending them. Provided it is sovereign and observes diplomatic obligations, a republic is as good a member of the comity of nations as a monarchy.[25]

It is easy to see how a foreign policy based on these principles could be regarded as 'liberal' by ultras at home and legitimists abroad. Episodes such as Canning's refusal to sanction interference in Spain to restore the Bourbons, his defence of Portugal against threats from France or Spain, and most of all his successful campaign in favour of the recognition of the former Spanish colonies in South America and of Brazil seemed to put Canning firmly in the camp of the liberal constitutionalists opposed to the pretensions of the Holy Alliance to police Europe and the wider world. It is important not to confuse cause and effect, however. Canning supported, for example, recognition of the independence of Spain's South American colonies, not out of an abstract commitment to republicanism or constitutionalism but as a consequence of his desire to preserve a peaceful balance in the world, and not only a balance of power but also a balance of principles. The Holy Alliance's power was to be broken, not from any desire to alter the internal organisation of its constituent parts, but from a desire to preserve the international peace. To this end Canning regarded Britain's role as one of occupying a middle position, as he noted. For example, in 1823, when he stated 'that there is a contest going on in the world, between the spirit of unlimited monarchy, and the spirit of unlimited democracy', adding later that Britain's role was 'essentially neutral: neutral not only between contending nations, but between conflicting principles'.[26] In particular, this idea of balance was most evident in Canning's attitude to North and South America. Thus in January 1824, shortly after the promulgation by the United States of the Monroe Doctrine, Canning noted that 'the effect of the ultra-liberalism of our Yankee co-operators, on the ultra-despotism of our Aix-la-Chapelle allies, gives me just the balance that I wanted'.[27] Later that year he stated that 'when he spoke of Europe and the world, the phrase had reference to Europe and America — the old world and the new — the different interests of which must be nicely balanced by every person who wished to attain the character of a British statesman'.[28] Further, in the debate in December 1826 on his decision to send troops to Portugal to forestall a Spanish strike, Canning gave full vent to this view. The conflict between Spain and Portugal was a conflict of opinions and 'if into that war this country shall be compelled to enter, we shall enter into it, with a sincere and anxious desire to mitigate rather than exasperate — and to mingle only in the conflict of arms, not in the more fatal conflict of opinions'. Canning was keen, therefore, to let 'the professors of violent and exaggerated doctrines on both sides' know that Britain was becoming involved in 'Portugal, not to rule, not to dictate, not to prescribe constitutions — but to defend and to preserve the independence of an ally'.[29] Despite Canning's disclaimer, Palmerston took a different message from Canning's speech. Writing to William Temple he stated that:

I confess I heard that speech with peculiar delight; it is most gratifying to hear avowed by the ministers of the country as the guide to their conduct those principles one feels & knows to be true ... The principles of constitutional freedom are not only the elements of strength to the country which carries them into practice, but the best guarantee of peace to neighbouring nations & it is much for our interest therefore to favour their extension on the Continent.[30]

This assertion, however, that Canning was in favour of constitutional freedoms *per se* was, it can be argued, a fundamental misreading of Canning's position. Later in this key speech on Portugal Canning uttered one of his most famous epigrams when he declared that 'I called the New World into existence, to redress the balance of the Old'.[31] Commentators at the time and since have tended to concentrate on what they saw as the vainglory in Canning's statement,[32] but the substantive point is not Canning's claim to have 'called the New World into existence' but his argument that he did it to restore the balance of power and principles in the world. Not only would France, which was in control of Spain at the time of recognition, not disrupt the balance of power by its control of Spanish colonies, but the establishment of constitutional republics in the former Spanish colonies would also balance the waxing power of authoritarian monarchism in Europe.

This search for balance meant that Canning was often seen as being on the side of the fledgling republics as a matter of principle and this gave his foreign policy a more 'liberal' reputation than it perhaps deserved. The *balance*, however, was the principle and measures such as recognition of the independence of Spain's colonies in South America were as much means to preserving that balance as ends in themselves. When it came to Europe Canning believed that it was 'not ... a British interest to have free States established on the Continent. Much better and more convenient for us to have neighbours, whose institutions cannot be compared with ours in point of freedom',[33] as thereby Britain's influence would be all the greater.[34] Moreover, Canning saw the preservation of monarchy in parts of the new world such as Brazil as desirable in that it 'would cure the evils of universal democracy, and prevent the drawing of the line of demarcation which I most dread — America *versus* Europe'.[35] This then is in clear contradistinction to Palmerston's principles as outlined in his letter to Temple, quoted above, and many of his later statements. In 1838, for example, Palmerston made the following distinctly un-Canningite statement in a letter to Frederick Lamb:

The system of England ought to be to maintain the liberties and independence of all other nations; out of the conflicting interests of other countries to secure her own independence; to throw her moral weight into the scale of any people who are spontaneously striving for freedom, by which I mean rational govt, and to extend as fast as possible civilization all over the world.[36]

This missionary zeal is clearly at odds with Canning's conception of Britain's role as a mediator of the balance of power and principles. Turning to another facet of Canning's foreign policy, it can be seen to have had a strong mixture of English or British nationalism in it, and in this respect at least Palmerston's approach has a greater degree of similarity. Thus, Canning stated in his Plymouth speech of 1823 that 'in the conduct of political affairs, the grand object of my contemplation is the interest of England', and he was able to refer in a debate on the Alien Bill in April 1824 to 'the shibboleth of his ... policy upon this and every other public question; and that word was "England"'.[37] This desire to consult only the interests of England was of a piece with the role he saw her occupying as a mediator between the two rival principles, autocracy and democracy. So when he said 'that for *Europe*, I shall be desirous *now* and *then* to read *England*',[38] or that 'in the substitution of one word for another — for "Alliance" read "England"', ... you have the clue of my policy',[39] he meant just that. He was not deserting the Holy Alliance to join the ranks of the democrats and republicans but rather to occupy the middle ground between them in order to preserve both the balance of power and of principles in the world. Palmerston, too, saw a particular role for Britain and invoked Canning in his assertion of it:

We have no eternal allies, and we have no perpetual enemies. Our interests are eternal and perpetual, and these interests it is our duty to follow … And if I might be allowed to express in one sentence the principle which I think ought to guide an English minister, I would adopt the expression of Canning, and say that with every British minister the interests of England ought to be the shibboleth of his policy.[40]

III

If, then, it is potentially misleading to describe Palmerston as a Canningite in domestic political terms and if such an ascription also requires modification with regard to the principles of their respective foreign policies, did they share any similarities in method, notwithstanding these differences in policy? There were clearly differences of approach which developed out of their differences of principle but which also reflect the different times in which each statesman practised his craft. Palmerston was much more inclined

to become involved in the affairs of Europe and to put much greater
store in the use of congresses than Canning, who deprecated the
'predominating *areopagitical* spirit' of such gatherings.[41] Palmerston, indeed, gave the impression of being so keen on congresses
that Metternich, in Webster's words, 'accused him of a design to
make the Belgian Conference a sort of permanent Council of
Europe'.[42] Webster in fact seems to consider Palmerston as a kind
of hybrid of Castlereagh and Canning in his methods: 'His attitude
towards Europe in these years [1830-41] was indeed more that of
Castlereagh than of Canning. But to Castlereagh's conception of a
concert of the great powers he added that protection of liberalism
which Canning had threatened but never carried out.'[43] Leaving
aside the question of whether Canning ever saw himself as a
defender of liberalism *per se*, it would clearly be a mistake to see
Palmerston as simply applying the methods of Canning to a new
era.

In one final area, that of the moulding of public opinion,
both for domestic political and for foreign policy ends, the names
of Canning and Palmerston have often been linked. Harold
Temperley has given a definitive account of Canning's relationship
with the press and the present author has written at length on the
broader relationship that Canning had with the concept of public
opinion.[44] Moreover, David Brown has, in two recent articles,
treated the issue of Palmerston's relationship with public opinion
in detail.[45] Consequently this section will confine itself to some
general remarks on the relationship between their approaches.

It is clear that both Canning and Palmerston recognised not
only the inescapable role of public opinion in early nineteenth-
century political life but also the consequent imperative to mould it.
To take one example from each: Canning's most revealing statement
about public opinion came during a speech in Liverpool in August
1822, when he referred to 'that mighty power of Public Opinion,
embodied in a Free Press, which pervades, and checks, and,
perhaps, in the last resort, nearly governs the whole', a power which

he likened to 'the power of STEAM'.[46] Similarly, for Palmerston, speaking in 1829:

There is in nature no moving power but mind, all else is passive and inert; in human affairs this power is opinion; in political affairs it is public opinion; and he who can grasp this power, with it will subdue the fleshly arm of physical strength … those statesmen who know how to avail themselves of the passions, and the interest, and the opinions of mankind, are able to gain an ascendancy, and to exercise a sway over human affairs, far out of all proportion greater than belong to the power and resources of the state over which they preside …[47]

Consequently, both would seek to harness this power via the press and other means: for example, both men dipped toes in the journalistic pond (and in Canning's case founded journals), and both spoke out-of-doors. The key point for our concerns here, however, is the extent to which Palmerston was influenced by Canning. David Brown states that 'Palmerston might have denied the link, but he was unquestionably influenced by the example of … Canning, in appreciating fully the importance of counting public opinion amongst one's allies'.[48] Undoubtedly, Palmerston would have been aware of the approach to cultivating public opinion that Canning took and to the extent that Palmerston adopted a similar approach there is a *prima facie* case for Canning influencing Palmerston in this matter. Nevertheless, it was not just a case of Palmerston copying Canning's tactics rather than, say, Castlereagh's, but rather a case of two highly astute politicians recognising the need to harness a new force in political life and having the imagination and energy to carry such a policy through. It may, therefore simply be an accident of chronology that makes Canning look like the innovator and Palmerston the disciple: had their situations been reversed, there is nothing lacking in Palmerston's intellectual capacity, political judgement or organisational ability that would have prevented him from taking similar strides without Canning's footsteps in which to follow.

Moreover, a biographical focus too rigidly applied can easily deceive us in this matter. Both Canning and Palmerston were part of a wider movement in early nineteenth-century political life which saw an increasing level of discussion and speculation about the impact of an emergent public opinion, for good and evil, on British politics and society. Examples of such discourse can be found widely spread in the private papers of politicians, in the press and in pamphlets of the time,[49] and the phenomenon of emergent public opinion has been much commented upon by historians since.[50] It thus trivialises the situation markedly simply to see Palmerston as picking up where Canning left off. Rather both inhabited, and contributed to, a developing discourse about public opinion which provided some of the causal conditions for their thoughts and actions.

IV

Palmerston himself appears, towards the end of his career, to have had some doubts about closely identifying himself with Canning. In 1860 a firm of publishers sent him a biographical sketch of himself for his comments. He deleted two passages that referred to Canning: the first claimed that 'it may be said with great truth that Canning the statesman made Palmerston a politician in reality and depth', while the second asserted that after May 1828 Palmerston 'aimed at acquiring the reputation of being Mr Canning's successor'.[51] It is perhaps understandable that a great statesman at the end of his career would wish to be thought of as his own man and not someone else's acolyte. Later historians, however, are not necessarily bound by such judgments and in thinking and writing about history one always has recourse to generalisations and shorthand formulations, and the description of Palmerston as a Canningite is no different from any other example: if used carefully and thoughtfully it poses no danger; if used unthinkingly it can obscure as much as it reveals. So, while not wishing to reject completely the utility of the description 'Canningite' for Palmerston, one must, alongside his rhetorical willingness to invoke the legacy of Canning, always remember the lateness of Palmerston's conversion to the cause; alongside his donning of Canning's mantle as the defender of England's interests, one must always remember the extent to which he developed beyond (or perhaps even misread) the essence of Canning's approach to foreign policy.

References

[1] *Edinburgh Review* 71 (Jul 1840) pp. 552-3.

[2] Canning MSS, 33, Leeds District Archives, Canning to Portland, 24 Mar 1809 [copy; original not sent until 2 Apr]. Reproduced by the kind permission of the Earl and Countess of Harewood and Trustees of the Harewood House Trust.

[3] For detailed references to these events see Stephen M. Lee, 'George Canning and the Tories, *c*.1801-27' (unpublished PhD thesis, University of Manchester, 1999) p. 57, n. 4.

[4] For which see Lee, 'George Canning', pp. 56-92.

[5] Kenneth Bourne *Palmerston: the early years 1784-1841* (London: Allen Lane, 1982) pp. 51, 76, 84, 228. There was also some talk, for example, of Palmerston becoming Canning's under-secretary at the Foreign Office in August 1807: see R. G. Thorne (ed.) *The House of Commons 1790-1820* (5 vols., London: Secker and Warburg, 1986) v, p. 349.

[6] Bourne, *Palmerston*, p. 90.

[7] The lateness of Palmerston's 'conversion' is attested to by Lady Palmerston herself: see Tresham Lever (ed.) *The letters of Lady Palmerston* (London: John Murray, 1957).

[8] Palmerston to Malmesbury, 18 May 1812, quoted in Bourne, *Palmerston*, p. 229. Palmerston added later: 'we must have Wellesley [and] Canning if we mean to go on, and surely the Prince will not keep them out from any fears about the Catholic question'. Palmerston was to be disappointed.

[9] Palmerston to Laurence Sulivan, 19 Aug 1822, quoted in K. Bourne (ed.) *The letters of the third Viscount Palmerston to Laurence and Elizabeth Sulivan 1804-1863* (London: Royal Historical Society, Camden 4th series, 23; 1979) p. 152.

[10] Bourne *Palmerston*, p. 239.

[11] Palmerston to Laurence Sulivan, 19 Aug 1822, quoted in Bourne (ed.), *Letters to Sulivan*, p. 152.

[12] Lee, 'George Canning', pp. 222-5.

[13] G.I.T. Machin *The Catholic question in English politics 1820 to 1830* (Oxford: Oxford University Press, 1964) p. 86.

[14] *John Bull*, 19 Jun 1826, p. 196.

[15] Henry Lytton Bulwer *The life of Henry John Temple, Viscount Palmerston: with selections from his diaries and correspondence* (3 vols., London: Richard Bentley and Son, 1870-4) i, pp. 160-73; Bourne, *Palmerston*, pp. 241-8 (p. 244

for the affair of the franks); Machin, *Catholic question*, pp. 80-3. For his part Canning declined to be returned for Harwich in 1826 due to the strength of the anti-Catholic feeling there (Stapleton to J. H. North, 31 May 1826, Canning MSS, 87c).

[16] Palmerston to William Temple, 17 Jul 1826, quoted in Bulwer, *Palmerston*, i, pp. 171-2.

[17] For detailed discussion of this episode see Bourne, *Palmerston*, pp. 252-65.

[18] Palmerston to Elizabeth Sulivan, 7 Aug 1827, quoted in Bourne (ed.), *Letters to Sulivan*, p. 190.

[19] Speech in the House of Commons on provision for Canning's family, 14 May 1828. Only a summary exists in *Parliamentary Debates*, n.s., xix, 722; the text quoted here is taken from George Henry Francis *Opinions and policy of the Right Honourable Viscount Palmerston* (London: Colburn and Co., 1852) p. 59.

[20] Quoted in Bourne, *Palmerston*, p. 296.

[21] Quoted in Bourne, *Palmerston*, p. 300.

[22] House of Commons, 3 Mar 1831, quoted in Francis, *Palmerston*, pp. 165-6. This text differs from *Parliamentary Debates*, 3rd ser., ii, 1322-3 in its details but the sentiment remains the same. The version presented here, with its Burkean overtones, reads better.

[23] For this split in the Canningites see A. Aspinall, 'The last of the Canningites' *English Historical Review* 50 (1935) pp. 638-69.

[24] i.e. no further Congresses.

[25] Harold Temperley *The foreign policy of Canning 1822-1827: England, the neo-Holy Alliance, and the new world*, (2nd edn., London: Frank Cass, 1966) pp. 470-1.

[26] R. Therry (ed.) *The speeches of the Right Hon. George Canning* (6 vols., London: J. Ridgway, 1828) v, pp. 126, 129.

[27] J. Bagot (ed.) *George Canning and his friends* (2 vols., London: John Murray, 1909) ii, pp. 217-8, Canning to Bagot, 22 Jan 1824. In a second letter of this date Canning went on to say 'if things are prevented from going to extremities it must be by *our* keeping a distinct middle ground between the two conflicting Bigotries and staying the plague both ways', *ibid.* ii, p. 222.

[28] Therry (ed.), *Canning Speeches*, v, pp. 165-6.

[29] *Ibid.* vi, pp. 90-2.

[30] Palmerston to William Temple, 26 Dec 1826, quoted in Bourne, *Palmerston*, p. 249.

[31] Therry (ed.), *Canning speeches*, vi, p.111.

[32] Mrs Arbuthnot thought Canning's performance 'abominable' (Francis Bamford and the Duke of Wellington (eds.) *The journal of Mrs. Arbuthnot 1820-1832* (2 vols., London: Macmillan, 1950) ii, p. 64); the Duke of Cumberland considered it 'ill-judged' (A. Aspinall (ed.) *The letters of King George IV 1812-1830*

(3 vols., Cambridge: Cambridge University Press, 1938) iii, p. 194); but John Cam Hobhouse thought it a 'masterpiece' (J. C. Hobhouse (Lord Broughton) *Recollections of a long life* ed. Lady Dorchester (6 vols., London: John Murray, 1909-1911) ii, p. 159); and Greville thought it 'brilliant' (Lytton Strachey and Roger Fulford (eds.) *The Greville Memoirs 1814-60* (8 vols., London: Macmillan, 1938) i, p. 161). For his part, Canning did not 'regret the extremity to which I was driven' (Canning to Granville, 14 Dec 1826, quoted in Augustus Granville Stapleton *George Canning and his times* (London: John W. Parker, 1859) p. 546).

[33] Memo by Stratford Canning of a conversation with Canning, 4 Dec 1824, quoted in Temperley, *Foreign policy of Canning*, p. 458.

[34] Therry (ed.), *Canning Speeches*, v, p. 125.

[35] Canning to William A'Court, 31 Dec 1823, quoted in Stapleton, *Canning and his times*, pp. 394-5.

[36] Palmerston to Frederick Lamb, 21 Mar 1838, quoted in Bourne, *Palmerston* p. 627.

[37] Therry (ed.), *Canning speeches*, v, pp. 252-3; vi, p. 421.

[38] Canning to Charles Bagot, 5 Nov 1822, quoted in Stapleton, *Canning and his times*, p. 364.

[39] Canning to Frere, 8 Aug 1823, quoted in Gabrielle Festing *John Hookham Frere and his friends* (London: J. Nisbet and Co., 1899) p. 257.

[40] *Parliamentary Debates*, 3rd ser., xcvii, 122-3 (1 March 1848).

[41] Therry (ed.), *Canning speeches*, v, p. 63. Canning, in this speech of April 1823, invoked Castlereagh's state paper of May 1820 as the justification for his antipathy to such gatherings.

[42] Charles Webster *The foreign policy of Palmerston, 1830-1841: Britain, the liberal movement and the eastern question* (2 vols., London: G. Bell and Sons, 1951) ii, p. 791.

[43] Webster, *Foreign policy of Palmerston*, ii, p. 781. See also Bourne, *Palmerston*, p. 349.

[44] Temperley, *Foreign policy of Canning*, pp. 297-316; Lee, 'George Canning', pp. 168-84.

[45] David Brown, 'Compelling but not controlling ?: Palmerston and the press, 1846-1855' *History* 86 (2001) pp. 41-61; *idem*, 'The power of public opinion: Palmerston and the crisis of December 1851' *Parliamentary History* 20 (2001) pp. 333-58.

[46] Thomas Kaye (ed.) *Speeches of the Right Hon. George Canning delivered on public occasions in Liverpool* (Liverpool: Baldwin, Craddock and Joy, 1825) pp. 363-5.

[47] Quoted in Bourne, *Palmerston*, p. 299.

[48] Brown, 'Compelling but not controlling ?', p. 45.

[49] See, for example, Peel's famous comments on public opinion being 'that great

compound of folly, weakness, prejudice, wrong feeling, right feeling, obstinacy, and newspaper paragraphs', (Peel to Croker, 23 Mar 1820, quoted in Louis J. Jennings (ed.) *The Croker papers: the correspondence and diaries of the late Right Honourable John Wilson Croker* (3 vols., London: John Murray, 1884) i, p. 170) or William Mackinnon's pamphlet *On the rise, progress and present state of public opinion in Great Britain and other parts of the world* (London: Saunders and Otley, 1828).

[50] For a discussion of public opinion during Wellington's ministry, but one which has considerable relevance to the early nineteenth century as a whole, see Peter Jupp *British politics on the eve of reform: The Duke of Wellington's administration, 1828-30* (Basingstoke: Macmillan, 1998) pp. 330-86. In addition see the other works referenced in Lee, 'George Canning', pp. 168-70 n. 26-n. 33.

[51] Herbert C. F. Bell *Lord Palmerston* (2 vols., London: Longmans, 1936) i, p. 59.

CHAPTER 2

Palmerston and the Church
John Wolffe

Palmerston's religious policy has tended to be a staple of caricature, almost from the time that his son-in-law,[1] the seventh Earl of Shaftesbury, wrote on his accession to office:

I much fear that Palmerston's ecclesiastical appointments will be detestable. He does not know, in theology, Moses from Sydney Smith. The vicar of Romsey, where he goes to church, is the only clergyman he ever spoke to; and as for the wants, the feelings, the views, the hopes and fears, of the country, and particularly the religious part of it, they are as strange to him as the interior of Japan.[2]

The way in which Palmerston subsequently took Shaftesbury himself into his confidence naturally caused the latter to revise his opinion, but has given rise to another caricature, of Palmerston as a mere puppet in ecclesiastical affairs, manipulated by Shaftesbury and an Evangelical clique. This is the view of Nigel Scotland in his recent book on the Palmerston bishops, following Jasper Ridley's judgement that Palmerston depended 'almost entirely' on Shaftesbury.[3] Archibald Campbell Tait, a future Archbishop of Canterbury, believed that the ultimate *eminence grise* behind Palmerston's church appointments was H.M. Villiers, successively Bishop of Carlisle and Durham, who 'pulled the strings' of Shaftesbury through their mutual friend A.F. Kinnaird, MP for Perth.[4] Meanwhile Palmerston emerged as the improbable hero of the Evangelicals, who felt that, despite himself, he gave them a belated place in the sun.

Both these images, of Palmerston as a religious ignoramus, and of him as the mere tool of the Evangelical party, are founded on the presupposition that he had no real interest or agenda of his own in church affairs, and that the consequent vacuum was filled by the ruthlessly pious Shaftesbury. It is certainly true that, like all contemporary prime ministers, with the partial exception of Gladstone, Palmerston was heavily dependent on informal advice to help him identify suitable men for senior church appointments. Nevertheless, in this chapter, it will be argued that Palmerston had coherent and firmly held views of his own on religious matters, which were reflected in the policies and appointments of his administrations. The church appointments between 1855 and 1865 will be reassessed below, but these first need to be set in a wider context. While the focus of the paper is on Palmerston's policy towards the Church of England, his attitudes to Nonconformity and Roman Catholicism will also be explored.

I

A trawl through *Hansard* shows that his interventions in debate on religious issues were, albeit infrequent, still cumulatively quite numerous. There were five before 1830, four in the 1830s, nine in the 1840s, and four between 1851 and 1854. In 1855 and 1856, the first two years of his premiership, there were no less than 14, and a further 11 between 1857 and 1865. The definition of religion used here is quite a broad one, including for example diplomatic relations with the papacy and university reform, as well as more narrowly ecclesiastical issues, but even on the latter he was by no means silent.

Palmerston was a consistent advocate of religious liberty, for both Roman Catholics and Dissenters. In 1828 he voted against the repeal of the Test and Corporation Acts, but only because he believed that Parliament should remove the real grievances of Catholics, before it tackled the nominal ones of Dissenters.[5] At the same time he was a firm advocate of the Church of England. In April 1824, he supported the building of new churches, explaining that, while he upheld principles of religious liberty, he still regretted the increasing numbers of Dissenters. He continued:

It was his wish to see that the established church should be the predominant one in this country; for nothing, he was persuaded, could tend more to the general tranquillity and happiness of a people, than a community of sentiment, as far as it could be obtained, without intolerance to any party, in matters of religious doctrine.[6]

It was a rather utilitarian argument for establishment, with an obvious lack of theological interest or spiritual fervour, but it was nonetheless sincerely and deeply held. In 1828 Palmerston argued that legislative props to defend the Church would be useless without the 'attachment and reverence of the people' founded on 'the purity of its doctrines, the piety and learning of its ministers, their moral conduct and exemplary lives.' Such a consciousness of the church as a catalyst for social harmony, provided it eschewed intolerance and its clergy set high standards of behaviour, ran through his career. He recognized moreover that religion was more than a matter of mere outward observance: in 1834 while supporting the admission of Dissenters to Cambridge degrees, he took the opportunity to question the value of compulsory chapel attendance. He wondered whether it was really in the interests of 'the Church and true religious feeling' that young men should be obliged to rush to morning prayers 'unwashed, unshaved, and half dressed' or to interrupt their evening drinking parties in order to do so.[7]

In 1837 Palmerston took a further opportunity to express his views on the church, at a meeting in Winchester to establish a Diocesan Church Building Society. Seconding the main motion proposed by the bishop, the Evangelical Charles Sumner, Palmerston agreed that there was an urgent call on members of the Established Church to contribute to the maintenance of its interests. Dissenters were building extensively, and the Church of England should emulate them. Indeed the increase in Dissent was hardly surprising when Anglican accommodation was so insufficient. Nevertheless he did not wish to be thought hostile to Dissenters. His own attachment to the Church of England stemmed from both education and conviction, and from a consciousness that it 'was founded on the mild spirit of toleration which it accorded to other sects'. Such toleration was 'nothing but charity', and its maintenance of this principle made its doctrines 'the purest form of Christian belief'.[8] Such sentiments, however, aroused the ire of the young Samuel Wilberforce, then an incumbent in the diocese, who made a vehement speech to the meeting, deprecating any approach to the voluntary support of religion, and accusing Palmerston of taking a line 'inconsistent with true Churchmanship'.[9] This early confrontation between Palmerston and the man who was to be the leading High Church bishop at the time he was Prime Minister highlights how his tolerant and liberal conception of the Church of England placed him at odds with those who held to a stronger and more belligerent sense of Anglican identity.

In relation to Ireland, Palmerston maintained in 1843 that the need for changes in the conditions of the Catholic and Protestant churches was a particularly pressing grievance. He did not want to subvert the Church of Ireland, but he thought that, despite the controversial reforms of the Irish Church Temporalities Act of 1833, it was still over-resourced. Meanwhile the Roman Catholic Church should be endowed as a means of conciliating the majority population: he noted approvingly that it was the practice of the state in other countries, for example Austria and Prussia, to provide for a variety of religious persuasions.[10] Accordingly, when in 1845 Peel, at odds with many of his own backbenchers, proposed permanent expanded statutory provision for the Roman Catholic seminary at Maynooth, Palmerston not only supported him, but argued that the necessary funds should come from the surplus revenues of the Church of Ireland.[11] He held that the points of agreement between Catholics and Protestants were of much greater importance than those of disagreement. He believed, therefore, that if the Irish could not be made Protestants, they should at least be made 'good Catholics', and that it was important not to forget 'as some men in their zeal seem to do, that Roman Catholics are Christians.' Such conciliation would greatly strengthen ties between England and

Ireland.[12] He also warmly supported the Peel ministry's subsequent proposals for 'Queen's Colleges', non-sectarian higher education in Ireland, believing that they would lay 'a foundation for concord between persons of different religious opinions'.[13]

Subsequent events, however, led Palmerston to a more negative view of Roman Catholicism. He was annoyed when Pope Pius IX condemned the Queen's Colleges, and alarmed by the growth of sectarian violence allegedly instigated by the priests. Following his return to office in 1846, he supported endeavours to establish formal diplomatic relations with the Holy See, with a view particularly to persuading the Pope to control the political activity of the Irish clergy. Meanwhile Russell and Clarendon pursued schemes for the state endowment of the Irish Roman Catholic clergy. Palmerston supported this policy, on the grounds that it would 'not tend to the propagation of what we consider religious error, but that it would tend to the diffusion of political contentment.' He did not, however, think there was any chance of such a measure being passed at present.[14] All these plans indeed came to nothing, and for Palmerston, as for his Cabinet colleagues, consequent frustration came to a head when, in the autumn of 1850, Pius IX restored a territorial hierarchy of Catholic bishops in England. Although Palmerston thought the 'thing itself ... little or nothing', he was offended by the 'insolent and ostentatious' manner in which it was announced, and by the Pope's failure to consult the British government. He also felt that the extent of the public outcry against the new bishops meant that the government must act against them.[15] At the same time, he remained committed to principles of liberal toleration and affirmed that he would never consent to a 'penal enactment'. His dilemma was a very genuine one. He prefaced his support in the Commons for the Ecclesiastical Titles Bill with the confession,

that he never remembered, since he had had the honour of a seat in that House, any discussion that had been so painful to the mind as that in which they were then engaged. He had hoped that when the disabilities were removed in the first place from the Dissenters, and afterwards from the Roman Catholics, that discussions and controversies on religious questions would never again be heard within the walls of Parliament.[16]

It is therefore a serious distortion to suggest, as some recent scholars do, that Palmerston was 'absurdly suspicious' of Roman Catholics in general.[17] His objection was not to Roman Catholicism *per se*, but to politicised religion, in which terms he saw both the Pope's restoration of the English hierarchy and the activities of the priests in Ireland. By the 1860s he came explicitly to see the Italian and Irish situations as linked, believing that the Pope encouraged the Irish priests to foster opposition to the British government, because of the latter's support for Italian unity.[18] On the other hand he thought it vindictive and impolitic to punish ordinary Catholics for the actions of their leaders.[19] Nor did he have a *prima facie* hostility to them. When Protestant agitators raised objections to the employment of William Turnbull, a Roman Catholic, in the State Paper Office to work on an edition of documents relating to the Reformation era, Palmerston was initially unpersuaded there was a problem.[20] Only when confronted by evidence from Turnbull's publications that showed that he indeed held a partisan Roman Catholic position, did he press for his transfer to other duties, provoking Turnbull's resignation.[21] Despite everything, at the end of his life Palmerston still regarded Catholic Emancipation as an 'act of sound policy and strict justice'.[22]

Palmerston's religious views were further illuminated by his stance as Home Secretary in autumn 1853, when a resurgence of cholera caused both the Church of Scotland and Free Church Presbyteries of Edinburgh to write to him to urge the calling of a Fast Day.[23] National Fasts had been called in response to previous epidemics and other national emergencies, in order to acknowledge the hand of God, and to pray for deliverance. On this occasion, however, Palmerston refused. Since the last cholera epidemic in 1848, understanding of the material causes of cholera had greatly increased, and he responded to the Scottish churchmen that God had established laws of nature, including the importance for health of avoiding overcrowded and unsanitary living conditions.

Providence gave men measures they could take for their own welfare, and steps must be taken to purify and improve the slums where
contagion festered. If this was not done, the disease would 'infalli-
bly' continue, 'despite all the prayers and fastings of a united but
inactive nation.' 'When', Palmerston concluded, 'man has done his
utmost for his own safety, then is the time to invoke the blessing of
Heaven to give effect to his exertions.'[24] Despite Palmerston's references to God and Providence, this letter outraged some Evangelicals, who saw it as a profane mockery of the idea of God's
intervention in human affairs, and as giving an impulse to the 'evil
heart of disbelief'.[25] For his part, the secularist leader George Jacob
Holyoake reportedly described it as a 'magnificent secular letter'.[26]
Shaftesbury, staunch Evangelical though he was, recognized,
however, that Palmerston had 'no intention to be irreverent' and
thought his letter contained 'abundant good sense and much truth.'[27]
Palmerston also received eloquent support from Charles Kingsley
who, in an article in *Fraser's Magazine*, defended his position as
orthodox and Christian, and believed that it reflected the common
sense view of the great majority of clergy and laity.[28]

II

Palmerston's approach to religion as Prime Minister thus combined
a deep-seated commitment to toleration as a worthy end in itself,
with a strong dislike of theological controversy, especially when it
became divisive and politicised. This was a view he restated twice
early in 1855, shortly after becoming prime minister. With reference
to Scottish education, he declared his respect for the
religious commitments of the various denominations, but still
thought it 'very desirable' that children should not 'be brought up
in religious antagonism to each other'.[29] The current contests over
church rates seemed to him 'very prejudicial … to the general
interests of the country, and … to the interests of religion itself'.
He was not sure of the best solution, but thought it would be a blessing if arrangements could be made to repair places of worship

without giving rise to religious controversy.[30] When, however, Sir William Clay brought forward a Bill for the abolition of church rates, he opposed it on the grounds that it was not a satisfactory basis for the settling the question. In particular he thought a distinction needed to be made between rates for the support of worship, to which he thought conscientious objection was understandable and legitimate, and payment for the maintenance of church buildings, which he thought should continue, provided these were viewed 'not as emblems of sectarian division, but as national fabrics applicable to the Christian worship of God.'[31]

Two further illustrations can be noted of Palmerston's view that the avoidance of religious conflict was a worthwhile end in itself. Regarding Sabbath observance, he made no secret of his own view that recreational non-religious activities were harmless and were even to be encouraged. He therefore allowed bands to play in London parks on Sundays.[32] Nevertheless, when in May 1856 he received strong representations from Archbishop Sumner of Canterbury reporting widespread outrage from people who believed this 'a vital question as regards the national religion' he immediately decided to have the performances discontinued.[33] He did not consider they offered sufficiently great advantages 'to compensate for the evil of running counter to the religious feelings of a large body of the community'.[34] Moreover he was now prepared to face down the radical advocates of the musical performances.[35] Similarly, although personally supportive of a proposed religious profession clause in the 1861 Census, he consented to its withdrawal 'in deference to the great and respectable Body of the Dissenters', who had opposed its inclusion.[36]

Palmerston wanted to see the Church of England pastorally effective, but with a view to conciliating rather than antagonising the Nonconformists. At the beginning of his premiership, he was interested in increasing the number of dioceses. Such a project would have been a logical continuation of the policy begun with the creation of the see of Ripon in 1836 and of Manchester in 1847. It would also have reinforced the process of diocesan revival which,

as Arthur Burns has shown, was central to the recovery of the
Church during the nineteenth century.[37] Palmerston consulted particularly on a proposal to divide London, which would have used
Westminster Abbey as the cathedral for a new diocese to cover the
western half of the metropolis.[38] Ideas for dividing Durham were
also actively under consideration.[39] The first step, however, was
to secure legislation to allow the current bishops of Durham and
London, both incapacitated by chronic illness, to resign. The
government brought forward this measure at the end of the 1856
parliamentary session, apparently expecting that the bill would be
seen as an unproblematic technicality. However, while no-one
disputed the timeliness of the specific resignations, they were seen
as setting potentially far-reaching precedents. The provision of generous pensions for the former bishops raised critical questions about
the appropriate use of church funds. There was also concern that
the measure would place two of the greatest plums of ecclesiastical
patronage in Palmerston's hands. Hence there was extensive debate,
and several votes in both houses before the bill passed.[40]

Palmerston proceeded to appoint energetic successors,
A.C. Tait to London and C.T. Longley to Durham, while making
their elevations conditional on their acceptance of any subsequent
divisions of their sees.[41] Subsequently, however, Palmerston concluded that piecemeal measures were not desirable, and that a full-
scale reorganization of dioceses would require additional funds,
which should not be taken from the existing bishops, nor from the
current revenues of the Ecclesiastical Commission.[42] The circumstances though were unpropitious. Not only did the Liberation
Society's continuing campaign against church rates suggest there
would be likely to be a hostile reaction to attempts to secure more
resources for the Church of England, but the contentiousness of the
seemingly trivial Bishops of London and Durham Resignation Bill
showed how politically complex church reform could rapidly
become. Accordingly Palmerston appears to have tacitly concluded
that he did not want to risk stirring up a parliamentary hornets' nest
with more far-reaching reform. For him antagonising Dissenters in

order to secure church reform would have been wholly counter-productive. He preferred for the present at least to leave things as they were, rather than have Bishops on 'half Pay and full Duty'.[43] Nevertheless, the measure of consideration given to the idea during Palmerston's ministries helped to prepare the ground for the subsequent enlargement of the episcopate, with the creation during the 1870s and 1880s of the sees of Liverpool, Newcastle, St Albans, Southwell, Truro and Wakefield.[44]

III

Palmerston in the meantime had decided that the best and most realistic means of strengthening the church was by improving its leadership rather than by changing its structures. He noticed that the advent of an effective new bishop of London had neutralised pressure for immediate division of the diocese, and sought to achieve similarly successful results elsewhere.[45] His correspondence bears extensive testimony to the care that he took with senior ecclesiastical appointments. While he noted unsolicited recommendations, he was scrupulous in avoiding prior commitments, or, except very rarely, in using church patronage for political purposes.[46] He was, though, preoccupied with ensuring an approximate balance between Cambridge and Oxford men, although even here he was flexible when circumstances and individuals warranted.[47] He was thus genuinely concerned to secure the best men, his key criteria being evidence of energy and efficiency in organization and pastoral oversight, and an absence of the kind of arrogance and intolerance that was likely to alienate Nonconformists and others from the church.[48] It was this latter concern, rather than theological antipathy as such, that led him to rule out Samuel Wilberforce and other more assertive High Churchmen. The care he took with appointments was further indicated by his evident frustration and disappointment on the rare occasions when preferred candidates turned down offers, as when Charles Vaughan declined Rochester in 1860 and Tait York in 1862.[49]

Shaftesbury was undoubtedly his key advisor, but he was no puppet master. His role deserves rather to be seen as having significant elements of that of a modern patronage secretary, ready to suggest candidates from a variety of ecclesiastical backgrounds, particularly once he had satisfied his own immediate agenda through the elevation of a few leading Evangelicals. Although it was family connection rather than spiritual affinity that accounts for Palmerston first turning to Shaftesbury for advice, there was more common ground than might appear at first sight.[50] Shaftesbury was a substantial and experienced politician in his own right, and although his commitment to philanthropic and religious causes had caused him to sacrifice conventional ambition, it had given him a sound political judgement. His commitment to Evangelicalism did not render him uncritical of his co-religionists, and he had no interest in promoting appointments that would risk significant embarrassment to either the government or the Evangelical party. Palmerston, for his part, while he might find the dogmatic side of their theology perplexing, saw Evangelicals as energetic and conscientious, representative of the great majority of Anglican lay opinion and likely to be much more conciliatory towards Nonconformists than were the High Churchmen. After the publication of *Essays and Reviews* in 1860, Shaftesbury and Palmerston appear to have found further common cause in strengthening resistance to that pioneering work of liberal theology. Palmerston's anxiety to avoid men who might be contentious and unsettling innovators here converged with Shaftesbury's concern to safeguard conservative doctrine.[51]

In addition to Shaftesbury, Palmerston also consulted his step-son William Cowper (later Cowper-Temple), who was a more liberal political and theological influence.[52] The Broad Church Bishop Tait, himself Palmerston's most significant early non-Evangelical appointment, felt himself to be used by the Prime Minister as a sounding board to ensure that proposed appointments were acceptable to other groupings within the church.[53] Other members of the government also tried to exert influence, particularly in seeking to mitigate Palmerston's perceived hostility to High Churchmen.[54] Gladstone could be pressing with unsolicited advice, most notably in strongly urging Samuel Wilberforce's translation from Oxford to York in 1862.[55] He was unsuccessful on this occasion, but Palmerston had previously followed his advice in moving Longley from York to Canterbury, and was again to do so in appointing William Jacobson to Chester in 1865.[56]

The Queen also tried to influence appointments. In November 1856 she fired a warning shot across Palmerston's bows, when approving the nomination of Robert Bickersteth to Ripon. She hoped that this selection of a strong Evangelical would be balanced by future appointments from other church parties.[57] In December 1860, she expressed concern that future episcopal appointments should include 'University men of acknowledged standing and theological learning' rather than just 'respectable parish priests'.[58] Palmerston sent a robust response, arguing that bishops were analogous to generals of districts in the army, that their chief duty was to oversee the clergy, and that they should accordingly have practical parochial experience. Theological bishops risked provoking contention — like Phillpotts of Exeter or Wilberforce of Oxford — or being inefficient in practical matters — like Thirlwall of St David's. Nevertheless in relation to the then current nomination to Worcester he appears to have been responsive to royal pressure.[59] Despite initial thoughts of appointing Emilius Bayley,[60] Rector of St George Bloomsbury, the eventual selection was the much more obviously academic Henry Philpott, a former vice-chancellor of Cambridge, whose cause had probably been advocated by the Prince Consort.[61]

After Albert's death in December 1861, Victoria became more abrasive in making her views known, sometimes before Palmerston even had time to make a recommendation, as in the choice of A.P. Stanley as Dean of Westminster in 1863,[62] or by refusing to endorse Palmerston's nominations, as with the proposed appointment of Samuel Waldegrave to York in 1862.[63] A sharp clash occurred over the appointment of a Regius Professor of

Ecclesiastical History at Oxford, to succeed Stanley, on the latter's elevation to Westminster. Victoria, apparently advised by Stanley himself, wanted George Granville Bradley, the headmaster of Marlborough, a man very much in the same theologically liberal mould. Shaftesbury and Palmerston were both dead set against such an appointment, the former from concern about Bradley's theology and from hostility to Stanley in effect nominating his own successor; the latter because he was determined to resist 'backstairs influence'. According to Tait, who heard the story from Stanley, Palmerston 'kept on submitting name after name to the Queen — Farrar, Lake, Shirley, resolved only on one point that Bradley should not have it.' Walter Waddington Shirley was eventually appointed.[64] In April 1864 relations deteriorated further when the Queen, again allegedly instigated by Stanley, initially resisted Palmerston's nomination of Francis Jeune to be Bishop of Peterborough, proposing instead Augustus Sanders or William Jacobson.[65] Shaftesbury complained to Palmerston of her 'unconstitutional' behaviour and alluded to current hopes that she would abdicate, while Palmerston angrily reminded her that the constitutional responsibility of advising her in such matters lay with the First Lord of the Treasury.[66] Victoria gave way over Jeune, but was evidently furious at the tone of Palmerston's letter.[67] Attitudes remained frosty, with Palmerston complaining to the Queen of the role of her 'irresponsible advisors in such matters'.[68] She retorted by pointing out that he consulted others on appointments, and she did not see why she should not also do so.[69] Possibly, though, his last appointment, that of Jacobson to Chester in June 1865, was an attempt to appease her as well as Gladstone.

In the midst of this complex web of consultation and influence, there can be little doubt that Palmerston himself rather than Shaftesbury made the real decisions. Certainly Evangelicals predominated among his episcopal appointments, but he had his own reasons for preferring them, and they consistently repaid his confidence by showing themselves conscientious, effective and uncontroversial bishops. His need, which Shaftesbury fully appreciated, to manage the Queen, Parliament and his Cabinet were all a constraint on giving undue preference to Evangelicals. Some of the most senior appointments he made, Tait to London, Longley successively to Durham, York and Canterbury, and Trench to Dublin, were not Evangelicals. Among the second tier of appointments, to deaneries and canonries, Broad Churchmen and moderate High Churchmen were proportionately more numerous.[70] In such roles men who were better scholars than the activist Evangelicals could be most effectively deployed.

IV

During his tenure as Prime Minister Palmerston made nineteen appointments to English bishoprics, six to Irish sees, and thirteen to English deaneries. Twenty-six different individuals were involved.[71] It was an impressive yield of patronage, meaning that by 1865 roughly half of the bishoprics and English deaneries, including all six senior sees,[72] were held by Palmerston appointees. He was proud of his stewardship, writing to the Queen in April 1864, when she questioned his choice for Peterborough:

In a body among the ranks of which such diversities of theological opinion exist, as in the ranks of the Church of England, it is perfectly impossible that any choice for dignities can be made which shall be approved by all parties, but Viscount Palmerston has the satisfaction of knowing, by many communications made to him by wholly disinterested persons, and by persons of many different political parties, that his recommendations to your Majesty for ecclesiastical appointments have been generally approved; and it has been acknowledged by all that these recommendations have not been suggested by personal partialities, or what is vulgarly called the spirit of job, but have arisen from an earnest desire to promote the character and interests of the Church.[73]

There is no space here to attempt any systematic assessment of the record and achievements of the men Palmerston promoted, but the research of other scholars indicates that they were indeed effective administrators, and energetic pastors.[74] Nor were the Evangelical appointees inflexible militants. Even Robert Bickersteth of Ripon, although an uncompromising opponent of Roman Catholicism, was not vindictive towards the Anglican High Churchmen in his own diocese.[75] Other more extreme, but undeniably energetic and effective, Evangelical clergy, such as Hugh McNeile of Liverpool and Hugh Stowell of Salford, were left in their parishes. Moreover with the exception of Jacobson, who had been pressed on Palmerston by both Gladstone and the Queen perhaps against his own better judgement, they were notably conciliatory towards Dissent, thus alleviating hostility to the Church of England on the ground. This attitude is a significant one in the light of the considerable pressure for disestablishment, in England as well as Ireland, in the 1860s, 1870s and 1880s. A more confrontational episcopate might well have heightened the pressure on the Church, rather than eventually neutralising it. Rather in the Palmerston years one can see the foundations being laid for the late nineteenth-century *de facto* acceptance by many Nonconformists of the continuing national role of the Church of England. This was exactly what Palmerston himself had sought to achieve. Furthermore there was a diffuse but even more important manner in which Palmerston's legacy was important for the situation of the Church. For this 'most English minister'[76] the Church of England merited support and attention as a central focus of national identity and cohesion. In obituary tributes to him it was therefore surprisingly easy to link the patriotic and the religious, an association that was central to the enduring prominence in the late nineteenth and earlier twentieth centuries of Christianity in general and the Church of England in particular.[77] The Evangelical R.W. Dibdin preached a funeral sermon on the question *The Patriot Palmerston: Was He Saved?* and concluded with a tentative affirmative.[78] The Broad Church Dean Stanley saw his life as an inspiration to reconciliation 'of things old with things new, of things common with things sacred, of class with class, or man with man, of nation with nation, of church with church, of all with God.' This he affirmed 'is the high calling of England'.[79] Like Melbourne before him and Disraeli after him, Palmerston was an unlikely church reformer, but a very successful one.

References

A revised and expanded version of this article appears in *The English Historical Review* (2005). This chapter is published here by kind permission of the editors of *EHR* and of Oxford University Press.

[1] Shaftesbury was married to Lady Palmerston's daughter, Lady Emily ('Minny') Cowper, born during her first marriage to Earl Cowper, but almost certainly the natural child of Palmerston himself.

[2] Quoted in E. Hodder *The life and work of the seventh Earl of Shaftesbury, KG* (London: Cassell, 1887) ii, p. 505.

[3] Nigel Scotland *'Good and proper men': Lord Palmerston and the bench of bishops* (Cambridge: James Clarke and Co, 2000); Jasper Ridley *Lord Palmerston* (London: Constable, 1970) pp. 499-501.

[4] Tait papers, Lambeth Palace Library, vol. 75, fol. 213v.

[5] *Parliamentary Debates*, 2nd series, xviii, 778-81 (26 Feb 1828).

[6] *Ibid.*, xi, 358-60 (9 Apr 1824).

[7] *Parliamentary Debates*, 3rd series, xxii, 898-702 (26 Mar 1834). For the wider context of the religious attitudes and policies of the Whig governments of the 1830s see R. Brent *Liberal Anglican politics: Whiggery, religion and reform, 1830-1841* (Oxford: Oxford University Press, 1987). Brent, however, offers only passing references to Palmerston.

[8] *Hampshire Chronicle*, 3 Apr 1837.

[9] *Ibid.*; A.R. Ashwell *Life of the Rt. Rev. Samuel Wilberforce, DD* (London: John Murray, 1880) i, p. 107.

[10] *Parliamentary Debates*, 3rd series, lxx, 1067-70.

[11] *Ibid.*, lxxix, 1301-5.

[12] Evelyn Ashley *The life and correspondence of Henry John Temple Viscount Palmerston (*2 vols., London: Richard Bentley and Son, 1879) i, pp. 485-8.

[13] *Parliamentary Debates*, 3rd series, lxxx, 405-9.

[14] *Speech of Lord Viscount Palmerston ... to the electors of Tiverton, on the 31st July* 1847 (London: Smith, Elder and Co, 1847); Ashley, *Palmerston*, ii, pp. 44-54; Donald Southgate *'The most English minister...': the policies and politics of Palmerston* (London: Macmillan, 1966) p. 407; John Wolffe *The Protestant crusade in Great Britain, 1829-1860* (Oxford: Oxford University Press, 1991) pp. 232-7. Cf. Donal A. Kerr *'A nation of beggars'?: priests, people and politics in famine Ireland, 1846-1852* (Oxford: Oxford University Press, 1994).

[15] Ashley, *Palmerston*, ii, pp. 172-5.

[16] *Parliamentary Debates*, 3rd series, cxv, 182-7 (18 Mar 1851).

[17] Ridley, *Palmerston,* pp. 500-1; Scotland, *'Good and proper men'*, p. 25. Scotland follows Ridley, whose source is Lord Rendel's report of Gladstone's recollections of 1864, recorded thirty years later (F. E. Hamer (ed.) *The personal*

papers of Lord Rendel (London: Ernest Benn, 1931) p. 120). Rendel's text, however, reads 'Lord Palmerston was violently anti-Papal', which even if it records Gladstone's exact words, has in the context of the Italian and Irish situations in 1864, a very different and more specific connotation from the view that Palmerston was 'absurdly suspicious' of Roman Catholics in general, which Ridley wrongly attributes to Gladstone.

[18] Palmerston to Chichester Fortescue, 10 Sep 1864, BP, LB/1.

[19] *Parliamentary Debates*, 3rd series, cxxi, 579-82 (11 May 1852).

[20] Palmerston to Sir John Romilly and C.N. Newdegate, 6 Nov 1859, BL Add. Ms. 48581, fol. 59v.

[21] Palmerston to Romilly, 13 Jan 1861, BL Add. Ms 48582, fol. 37. For further extensive correspondence regarding Turnbull see BP, HA/L/4.

[22] Palmerston to Fortescue, 10 Sep 1864, BP, LB/1.

[23] Wm K. Tweedie and W.H. Gray to Palmerston, both 15 Nov 1853, TNA, HO 45/4548.

[24] Robert Buchanan *The waste places of great cities, or, the voice of God in the cholera. With remarks on the recent letter upon that subject of the Right Hon. Lord Palmerston* (Glasgow: Blackie and Son, 1853) pp. 5-6. The manuscript correspondence is in TNA, HO 45/4548, and shows that Palmerston drafted his reply himself. It was a symptom of changing evangelical attitudes to Palmerston that the writer of his obituary in *The Record* in 1865 attributed it to a 'flippant Under-Secretary' (*Record*, 20 Oct 1865).

[25] *The Record*, 31 Mar 1853; Buchanan, *Waste places*, p. 14.

[26] Quoted in Buchanan, *Waste places*, p. 13.

[27] Hodder, *Shaftesbury*, ii, p. 457.

[28] *Fraser's Magazine* 49 (1854) pp. 47-53. For the authorship of the article see F. Kingsley *Charles Kingsley: his letters and memories of his life* (London: H.S. King and Co., 1877) i, p. 414.

[29] *Parliamentary Debates*, 3rd series, cxxxvii, 1011 (23 Mar 1855).

[30] *Ibid.*, cxxxvii, 1367-8 (29 Mar 1855).

[31] *Ibid.*, cxxxviii, 686-90 (16 May 1855).

[32] *Ibid.,* cxl, 1113-5 (21 Feb 1856); Palmerston to Sumner, 10 May 1856, BP, GC/CA/319.

[33] Sumner to Palmerston, 10 May 1856, BP, GC/CA/315. Sumner's intervention was instigated by Shaftesbury, who also spoke directly to Palmerston (Hodder, *Shaftesbury*, iii, pp. 31-2).

[34] Palmerston to Sumner, 10 May 1856, BP, GC/CA/319.

[35] Palmerston to Sir Benjamin Hall, 24 May 1856, BL Add. Ms. 48,580.

[36] Memorandum by Palmerston, 8 Jun [sic, pencilled 'July?'] 1860, BP,CAB/132. Dissenters feared that the probable tendency for 'Church of England' to be the default response would lead to an exaggerated impression of Anglican strength.

[37] Arthur Burns *The diocesan revival in the Church of England c.1800-1870* (Oxford: Oxford University Press, 1999).

[38] Archbishop Sumner had in June 1853 sent Palmerston (then Home Secretary) a scheme for the division of the diocese of London (BP, CAB/312). On 15 December 1855 Palmerston wrote positively to the Archbishop about the proposal (BL Add. Ms. 48,579, fol. 89) and on 7 July 1856 he wrote to the Earl of Chichester, the First Church Commissioner 'I much wish to insert in that Bill [the Bishops of London and Durham Resignation Bill, shortly to be brought forward in the House of Lords] an actual division or power to divide London into two' (BL Add. Ms. 48,580, fol. 104).

[39] BP, HA/H/5 contains suggestions for appointments from Shaftesbury based on the assumption that both Durham and London were about to be divided.

[40] *Parliamentary Debates*, 3rd series, cxliii, 546-9, 814-42, 948-64, 1094-1102, 1171-2, 1266-73, 1276-1346, 1355-84, 1408-16, 1429-30, (10-25 Jul 1856).

[41] Palmerston to Tait, fol. 277, Palmerston to Longley, both 15 Sep 1856, BL Add. Ms., 48,589, fol. 138.

[42] Palmerston to Lord St Germans (who had written concerning a proposed division of the diocese of Exeter), 26 Jan 1861, BL Add. Ms., 48582, fol. 38.

[43] *Ibid*.

[44] Cf. Burns, *Diocesan revival*, pp. 197-205.

[45] Palmerston to Sir George Grey, 6 Jul 1863, BP, LB/1, pp. 99-100.

[46] For examples of Palmerston's responses to recommendations see BL Add. Mss. 48,579, fol. 16; 48,580, fol. 381; 48581, fol. 44. The only apparent instances of political calculation in appointments were Palmerston's offer of a living to the brother of George Denman, his fellow MP for Tiverton (BL Add. Ms. 48,582, fol. 51) and the elevation of William Jacobson to be bishop of Chester in the hope that it would assist Gladstone's campaign for re-election at Oxford (BL Add. Ms. 48, 583, fol. 9). While Henry Montagu Villiers (Carlisle and Durham) and Charles Thomas Baring (Gloucester and Bristol and Durham) were the brothers respectively of the Earl of Clarendon (Foreign Secretary 1853-8) and of Sir Francis Baring, a former Whig minister, there is no evidence that their selections were attributable to such connections. Indeed on Baring's appointment to Durham Palmerston wrote to Sir Francis affirming that his brother was indeed 'the Bishop most worthy of being so advanced.' (BL Add. Ms. 48,582, fol. 83).

[47] Palmerston to Lord Dudley, 11 Dec 1860, BL, Add. Ms. 48582, fol. 29. On this occasion, Palmerston appeared to be using the perceived need to balance appointments between Oxford and Cambridge as a convenient excuse for rejecting Dudley's recommendation for Worcester of Thomas Legh Claughton, an Oxford graduate, whom Shaftesbury had warned was 'of the very ultra school, and would be a most ready and effective supporter of the Bishop of Oxford on the Episcopal Bench' (Shaftesbury to Palmerston 9 Nov 1860, BP, GC/SH/42). The

fact that he was a Cambridge graduate seems to have been a significant factor in Robert Bickersteth's elevation to Ripon in 1856 (Hodder, *Shaftesbury*, iii, p. 198). In fact the balance of Oxford and Cambridge men was uneven: of the fourteen individuals he appointed to English sees nine were Oxford graduates and only five Cambridge men.

[48] Palmerston to Sir Charles Wood, 20 Nov 1856, BL Add. Ms. 48,580, fol. 154v. Palmerston's on-going concern about the socially and politically divisive potential of High Anglican pretensions was illustrated by his hostility to proposals to give clergy greater powers to scrutinise the spiritual credentials of potential godparents, and by his feeling that Convocation was in danger of becoming a 'nuisance' (Palmerston to Sir George Grey, 5 Mar 1865, BP, LB/1, pp. 285-6; Palmerston to Sir George Grey, 24 May 1865, BL Add. Ms. 45,583, fol. 6).

[49] Palmerston to Vaughan, 29 Feb 1860, BL Add. Ms. 48,581, fol. 71; Lambeth Palace Library, Tait Papers, vol. 80, fols. 127, 145, 159-60, 169-72. Palmerston initially offered York to Tait on 27 September; Tait responded in the negative on 5 October; Palmerston wrote by return (6 October) urging him to reconsider; Tait again refused on 8 October, although acknowledging the attractions of York as a post 'at once of greater dignity and less work' relative to London.

[50] Hodder, *Shaftesbury,* iii, pp. 196-7.

[51] Tait Papers, vol. 75, fols. 218-9.

[52] G.B.A.M. Finlayson *The seventh Earl of Shaftesbury* (London: Eyre Methuen, 1981) pp. 378-9. Like his sister Lady Shaftesbury, Cowper was almost certainly Palmerston's own natural child.

[53] Tait Papers, vol. 75, fols. 160-4. BL Add. Ms. 48,581, fol. 86, Palmerston to Sidney Herbert, undated memorandum. Tait noted that Palmerston ceased to consult him after the *Essays and Reviews* furore broke, he assumed because Broad Church influences then became more suspect.

[54] Palmerston to Sir Charles Wood, 20 Nov 1856, BL Add. Ms. 48,580, fol. 154; Palmerston to Herbert, 20 Jun 1860, Add. Ms. 48,581, fol. 86.

[55] Philip Guedalla *Gladstone and Palmerston* (London: Victor Gollancz, 1928) pp. 236-9.

[56] *Ibid.* pp. 231-2, 338-9.

[57] A.C. Benson and Viscount Esher (eds.) *The letters of Queen Victoria: a selection from Her Majesty's correspondence between the years 1837 and 1861* (3 vols., London: John Murray 1907) iii, p. 276.

[58] *Ibid.,* iii, p. 529.

[59] *Ibid.,* iii, pp. 530-1.

[60] Bayley, although an Evangelical, was not the preference of Shaftesbury, who had previously recommended William Broderick (Shaftesbury to Palmerston, 9 Nov 1860, BP, GC/SH/42).

[61] Tait papers, vol. 75, fol. 218.

[62] Tait papers, vol. 75, fol. 221.

[63] H. Kirk-Smith, *William Thomson Archbishop of York* (London: SPCK, 1958) p. 15. It was on this occasion that, already frustrated by Tait's refusal, an exasperated Palmerston reputedly handed the Queen a list of all the bishops and invited her to make her own choice for York (*ibid.*). This story appears implausible, even if the eventual choice of William Thomson was as much her preference as Palmerston's, although Palmerston himself had appointed him to Gloucester and Bristol in the previous year.

[64] BP, GC/SH/56-8, Shaftesbury to Palmerston, 15, 20, 22 Nov 1863; Tait papers, vol. 75, fol. 222.

[65] Sir Charles Phipps to Palmerston, 28 Apr 1864 in G.E. Buckle *The letters of Queen Victoria, second series: a selection from Her Majesty's correspondence and journal between the years 1862 and 1878* (3 vols., London: John Murray, 1926) i, p. 177.

[66] Shaftesbury to Palmerston, 29 Apr 1864, BP, GC/SH/64/1; Palmerston to the Queen, 29 April 1864, Buckle, *Letters of Queen Victoria*, i, pp. 178-9.

[67] The Queen to Palmerston, 2 May 1864, *ibid.* i, p. 179.

[68] Palmerston to the Queen, 5 Jul 1864, *ibid.* i, p. 236.

[69] The Queen to Palmerston, 7 Jul 1864, *ibid.* i, p. 239.

[70] See Shaftesbury's review of Palmerston's appointments, 18 Nov 1862, BP, GC/SH/50.

[71] Palmerston translated five bishops he had earlier appointed (Baring, Fitzgerald, Longley (twice), Thomson and Villiers), three deans (Ellicott, Jeune and Trench) were subsequently elevated to the episcopate, one dean (Garnier) was successively appointed to two different deaneries.

[72] Canterbury, York, Armagh, Dublin, London and Durham.

[73] Buckle, *Letters of Queen Victoria*, i, pp. 178-9.

[74] Scotland, '*Good and proper men*'; D.N. Hempton, 'Bickersteth, Bishop of Ripon' *Northern History* 17 (1981) pp. 183-202; A.F. Munden, 'The first Palmerston bishop: Henry Montagu Villiers, Bishop of Carlisle, 1856-60 and Bishop of Durham 1860-1861' *Northern History* 26 (1990) pp. 186-206.

[75] Hempton, 'Bickersteth', pp. 191-2, 195-6.

[76] *Daily Telegraph* obituary, quoted in Donald Southgate, '*Most English minister*', p. xxviii.

[77] For the wider context of this judgement see John Wolffe *God and Greater Britain: religion and British life, 1843-1945* (London: Routledge, 1994) and *Great deaths: grieving, religion and nationhood in Victorian and Edwardian Britain* (Oxford: Oxford University Press, 2000).

[78] R.W. Dibdin *The patriot Palmerston: was he saved ?* (London: James Nisbet and Co., 1865).

[79] A.P.Stanley *Sermons on special occasions* (London: John Murray, 1882) p. 126.

CHAPTER 3

Palmerston as Public Speaker
Joseph S. Meisel

Oratory is widely acknowledged to have been a crucial element in the careers of many of Britain's leading political figures, including the elder and younger Pitts, Gladstone and Disraeli, Lloyd George and Churchill, among the most notable. In Lord Palmerston's case, however, the general view is that he was not 'born to sway senates by the force or grace of … eloquence'.[1] Biographers mention his speech-making to a greater or lesser extent, but rarely consider its role in his career or connect it with broader trends in nineteenth-century British politics. Those who study political speeches have barely taken notice of Palmerston if they mention him at all.[2]

Speeches were central to Victorian public life.[3] In light of this, and of his importance in the history of Victorian politics, it is not necessary to claim a place for Palmerston in the front rank of British orator-statesmen in order to justify a more intensive inves-tigation of his speech-making. Studying this neglected aspect of Palmerston's career offers new perspectives on his reputation and achievements, with broader implications for understanding the structures of politics and the evolution of British political culture in the nineteenth century.

I

Young Harry Temple received some preparation for what would become a life of making speeches at all three of the institutions at which he was educated. At Harrow School, he performed in the school's public declamation exercises on at least three occasions.[4]

At the University of Edinburgh, he did not join the debating societies that were so prominent in the city's intellectual life, although his teacher, Dugald Stewart, was a member of the best known of these organizations, the Speculative Society. Instead, he participated in the 'debates' organized by Stewart for his students and children in which one participant would read a prepared essay and the others would respond. Palmerston read essays on five known occasions in 1800-1, but seems to have discontinued this activity during his remaining two years in Edinburgh.[5]

On going up to Cambridge in 1803, Palmerston joined a small collegiate essay club named the 'Speculative' after the Edinburgh society, but which he called the 'Fusty'. He is recorded as having read only five essays during his time at the University, but his correspondence clearly reveals his considerable enthusiasm for the club. Serious young man that he was, Palmerston liked the fact that all members (numbering as few as six) were required to respond to the essay and thus had to be properly prepared to speak. He became a dominant figure in, and possibly president of, the Fusty, and often hosted meetings in his rooms. At times, his letters show him anticipating the meetings with relish. At other points, however, he thought the Fusty 'rather drooping'.[6] Later, the club was absorbed into the Cambridge Union Society (founded in 1815), which, despite Palmerston's description of it as 'the enlarged Fusty',[7] ultimately offered a parliamentary model of debating.

Compared to the early years of some other prime ministers, Palmerston's youthful cultivation of his oratorical skills seems modest. Unlike the younger Pitt, a great orator of a father did not train him for a brilliant future as a parliamentary debater. Unlike Gladstone's and later generations, he was born too early to join the hothouses of youthful oratory that sprang up at both public schools and the universities in the early nineteenth century. And unlike Churchill, he did not dedicate himself, with the assistance of speech therapists, to building up his declamatory powers. Nothing about Palmerston's early life was the stuff out of which later oratorical legends could be made. Indeed, to the extent that Palmerston made youthful forays into public speaking, they were no more than what was typical for a serious-minded aristocratic youth of that time.

His studiousness notwithstanding, Palmerston was a young gentleman of wealth, position, and fashion. It was natural for him, like many an aristocratic scion, to enter Parliament (as his father and great-grandfather had before him), although *noblesse oblige* hardly promised an extensive and important future in public life. Certainly, he neither appears to have been eager to make his mark in parliamentary debates, nor, at the outset of his career, did he express confidence that he ever would. While it was not his intention 'to run mute always in the St Stephen's covers', he was concerned about 'the loss of character the Fusty may sustain' as a result of opening his 'potatoe trap'.[8] Of his maiden speech (February 3, 1808), Lady Holland recorded that it 'was not attended either with the bad or good qualities of a young beginner; he had practised in debating societies, and formed an unimpressive, bad manner.'[9] It would be another two years before the House heard from Palmerston again.

II

Palmerston came of age during what came to be viewed as the golden age of parliamentary speech, which reached its zenith with the political and oratorical rivalry between the younger Pitt and Charles James Fox. This was a time of highly charged debates over great issues in which the number of active speakers in Parliament was relatively small.[10] 'Any great affair', wrote Henry Lytton Bulwer, 'was debated in a great manner by the leading men'.[11] When offered the post of Chancellor of the Exchequer in 1809, Palmerston turned it down in part because he felt he did not measure up to the oratorical standards exemplified by Pitt and Fox.[12] By the end of Palmerston's life, the oratorical constitution of the House — like the constitution itself — had altered considerably and was in the process of further change. In his later years, Palmerston appreciated the changed character of debates. As he said in 1863, opposing a motion to limit the length of members' speeches:

There are more Members capable of speaking with credit to themselves and with advantage to the House than used to be the case in former times. Formerly, when a debate took place, it was merely a combat between two or three of the leaders on one side and two or three on the other, and the rest of the House were not expected to take any part in it; but now the House has an abundance of Members possessing great talent and knowledge and learning, who can give useful information on all matters that come under the consideration of Parliament, and though we may suffer from the length to which our debates are in consequence carried, yet that by no means ought to be considered an evil.[13]

Palmerston was not simply an observer of the changing patterns of parliamentary speech-making. To better understand his long career in the context of these broad changes, it is necessary to know more about his contributions to debates, his reputation as a speaker, and his style of speaking in the Commons.

III

The study of Palmerston's parliamentary speeches is facilitated by the annotated list compiled from *Hansard* by Michael and Karen Partridge.[14] The list records that, over his 58 years as an MP, Palmerston 'got on his legs' a total of 1,335 times, an average of 23 utterances per year. Following a gradual rising trend through the early 1850s, as Figure 3.1 shows, Palmerston's annual output of speeches increased substantially beginning with his tenure of the Home Office and even more so after assuming the premiership. Between 1807 and 1852, Palmerston made an average of 12 parliamentary utterances per year. Between 1853 and 1864, the average increased more than five-fold to 64. Palmerston held government office for 48 years, or 83 percent of his parliamentary career. In almost exact correspondence, he delivered 84 percent (1,125) of his speeches while in office.

Palmerston's speeches in the House of Commons

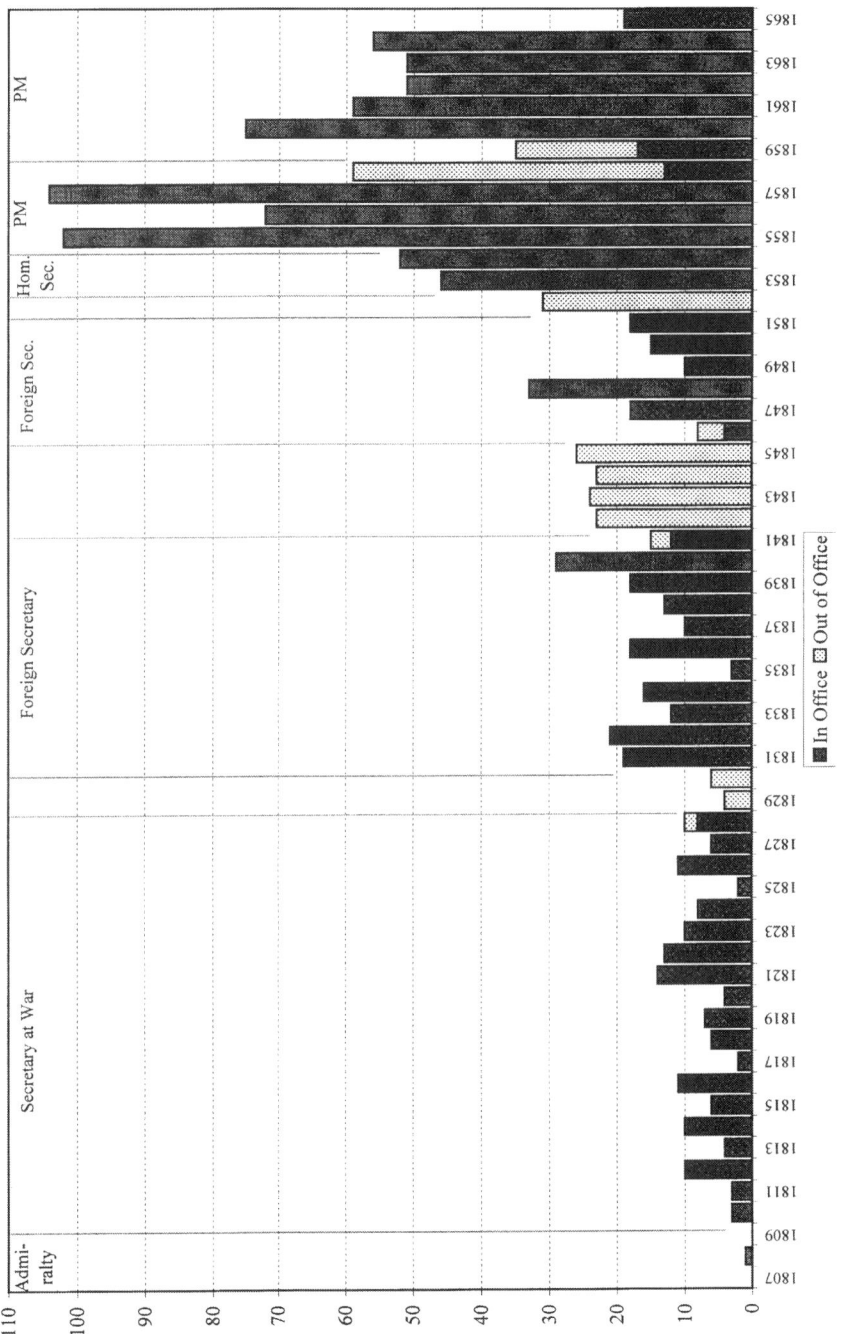

Source: Data assembled from M.S. Partridge and K.E. Partridge *Lord Palmerston, 1784-1865: a bibliography* (Westport, Conn.: Greewood Press, 1994)

The Partridges' list also includes the *Hansard* columns on which Palmerston's utterances begin and end, from which it is possible to calculate the approximate length of each speech (rounded on either side to the nearest whole column). Overall, his parliamentary speeches averaged 4.1 columns. In office, when he was obliged to make numerous brief responses to questions or other kinds of short interjections on matters relating to his department, his speeches averaged 3.8 columns. Out of office, he was at greater leisure to speak on the subjects he chose (often defending his record), which naturally led to a preponderance of more substantial statements averaging 5.8 columns. The relative brevity of his speeches in office may also indicate that Palmerston sought to say only as much as was necessary on a given subject, thereby giving his opponents as little material as possible to use against him while also leaving himself greater room for later manoeuvre. At least 148 (11 percent) of Palmerston's Commons speeches are no greater than one column in length; 141 of these were delivered while in office.[15]

Dividing Palmerston's parliamentary speeches into broad subject categories, the largest group deals with foreign affairs and war (39 percent), including statements relating to diplomacy, events overseas, and active military conflicts. Nearly as numerous are speeches on domestic and general subjects (36 percent), including 31 statements on the address (which cover a range of domestic, foreign, and imperial subjects). The next largest category consists of speeches on defence matters (18 percent), including 104 statements on the army estimates. Last are speeches dealing with the Empire and Ireland (7 percent). The distribution and timing of these subjects correspond to the three major blocks of his career. While Secretary at War, he focused on military questions and otherwise voiced his support for government measures. As Foreign Secretary, his speeches dealt overwhelmingly with foreign affairs. As Prime Minister, he spoke on domestic, foreign affairs, and defence matters, with a spike in imperial speeches in the 1850s prompted by the Indian revolt and the subsequent legislation for the government of India.

Toward the end of his life, Gladstone observed that 'my profession has been that of politicians, or more strictly ministers of state, an extremely short-lived race, when their scene of action has been in the House of Commons: Lord Palmerston being the only complete exception.'[16] Palmerston's 58 years in Parliament fall just short of Gladstone's 61. Among later Prime Ministers who spent their entire career in the Commons, only Winston Churchill, with 62 years, can be placed alongside the two nineteenth-century titans. Because of the great differences among the most readily available data sources, and because of the evolving nature of *Hansard* reports — from incomplete summaries, to fuller but still incomplete texts, to verbatim reports — comparisons of oratorical productivity can only be taken so far. Nevertheless, the figures are suggestive.[17] Gladstone delivered no fewer than 1,796 Commons speeches — 35 percent more than Palmerston. But Palmerston appears to have outspoken Churchill, whose eight-volume 'complete' speeches contains 1,040 parliamentary utterances. Palmerston's average of 23 utterances per year falls well behind Gladstone's average of 30, but is ahead of Churchill's 19.

The difference between Palmerston's speech-making in the Commons and Gladstone's is even greater when measured by *Hansard* columns. Gladstone's parliamentary utterances occupy some 15,000 columns. Palmerston produced at the outside 5,458 columns, or approximately one-third the amount for Gladstone. Gladstone delivered 17 speeches taking up 40 or more columns, including four speeches at least 60 columns long. Churchill produced five speeches of at least 40 columns, but the longest of these were 42 columns. Palmerston, by comparison, delivered only three speeches longer than 40 columns: the 1850 Don Pacifico speech (65 columns); a refutation in 1848 of charges that he was working in the Russian interest (58 columns); and a denunciation of the 1843 Webster-Ashburton treaty (57 columns). At the other end of the scale, 42 percent of Palmerston's parliamentary speeches are two columns or fewer, close to double the corresponding figure of 23 percent for Gladstone. Churchill's *Complete Speeches* does not provide *Hansard* column references, but 85 percent of the 1,040 parliamentary utterances reproduced in those volumes are two pages or fewer in length.

Although all three had parliamentary careers of around 60 years, Gladstone and Churchill held government office for less than 60 percent of the time that Palmerston did (the equivalent of 28 and 29 years, respectively). The changing oratorical demands of office-holding from the early nineteenth century to the mid-twentieth can be observed by comparing their time in office to speeches made while in office. As already noted, Palmerston held office for 83 percent of his career and delivered 84 percent of his speeches while holding office. Gladstone spent 46 percent of his parliamentary career, but made 65 percent of his speeches, in office. The corresponding figures for Churchill are similar: 47 percent and 61 percent.

While analyzing the quantitative record of Palmerston's parliamentary speeches and comparing it to those of other figures is revealing, these data need to be understood in the context of how contemporaries rated Palmerston as a parliamentary speaker and evaluated the qualities of his speech-making.

IV

Although Palmerston became Secretary at War shortly after entering Parliament and held that brief for 18 years under five successive Prime Ministers, he emerged only later as a major figure in politics. Earl Russell quipped in 1863 that 'Mr Pitt matured at *24* & Lord Palmerston at *74*.'[18] Several years later, Francis Galton noted that the late premier was 'singularly slow in showing his great powers ... He was fully 45 years old before his statesmanlike powers were clearly displayed.'[19] Palmerston's reputation as a speaker follows a similar pattern. According to a parliamentary colleague, before he became Foreign Secretary 'I do not recollect an occasion of his opening his lips on any except the ordinary business of his office'.[20] Even by 1835, wrote another observer, he was 'by no means active in defence either of his principles or his friends. Scarcely anything calls him up except a regular attack on himself, or on the way in which the department of the public service with which he is entrusted, is administered.'[21]

A decade later, assessments were quite different. By 1846, a few months before Palmerston would become Foreign Secretary for the third time, it could be said that, after many years 'as a speaker ranked with the steady-paced humdrums', he suddenly 'astonished his contemporaries by the display of vigour which neither his youth nor middle age had shewn; he entered the lists alike with the veterans and the young, ardent spirits of the House of Commons, proving himself a very master of the art which he had thus with so tardy a haste essayed, and raising himself to a level with the very best speakers.'[22] Palmerston's emergence as a notable parliamentary speaker was seen to have commenced with his passionate speech in March 1829 supporting Catholic Emancipation.[23] Sir Horace Twiss, considered to be one of the best orators then in the Commons, thought it 'one of the ablest [speeches] ever delivered upon that or upon any question', and told Palmerston he had been 'doing a great injustice to yourself & to the country, by keeping your parliamentary talents so much in the shade'.[24]

Although not the period in which he produced the greatest number of speeches, the years between 1829 and 1851 — during most of which he was Foreign Secretary — were oratorically fertile in other ways. He produced not only his longest speeches, but also some of his most ringing, including the famous 1848 declaration that 'We have no eternal allies, and we have no perpetual enemies. Our interests are eternal and perpetual, and those interests it is our duty to follow.'[25] The enduring high point of Palmerston's speaking career, however, was his five-hour 'Civis Romanus sum' speech of 1850 defending his gunboat diplomacy in Greece. It has been said that, 'Like so many parliamentary orators before him,

Palmerston used a resounding classical analogy to get himself out of trouble.'[26] But the Latin tag, like his peroration of two years before, adorned a mammoth effort of parliamentary persuasion and political self-defence. Lord Stanley (later fifteenth Earl of Derby) recorded that it was a speech of 'extraordinary talent and power'; 'in style and arrangement it appeared absolutely faultless: no other man in the Commons could have made it.'[27] Indeed, this great debate seems to have returned the Commons for a brief moment to the golden age. As Stanley noted, 'this great struggle has raised the reputation of the House for talent, a reputation of late years somewhat diminished. Scarcely any of the rank and file spoke: all was left to the leaders: and they had prepared themselves with unusual care.'[28] Viewed in the broader context of Palmerston's oratorical reputation, however, the Don Pacifico speech, like the Catholic Emancipation and 'eternal allies' speeches earlier, was an exception that proves the rule. Contemporary commentators are in general agreement that his overall success as a speaker owed far more to the manner than the matter. Even if the mid-nineteenth century was not regarded as a golden age of parliamentary eloquence, successful speech-making in the House was crucial in political life — especially for the leadership. Success was not, however, necessarily synonymous with great oratory. Since Palmerston was not regarded as a great orator, it is necessary to understand how his manner of speech contributed to his notable political achievements.

V

Contemporaries thought Palmerston's speaking voice strong, but also lacking in tone. According to an account from 1835, 'he often stutters and stammers to a very unpleasant extent, and makes altogether an indifferent exhibition. His voice is clear and strong, but has a degree of harshness about it which makes it grate on the ear.'[29] A decade later, another writer described 'the peculiar intonation of his voice, which has a hollow and fluty sound.'[30] After meeting Palmerston in 1862, Henry Adams noted his 'singular, mechanical, wooden' laugh.[31]

As a parliamentary speaker, Palmerston was generally regarded as effective, rather than eloquent. Disraeli, after witnessing a 'triumphant speech', observed that 'Palmerston said nothing, as usual, rich or rare; but there was noise, gaiety, health'.[32] Evelyn Ashley indirectly contrasted his step-father's abilities with those of Gladstone and Disraeli: 'As a public speaker, Lord Palmerston's success was very great, and surely results are good tests in the art of persuasion. He certainly never aspired to the lofty rank of a great orator nor to the magic wand of a great master of phrases; but in the power of conveying abundant knowledge in an apt, logical, and convincing form, he yielded the palm to none.'[33] According to the radical *Morning Star*, Palmerston 'was not an orator in any critical sense of the word. He never made the slightest attempt to rival such men as Pitt and Fox, as Gladstone and Bright, in eloquence. But few men were ever more successful in effecting, by means of public speaking, the objects at which they aimed.'[34]

Descriptions of Palmerston in the Commons emphasise his skills in the cut and thrust of debate. At least one observer was willing to assert that he was 'perhaps the best debater among the Whig leaders of the House of Commons'.[35] John Bowring recalled Palmerston's 'singular felicity for either warding off or replying to attacks and questionings in the House of Commons'.[36] The American historian and diplomat John Lothrop Motley wrote of his:

rattling, vigorous, juvenile, slashing speeches which ring through the civilised world as soon as uttered. I told him that it seemed to me very difficult to comprehend how any man could make those ready impromptu harangues in answer always to things said in the course of the debate, taking up all the adversary's points in his target, and dealing blows in return, without hesitation or embarrassment. He said very quietly that was all a matter of habit; and I suppose that he really does it with as much ease as he eats his breakfast.[37]

Connoisseurs of parliamentary oratory, however, tended to

view skill in debate as a secondary accomplishment next to the kind of true eloquence that gives speeches enduring value. MPs from the legal profession, for example, were often regarded as good debaters, but almost never as great orators.[38] This was connected to a more general Victorian anxiety over barristers' ability to persuade without necessarily believing in the cause they advocated.[39] Some likened Palmerston's debating style to that of lawyers. Ashley, as already noted, stressed Palmerston's powers of persuasion — successful advocacy — as the true test of effective speech-making. George Henry Francis, author of numerous articles on both political and legal oratory, described Palmerston's speaking abilities using legal terminology, and made comparisons with Lord Chancellor Lyndhurst.[40] He wrote of Palmerston as he would of a leading counsel: 'gladiator-like, he inquires little whether the cause he fights in be the cause of truth, being only anxious to shew his own skill and overcome his rival'.[41]

Like his debating skills, Palmerston's use of humour is a recurring theme in accounts of his speech-making. As recorded by Sir John Trelawny: 'P. spoke in his usual manner … boasting, bantering, jesting.' 'He was very sparkling & facetious — creating amazing merriment.' 'Cheers & laughter followed almost every sentence.'[42] All this humorousness had a serious purpose, however, by enabling Palmerston to beguile his parliamentary audiences, to deflect attacks, and to ridicule his opponents without engaging in 'personalities'. Ashley described 'the jocular hits in which Lord Palmerston so commonly delighted', and how, 'When argument failed, he employed broad, rough English satire.'[43] According to Francis, Palmerston:

possesses himself considerable power of ridicule; and when he finds the argument of an opponent either unanswerable, or that it could only be answered by alliance with some principle that might be turned against himself, he is a great adept at getting rid of it by a side-wind of absurd allusion. He knows exactly what will win a cheer and what ought to be avoided as calculated to provoke laughter in an assembly where appreciation of what is elevated in sentiment is by no means common.[44]

Of Palmerston's parliamentary style, Anthony Trollope wrote that he 'was brought up in that school of politicians in which a man uses his power of speech, or used to use it, not as a woman uses her teeth, for ornament, but as a dog does, for attack and defence.'[45] His debating skills combined with his good-natured manner, as Jonathan Parry has written, 'disguised reversals of position, ignorance of detail and occasional outright lies' and enabled him to absorb no fewer than 112 parliamentary defeats whilst Prime Minister with a minimum of damage.[46] In these ways, his abilities as a speaker played an important role in sustaining him in office for so much of his career.

Palmerston's work as a politician and a public speaker was hardly confined to the Commons chamber. A crucial factor in his later career was that, on the occasions when his charm and skill proved insufficient in the House, he was able to draw strength from popular support. This support was cultivated, in part, through extra-parliamentary speeches, which no account of Palmerston's oratorical record can overlook.

VI

Historians have discussed the extent to which Palmerston was influenced by Canning's political legacy. With respect to speech-making, Canning was described as the last of the 'golden age' orators. Some of Palmerston's early 'big' speeches in Parliament emulated his style, but Canning's legacy may have had a far more significant influence later on as an early example of a leading minister who promoted his policies through speeches to popular audiences.[47] Speeches 'out of doors' come in two major forms: those made on the hustings at elections, and those made on non-electoral occasions or outside one's constituency. Palmerston's experience with both reveals much, not only about his own career, but also about the evolving relationship between politics and political communication in nineteenth-century Britain.

On the hustings, as in Parliament, Palmerston was some-thing of an oratorical late bloomer. The reasons why, however, were quite different. In the Commons, speeches were not the means by which Palmerston chose to make his reputation. With respect to the hustings, however, circumstances rather than choice required little in the way of electoral speech-making for the first half of his career. His first seat, Newport, Isle of Wight, was purchased for him in 1807 following an agreement with the proprietor that he 'should never set foot in the place'.[48] From 1811 to 1831, Palmerston represented Cambridge University, where tradition dictated that candidates state their positions only in writing. Thus, like obtaining the representation of a borough through purchase, sitting for a university constituency required friends and funds, but not speeches.

Rejected by the University for his support of Reform, Palmerston purchased a seat for Bletchingley, Surrey, which he held for a year until the constituency was eliminated. For the election of December 1832, he accepted the offer to stand for South Hampshire but informed his supporters that the pressures of office would pre-vent him from campaigning in person to any great extent. By his own account, Palmerston did not canvass a single vote.[49] During the polling, he made a 'quiet and unprovoking speech' at nomina-tion and six more relatively insubstantial market-place speeches.[50] Palmerston lost his seat in the general election of 1834 and was out of Parliament until July 1835, when he was elected for Tiverton — his constituency for the remaining 30 years of his life. His candi-dacy was unopposed and the election was 'a very quiet affair'.[51] In sum, therefore, Palmerston had at best a minimal engagement with the electoral hustings for the first three decades of his public career.

Only beginning with the general election of 1837 was Palmerston obliged to become a regular hustings speaker. By that time, he had established himself as an assured and vigorous speaker in the Commons, and brought these qualities to the electors of Tiverton. In a summary of his 1837 address titled 'Palmerston's Soft Soap', he is described as delivering a 'harangue of considerable length and vivacity' that touched on a great many topics. Appealing to the recently enfranchised electors of the borough, he hammered away on the benefits of Whig reforms which the Tories would have withheld and, with a deftly humorous popular touch, discoursed upon how the sheep of Old Sarum — the quintessential rotten borough — would have enjoyed greater rights than the people of Tiverton.[52]

Although he got a late start in speaking to 'the people', as MP for Tiverton Palmerston readily grasped the importance of 'homely' local appeals to the expanding electorate. The ageing Lord Cupid 'seldom failed to pay some compliment to the ladies among his audience'.[53] His common touch also extended to other natural features of the locality. In 1849, for example, he told his con-stituents: 'With regard to the re-imposition of import duties on corn for the purpose of protection ... I venture, with all humility, to say, that when you see the River Exe running up from the sea to Tiver-ton, instead of running down from Tiverton to the sea, you may then look upon it that protection is near at hand.'[54]

Electoral soft soap notwithstanding, the Tiverton hustings also provided Palmerston with the opportunity to say things he thought he should not in Parliament. Indeed, hustings speeches could be vehicles of the autonomy with which he sought to conduct foreign policy. In the general election of 1841, for example, he deliberately used his speech to the electorate to comment upon the French army's harsh treatment of Algerians. As he wrote to Lytton Bulwer:

I felt that the English Government could not with propriety say anything on the subject to the Government of France. For a like reason I could not in my place in Parliament advert to it; but I thought that when I was standing *as an individual* on the hustings before my constituents, I might use the liberty of speech belong-ing to the occasion in order to draw public attention to proceedings which I think it would be for the honor of France to put an end to ...[55]

Palmerston's evident belief that statements made by a prominent ex-minister during an election were wholly independent from his party or a prospective government of which he might be part indicates that the extra-parliamentary platform was not yet the major extension of national and party politics it would later become.

On the hustings as in Parliament, Palmerston was always ready to defend his own conduct and policies, and to use his debating skills to undermine his opponents' position. When, in 1847, the Chartist candidate George Julian Harney added to his critique of Palmerston's conduct in office the accusation of manipulating the parliamentary machinery, 'it roused Lord Palmerston's wrath. Hence he set himself the task of replying with unwonted vigor, speaking for upwards of an hour on the foreign and domestic policy of the government, and winding up with an attack on the Charter in all its "points."'[56] Palmerston's ability to persuade on this occasion may be questioned. Harney was favoured by a show of hands, but withdrew from the contest before the official ballot.

Typically, however, Palmerston's hustings performances, even more than his parliamentary speeches, were distinguished by a 'jovial and rollicking' style and 'good humoured cleverness.'[57] Even Harney, who endured Palmerston's verbal cannonade in 1847, would later describe his erstwhile opponent as 'dowered with the gifts of witty repartee and keen, but never ill-natured, sarcasm; [and] … an air of easy nonchalance and winning bonhomie.'[58] When Palmerston's ire was aroused, he still replied to attacks from his opponents on the hustings, as one witness recorded, 'with perfect good temper, causing roars of laughter from his audience.'[59] And, as Trollope observed, 'he could answer a rowdy at the hustings with rough, easy fun, in a manner that, with such an audience, was found to be successful.'[60] These qualities, too, sustained his personal popularity in Tiverton, and beyond.

VII

Palmerston's sensitivity to public opinion was well recognized in his time. His discovery of the platform, like his earlier cultivation of the press (discussed below), served both to bolster and to communicate his personal popularity. As Muriel Chamberlain has observed, this development took hold following the Continental upheavals of 1848-9: 'suddenly he found that he had tapped an unexpected vein of popularity at home by speaking forcefully even when he could not act forcefully.'[61] Even other, ostensibly non-political occasional or ceremonial speeches (at the Lord Mayor's banquet, for example) provided opportunities to project and enhance his public persona.

Palmerston was first and foremost a man of the House (especially since he held office for so much of his career), and the practice of Cabinet ministers making political speeches in public without necessarily being prompted by a general election became a fixture in British politics only after his passing.[62] But, as Colin Mathew has written, 'Palmerston, following his mentor Canning, was an unsung pioneer' of these developments.[63] That his activities as a platform speaker have been overlooked until recently must be attributed, at least in part, to the fact that oratorical power has hardly figured in his wider reputation.[64] That reputation is also based to a very large extent on his years as Foreign Secretary, and his greatest extra-parliamentary speaking efforts came afterwards.

In the 1860s, Gladstone emerged as the 'People's William' following speaking tours in the industrial north. His appearances in Tyneside (1862) and Lancashire (1864) foreshadow the barnstorming Midlothian campaigns of 1879 and 1880, which are widely regarded as ushering in a new era of mass politics. Around the same time, John Bright, the 'Tribune of the People', returned to the platform, on which he had gained fame in the struggle to repeal the corn laws, to press the case for a new measure of reform at a succession of large meetings in great urban centres.[65] As Antony Taylor has stated, however, 'Gladstone and Bright did not invent the popular Liberal rally of the 1860s. Palmerston was a consummate platform performer and addressed a large number of public meetings in the period 1850-65.'[66]

Palmerston's platform activities took a number of forms and were directed at different immediate objectives, but the larger purpose was always to maintain his position of power. On occasion, he thought it prudent to explain his actions to his constituents. In 1838, for example, he went before the people of Tiverton to explain why he had voted against the abolition of Negro apprenticeship, despite the fact that he had received a petition supporting abolition signed by more than 1,500 of the borough's inhabitants. In no fewer than fourteen speeches to different gatherings, his explanation — that the government, of which he was part, had to honour an earlier compromise between abolitionists and slave owners — appears to have appeased his critics. [67] Similarly, he went before the people of Tiverton in 1858 to defend his administration's conduct in sheltering the fugitive would-be assassins of Napoleon III.[68]

As an embattled Foreign Secretary, and particularly following his enforced move to the Home Office at the end of 1852, Palmerston intensified his extra-parliamentary efforts to cultivate a popular following. He spoke at labourers' meetings, and also started receiving deputations of Radicals, Chartists, and working men. Contemporaries like Lord John Russell also sought to reach out to a wider public, but lacked the common touch.[69] Palmerston, however, distinguished himself by the courtesy with which he received deputations, and his jocularity in entertaining them. Yet, while charming and flattering these groups, he was careful to keep himself at a distance from their causes. In 1851, for example, he received an address in support of Kossuth, the Hungarian patriot leader, from a deputation of radicals. He complimented them on their efforts, but stressed that as a member of Her Majesty's government he could not be expected to concede in every point.[70]

According to Trollope, it was around this time, the early

1850s, that Palmerston 'became a notorious joker. He passed on from the light, courteous *persiflage* of the Foreign Minister to the common John-Bull fun of an English magistrate, without an apparent effort…. and when the world of deputations has been made to laugh, much has been achieved.'[71] On another level, as Taylor states, Palmerston's jocular banter helped him avoid discussion of the issues on which deputations sought to press him: 'He stonewalled, chatted of irrelevancies, dissembled, and sent them away with nothing but still managed to seduce them.'[72]

Palmerston's most significant extra-parliamentary speaking efforts took place after he attained the premiership. In November 1856, he made speeches in Salford, Manchester, and Liverpool on patriotic themes. His opponents expressed their disapproval of these appearances, not least because of their success. Richard Cobden, for one, wrote of Palmerston's 'imposture' at appropriating this technique of popular protest. When the Prime Minister spoke at the newly rebuilt Manchester Free Trade Hall, he complained to Bright about Palmerston's 'glorification' in a venue where the two heroes of the free trade movement had yet to appear.[73]

In the early 1860s, Palmerston returned repeatedly to the North to speak at large public meetings in Leeds (1860), Sheffield (1862), and Glasgow (1863). Closer to home, he also made speeches at the Mansion House (1864), Lambeth (1865), and on numerous occasions in Romsey. Of the Glasgow trip, Trelawny wrote, 'Palmerston's holiday is to be spent in making speeches at dinners in Scotland. Fine old fellow ! What a slave to his duty !'[74] Lord Clarendon marvelled at the spectacle of a man Palmerston's age journeying 400 miles to make ten speeches 'when most men at my period of life wd. prefer to walk the distance *not* to make such speeches.'[75]

Colin Matthew characterizes Gladstone's speaking tours of the 1860s as 'celebrations of achievements, not campaigns for a better future',[76] which could also describe Palmerston's own 'stumping'. Indeed, as historians increasingly recognise, Gladstone's performances of the 1860s were in some senses part of a Liberal double act, with Palmerston's own speech events topping the bill.[77] It was, however, hardly a co-ordinated or harmonious double act. The Prime Minister and his Chancellor of the Exchequer held opposite views on two major policy questions, Reform and military expenditure. Understandably, Palmerston wanted Gladstone to avoid making public statements that strayed from the official line, or that would get the people stirred up. Before Gladstone departed for the north in 1862, Palmerston asked that he 'not be too sympathising with the Tax Payer, nor tell the Country that they are paying too much Taxation, have too large [military and naval] Establishments, and ought to agitate to bring the House of Commons and the Government to more Economical ways & Habits. Those Topics suit best Cobden & Bright and their Followers.'[78] In 1864, he was even more blunt: 'it is undesirable that a Member of the Government ... should Endeavour to excite Agitation out of Doors for the Purpose of forcing upon the Government, Measures which the Parliament may not be disposed to adopt, & which the Government upon a review of the State of Things, may not think it advisable to propose.'[79]

Reflecting the sources of his popularity, Palmerston's public appearances were typically characterized by patriotic display. When Palmerston spoke at Glasgow in 1863, Sir Denis Le Marchant was amused by his 'ovation in the North', but expected that the speeches would be forgotten before long.[80] And as Lord Clarendon wrote a month later, the Glasgow speeches gave Palmerston

a fresh success & will I think make him politically stronger as no one will wish to disturb such a 'fine old English Gentleman'. For a man who has not thought on such matters I must say that his speech to the university was an unremarkable performance as respects both the selection of subjects & their arrangement. It must have required thought & when cd. he find time to think.[81]

Addressing mass audiences was an extraordinary (if not unprecedented) activity for a sitting Prime Minister. As these comments show, although experienced politicians might smirk at the content of the speeches, they recognized the phenomenon Palmerston was creating through his appearances. By demonstrating that public opinion was with him, Palmerston's appearances helped him maintain his base of support in Parliament.[82] Indeed, some viewed Palmerston's platform speeches as bypassing Parliament, not merely to promote his policies, but also to suggest a more direct connection between the premier and the public.[83] More broadly, it has been argued, the new political style he embraced and the emphasis he gave in his speeches to collaboration among the classes helped to reduce public and parliamentary pressure for a new measure of reform.[84]

If Palmerston's aim was to identify himself with patriotism (and vice versa) while setting aside questions of domestic reform, it is ironic that his approach was based on adapting 'the formula of local flattery and homilies to civic pride' from the radical orators of the early nineteenth-century's mass protest movements.[85] In adapting the form of the radical mass meeting as a means of keeping public opinion with him and solidifying his position, Palmerston pointed the way to the future of British political culture and to the greater democratization achieved after his death.

VIII

The history of the extra-parliamentary platform is closely connected with the history of the political press. As is well known, Palmerston was a careful and skilful cultivator of relationships with the press through providing special access and privileged information. In turn, favourable coverage in the newspapers helped shore up and extend his base of popular support and withstand often intense opposition in Parliament and from the Crown. According to David Steele, Palmerston's extra-parliamentary speaking when Prime Minister was 'a development of the tendency, strongly marked in his case before the premiership, to address a larger audience through the newspapers.'[86] But the connection between his platform and press activities operated on an even deeper level.

Palmerston's press relationships — a major part of his efforts to ride, and at times to steer, the tiger of public opinion — date back at least as far as the 1830s to the beginning of his close association with the *Morning Chronicle*. By the time he was Prime Minister, his influence extended across a broad swath of major papers representing many shades of opinion.[87] Most discussions of Palmerston and the press focus on his relationships with editors and proprietors, which are crucial for understanding the general promotion of his policies and influence. Examining Palmerston's extra-parliamentary speaking reveals that his cultivation of the press was hardly limited to the men at the top.

As Britain entered the era of mass democracy, the expanding number and circulation of newspapers (spurred by Gladstone's rescinding the 'taxes on knowledge' beginning in 1853) was fuelled by speech-making.[88] The emerging practice of leading politicians making extra-parliamentary speeches was an important part of these developments. Such events were regularly attended by reporters — sometimes dozens of them — who recorded the speeches in shorthand. Long before it would become a routine feature of late-Victorian politics, Palmerston understood well the connection between speech-making and what we today call the 'news cycle', and he took special care to win over the corps of reporters that covered his platform speeches.

When reporters from London appealed to him because they would be unable to get a report of his speech into the next morning's papers, he sought to change the schedule of events in order to accommodate their deadlines. If arrangements could not be altered, he provided reporters with an outline of what he intended to say. As one newspaperman recalled, 'It was not to be wondered at that Lord Palmerston should have been a very special favourite with the reporters — for no man was ever more courteous or kind to them than he was.'[89] Even when schedules did not have to be altered,

Palmerston was mindful of press deadlines. During one of his Tiverton re-election campaigns, for example, he was careful to limit the length of his speech from the window of the old Town Hall to exactly twenty minutes ('to a tick') so that the reporters seated in a wagon beneath the window could 'get away with their copy by an early train, so as to have the speech inserted on the following morning'.[90]

The courtesies Palmerston showed to the gentlemen of the press may have helped ease the burdens of their professional lives, and likely further increased his personal popularity among reporters. 'The reporters of all papers, without reference to the point as to whether the paper they represented were favourable or opposed to his Government, vied with each other in their anxiety to pay every attention to whatever he said.'[91] Since the editors and proprietors of the papers for which the reporters worked had already determined their papers' stances for or against him, Palmerston's attentiveness to reporters served an even more important political purpose by ensuring that his words would reach a wider public without delay.

IX

On one level, examining Palmerston's speech-making in detail tends to vindicate those who have given little consideration to this aspect of his career. He was neither specially endowed by nature, nor expressly trained in youth for oratory. His early ambivalence toward speaking carried through a substantial portion of his public life. In Parliament, the number of his annual contributions to debates remained relatively small until he was nearly 70 years old. Outside Parliament, the character of the constituencies he represented for the first half of his career required only minimal oratorical exertions. The rising number of speeches in his later years can be seen as no more than a functional necessity of high office in a democratizing political system.

But upholding Palmerston's scant reputation as a public

speaker is too limiting a conclusion, particularly in light of what we know about the growing importance of speech-making in British political culture over the course of the nineteenth century. Indeed, it is because Palmerston has not been counted among the great orator-statesmen that examining his record of speech-making offers perspectives on the character of public life that similar studies of the Gladstones of the world do not. Speech-making was more than merely a necessary function of Palmerston's outsized career. If he did not gain a reputation for great oratory, Palmerston used speeches to notable practical effect — to position himself as a natural choice for the Foreign Office, to extricate himself from serious parliamentary challenges, and to build up a base of popular support. Moreover, he could make speeches of Gladstonian length when circumstances required; he could amuse his audiences at least as well as Disraeli; and he could attract crowds at his public appearances to rival those that went to hear Bright.

Looked at from the broader perspective of the evolving role of political oratory, Palmerston's great achievement as a public speaker was to bend, in new ways, the necessity and conventions of speech-making to his own purposes. Although his formative years were spent in the golden age of parliamentary eloquence and his sometime model, Canning, was deemed the last of the great orators, Palmerston's public speaking shows that he was not, as sometimes asserted, a holdover from the eighteenth century. In Parliament, instead of great set-piece oratorical battles, his style of speech favoured a modern, highly mobile offence capable of covering tactical retreats and, with humour, disarming antagonists. In several key respects, he contributed to establishing new patterns of political communication, particularly through his close relationship with the press and his skilful use of extra-parliamentary speech events for mass audiences. Ultimately, speech (including its printed forms) was a crucial medium through which he was able to project the kind of winning image that strengthened his personal position in the country, and consequently in Parliament.

As stated at the outset, the purpose of this essay is not to argue that Palmerston should be placed in the pantheon of orator-statesmen, either with respect to the importance of speech-making in his career, or to the qualities of his speeches. Few of Palmerston's speeches could be considered to have an epochal character. As a public speaker, he offered little of the self-conscious transcendence that Pitt, Gladstone, and Churchill brought to so many of their performances. Nevertheless, even if it is fair to conclude that public speaking was not the *most* notable aspect of Palmerston's remarkable career, it should not be denied its rightful place. A full accounting of that career, and what made it so remarkable, must include Palmerston's considerable record of speech-making understood in the broader context of nineteenth-century public life.

References

[1] *The Cambridge history of English literature*, vol. XIV: *the nineteenth century* ed. A. W. Ward and A. R. Waller (Cambridge: Cambridge University Press, 1917) p. 138. One indication that Palmerston's contemporaries did not regard oratory as a major feature of his career is that, unlike many other major Prime Ministers and leading political figures with a following, there is no substantial published edition of his speeches. The volume of extracts from his speeches covers the years 1808 to 1851, thus excluding his years as Home Secretary and Prime Minister: *Opinions and policy of the right honourable Viscount Palmerston, G.C.B., M.P. as minister, diplomatist and statesman during more than forty years of public life* ed. George Henry Francis (London: Colburn and Co., 1852).

[2] See, e.g., Abraham Hayward 'The British Parliament: its history and eloquence' *Quarterly Review* 132 (1872) pp. 450-95; Robert Craig *A history of oratory in Parliament, 1213-1913* (London: Heath, Cranton, & Ousley, 1913); Earl Curzon of Kedleston *Modern parliamentary eloquence: the Rede lecture delivered before the University of Cambridge, November 6, 1913* (London: Macmillan, 1913); Robert T. Oliver *Public speaking in the reshaping of Great Britain* (Newark: University of Delaware Press, 1987); Joseph S. Meisel *Public speech and the culture of public life in the age of Gladstone* (New York: Columbia University Press, 2001).

[3] See, e.g., Colin Matthew *The nineteenth century* (Oxford: Oxford University Press, 2000) p. 106.

[4] Kenneth Bourne *Palmerston: the early years, 1784-1841* (London: Allen Lane, 1982) pp. 8-9.

[5] Bourne, *Palmerston*, p. 29.

[6] K. Bourne (ed.) *The letters of the third Viscount Palmerston to Laurence and Elizabeth Sulivan, 1804-1863* (London: Royal Historical Society, Camden, 4th series, 23; 1979) pp. 8-12, 33, 38-40, 47; Bourne, *Palmerston*, pp. 42-3.

[7] *Letters to Sulivan*, p. 177.

[8] *Letters to Sulivan*, p. 92.

[9] Quoted in Bourne, *Palmerston*, p. 82.

[10] See Linda Colley *Britons: forging the nation, 1707-1837* (New Haven and London: Yale University Press, 1992) pp. 151-2; and Meisel, *Public speech* pp. 72-3.

[11] Henry Lytton Bulwer *The life of Henry John Temple, Viscount Palmerston: with selections from his diaries and correspondence* (3rd ed., 3 vols., London: Bentley, 1871-4) i, p. 79.

[12] Expressed in a letter to Lord Malmesbury, 16 Oct. 1809, reproduced in Bulwer, *Palmerston* i, p. 79.

[13] *Parliamentary Debates*, 3rd ser. cxliii, 1231 (22 Jun 1856). See also Palmerston's later response to Disraeli on a similar motion: *ibid.* 3rd Series, clxv, 60 (11 Feb 1862).

[14] Michael S. Partridge and Karen E. Partridge *Lord Palmerston, 1784-1865: a bibliography* Bibliographies of British Statesmen, No. 16 (Westport, Conn.: Greenwood Press, 1994) pp. 103-82.

[15] Some of these approach a full column of reported speech, while others are briefer. It is also the case that some of the 419 (31 percent) of Palmerston's speeches printed across two columns were brief. For the present purposes, I have assumed that the long 'one column' speeches are in rough measure cancelled out by short 'two column' speeches.

[16] *The Gladstone diaries* ed. M.R.D. Foot and H.C.G. Matthew (14 vols., Oxford: Oxford University Press, 1968-94) xiii, p. 428 (29 Dec 1896).

[17] Statistics for Gladstone's and Churchill's speeches are presented in greater detail in Joseph S. Meisel, 'Words by the numbers: a quantitative analysis and comparison of the oratorical careers of William Ewart Gladstone and Winston Spencer Churchill' *Historical Research* 73 (2000) pp. 262-95.

[18] *Disraeli's reminiscences* ed. Helen M. Swartz and Marvin Swartz (New York: Stein and Day, 1976) p. 74. Emphasis in original.

[19] Francis Galton *Hereditary genius: an inquiry into its laws and consequences* (1869; Cleveland and New York: Meridian Books, 1962) p. 168. The emergence of Palmerston's talents, even if somewhat belated, was fully consistent with Galton's theories about the inheritance of talent. Of great-great-grandfather Sir John Temple, Master of the Rolls in Ireland, he wrote, 'even he was not the first of this family that showed ability.'

[20] Quoted in *The history of Parliament: the House of Commons, 1790-1820*

ed. R. G. Thorne (5 vols., London: Secker & Warburg) v, p. 350.

[21] James Grant *Random recollections of the House of Commons, from the year 1830 to the close of 1835, including personal sketches of the leading members of all parties* (London: Saunders and Otley, [1837]) p. 226.

[22] George Henry Francis 'Contemporary orators, no. viii: Lord Palmerston', *Fraser's Magazine* 33 (Mar 1846) pp. 317-18.

[23] See, e.g., Herbert C.F. Bell *Lord Palmerston* (2 vols., London: Longmans, Green, 1936) i, pp. 78ff.

[24] Sir Horace Twiss to Palmerston, 29 March 1829, BP, SP/A/11.

[25] *Parliamentary Debates* 3rd ser. xcvii, 122 (1 March 1848).

[26] Norman Vance *The Victorians and ancient Rome* (Oxford: Blackwell, 1997) p. 225.

[27] *Disraeli, Derby, and the Conservative party: journals and memoirs of Edward Henry, Lord Stanley, 1849-1865* ed. John Vincent (Hassocks: Harvester Press, 1978) pp. 21, 23.

[28] *Disraeli, Derby, and the Conservative party* pp. 22-3.

[29] Grant, *Random recollections* p. 226.

[30] Francis, 'Contemporary orators' p. 322.

[31] Henry Adams *The education of Henry Adams: an autobiography* (Boston and New York: Houghton Mifflin Company, 1918) p. 135. Lytton Strachey somewhat mis-characterises Adams's description. Lytton Strachey *Queen Victoria* (London: Chatto & Windus, 1921) p. 240.

[32] *Disraeli's reminiscences* p. 62.

[33] Evelyn Ashley *The life of Henry John Temple, Viscount Palmerston, 1846-1865: with selections from his speeches and correspondence* (2 vols., London: Bentley, 1876) ii, p. 310.

[34] Quoted in Ashley, *Palmerston* ii, p. 311.

[35] Francis, 'Contemporary orators' p. 318.

[36] John Bowring 'Recollections of Lord Palmerston' *Fortnightly Review* 3 (1865) p. 8.

[37] *The correspondence of John Lothrop Motley, D.C.L.* ed. George William Curtis (2 vols., New York: Harper & Brothers, 1889) i, p. 255.

[38] See Meisel, *Public speech* pp. 212-19.

[39] See Meisel, *Public speech* pp. 186-195.

[40] Francis, 'Contemporary orators' p. 318.

[41] Francis, 'Contemporary orators' p. 319.

[42] *The parliamentary diaries of Sir John Trelawny, 1858-1865* ed. T. A. Jenkins (London: Royal Historical Society, Camden, 4th series, 40; 1990) pp. 279, 83, 128.

[43] Ashley, *Palmerston* ii, pp. 311-12.

[44] Francis, 'Contemporary orators' pp. 319-20.

[45] Anthony Trollope *Lord Palmerston* (London: William Ibister Limited, 1882) p. 24.

[46] Jonathan Parry *The rise and fall of liberal government in Victorian Britain* (New Haven and London: Yale University Press, 1993) p. 192.

[47] See, e.g., Bulwer, *Palmerston* i, p. 147; Bell, *Lord Palmerston* i, p. 60. On Canning's extra-parliamentary speaking, see Meisel, *Public speech* pp. 229-31.

[48] Quoted in *The history of Parliament: the House of Commons, 1790-1820* v, p. 349.

[49] David Brown *Palmerston, South Hampshire and electoral politics, 1832-1835* (Winchester: Hampshire County Council, 2003) pp. 7, 16.

[50] Bourne, *Palmerston* p. 538.

[51] F. J. Snell *Palmerston's borough: a budget of electioneering anecdotes, jokes, squibs, and speeches* (London: Horace Marshall & Son, [1894]) p. 47.

[52] Snell, *Palmerston's borough* p. 51.

[53] Snell, *Palmerston's borough* p. 71.

[54] Snell, *Palmerston's borough* p. 73.

[55] Letter dated 17 Aug 1841, reproduced in Bulwer, *Palmerston* ii, pp. 382-3. Emphasis added.

[56] Snell, *Palmerston's borough* p. 80.

[57] Snell, *Palmerston's borough* p. 89.

[58] Snell, *Palmerston's borough* pp. 84-5.

[59] John Sharland *Recollections of the great Lord Palmerston and old times in Devon* (Tiverton: Gregory & Son, 1898) p. 9.

[60] Trollope, *Lord Palmerston* p. 15.

[61] Muriel E. Chamberlain *Lord Palmerston* (Washington, D.C.: The Catholic University of America Press, 1987) p. 123.

[62] See Meisel, *Public speech*, ch. 5.

[63] H.C.G. Matthew 'Gladstone, rhetoric and politics' in Peter J. Jagger (ed.), *Gladstone* (London: Hambledon, 1998) p. 219.

[64] The neglect of Palmerston's extra-parliamentary activities began early. Henry L. Jephson *The platform: its rise and progress* (2 vols., London: Macmillan, 1892), a compendious study of its subject, mentions Palmerston only once, and then only in passing.

[65] See Meisel, *Public speech* p. 238.

[66] Antony Taylor 'Palmerston and radicalism, 1847-1865' *Journal of British Studies* 33 (1994) p. 177.

[67] Snell, *Palmerston's borough* p. 68.

[68] Snell, *Palmerston's borough* p. 98.

[69] Taylor, 'Palmerston and radicalism' p. 176.

[70] Lord Lyndhurst to Lord Brougham, 20 Nov 1851, Brougham papers 13271, University College London.

[71] Trollope, *Lord Palmerston* pp. 148-9.

[72] Taylor, 'Palmerston and radicalism' p. 177.

[73] E. D. Steele *Palmerston and liberalism, 1855-1865* (Cambridge: Cambridge University Press, 1991) p. 120.

[74] *Parliamentary Diaries of ... Trelawny* p. 239.

[75] Lord Clarendon to Lord Brougham, 4 April 1863, Brougham papers 38733, University College London.

[76] H.C.G. Matthew *Gladstone, 1809-1874* (Oxford: Clarendon Press, 1986) p. 133.

[77] See Parry, *Rise and Fall of Liberal Government* pp. 168-9; Steele, *Palmerston and Liberalism* pp. 35-7.

[78] *Gladstone and Palmerston: being the correspondence of Lord Palmerston with Mr Gladstone, 1851-1865* ed. Phillip Guedalla (London: Gollancz, 1928) p. 233.

[79] *Gladstone and Palmerston* p. 237.

[80] Sir Denis Le Marchant to Lord Brougham, 8 Mar 1863, Brougham papers 34854, University College London.

[81] Lord Clarendon to Lord Brougham, 4 Apr 1863, Brougham papers 38733, University College London.

[82] Parry, *Rise and fall of liberal government* p. 192.

[83] Steele, *Palmerston and liberalism* p. 7.

[84] Steele, *Palmerston and liberalism* pp. 8, 35.

[85] Taylor, 'Palmerston and radicalism' p. 178.

[86] Steele, *Palmerston and liberalism* p. 15.

[87] See Stephen Koss *The rise and fall of the political press in Britain: the nineteenth century* (Chapel Hill, University of North Carolina Press, 1981) pp. 74-7 and ch. 4.

[88] See Meisel, *Public speech* ch. 5.

[89] James Grant *The newspaper press: its origin—progress—and present position* (2 vols., London: Tinsley, 1871) ii, p. 207. See also David Brown 'Compelling but not controlling ?: Palmerston and the press, 1846-1855' *History* 86 (2001) pp. 41-61.

[90] Snell, *Palmerston's borough* p. 97.

[91] Grant, *Newspaper press* ii, p. 206.

CHAPTER 4

Palmerston and the 1850s
David Brown

W. L. Burn, ruminating on the most apposite label for the mid-Victorian period, before settling on 'the age of equipoise', toyed briefly with the idea of 'the age of Palmerston' given that Palmerston had 'not merely touched but handled life at so many points'. He rejected the term, however, on the grounds, as he put it, of Palmerston's 'lack of the sober, serious, conscious thoughtfulness so characteristic of the age he lived into; and the sense that there was, at the bottom of him, a moral vacuum.'[1] The impression that Palmerston was a man out-of-tune with his times goes to the heart of important debates about his place in Victorian Britain: whether he was an irredeemable and antediluvian reactionary or, by contrast, in fact a progressive visionary. He was often taken to be, as Philip Guedalla put it in 1926, 'the last candle of the Eighteenth Century', a throw-back to a bygone age, yet as E. D. Steele has more recently suggested, his later career might sustain a quite different inter-pretation, in which he is presented as the possessor of a 'genius for adaptation' whose governments in the 1850s and 1860s were in fact a 'conscious introduction to the new era' of democratic politics.[2]

It is during the 1850s that what might be termed the many faces of Palmerston are clearly visible. It was a decade of contrasts for Palmerston, one that began in unpromising fashion as the Queen and senior Cabinet colleagues sought to remove him from the Foreign Office, and indeed succeeded in December 1851, sacking him after he had unofficially approved of Louis Napoleon's *coup d'état*; and yet it ended with him at the head of his own goverment.

From the gunboat diplomat, not long since derided by German conservatives as the 'Devil's son',[3] to reforming Home Secretary, to wartime premier, Palmerston would be, by 1859, not just Prime Minister for the second time but, significantly, also the first Liberal one. It was all a far remove from the days of the young Tory beau who had been accommodated only reluctantly, so the conventional Whig history had it, within the government of the second Earl Grey and whose bellicosity and abrasive manner throughout the 1830s and 1840s had made him, within the Whig family, most decidedly the troublesome in-law.

One of the curious features of Palmerston's career is that while he was consistently recognised as central to political life, his particular place within it was open to almost constant debate. Early Whig colleagues suspected him for his Tory roots and patrons; Tories were wary of the man who had deserted them and run away to join Mr Canning's liberal circus in the late 1820s and had subsequently fallen in with the Whig establishment in the 1830s, even to the extent of marrying into the Lamb family in 1839; and yet, his supposed vacillation and opportunism did not diminish his potency. By the 1840s the Whigs were not entirely comfortable with him but his perceived attractiveness to radical opinion saved his position within Russell's government on more than one occasion. And in 1852, after 22 years in which he had been at the heart of Whig politics, Disraeli and Derby could still look to Palmerston as a possible recruit to the Protectionist ranks. Often, both at the time and subsequently in secondary literature, this fluidity in Palmerston's political affiliations appeared to signal a certain pragmatism, or even cynicism, as Palmerston worked to serve the interests of no particular party or group consistently, save, perhaps, those of Henry Temple. At best, historians have sought to reconcile the tensions in his career with the convenient and plausible, though ultimately rather bland, suggestion that he was a conservative at home and a liberal abroad, but ultimately this serves only to make it more difficult to locate him within the parameters of Victorian politics. Arguably, however, he was more than the Machiavellian political adventurer of conventional accounts. While some historians have been content to explain Palmerston's shift to the Whig camp in the late 1820s and early 1830s as little more than political opportunism, conveniently facilitated by the blurring of Tory identity by Canning, when read in the context of Palmerston's Edinburgh education, where he had imbibed traditional Whig ideas of political economy and notions of constitutional government at the hands of Dugald Stewart, himself a former pupil of Adam Smith,[4] it might be that it is rather Palmerston's Tory apprenticeship between 1806 and the later 1820s that appears opportunistic or anomalous, and the re-alignment with the Whigs after 1830 the more natural accommodation of Palmerston's political outlook. Yet, Palmerston, despite his marriage to Emily Cowper (*née* Lamb) in 1839, did not enjoy the blood ties that bound together so many of the Whig grandees. His claim to a place at Whig Cabinet tables was earned rather than inherited.

I

Despite the relatively slow start to his ministerial career (Palmerston was already 45 by the time he took up the seals of the Foreign Office for the first time) he was, nonetheless, ambitious. In a political world increasingly defined by an emergent party system, advancement depended upon position and connection and thus were Palmerston's fortunes tied very much to those of the Whigs. However, there remained considerable ambivalence towards Palmerston's ascendancy within Whig circles and this was embodied nowhere more clearly than in the person of Lord John Russell. As Jonathan Parry shows, this personal rivalry defined the character of, and the divisions within, Whig politics for much of the mid-Victorian period.[5] Palmerston's politics at this time might, then, be read as having been conceived, in part, in reference to Russell, by way of separating them within the Whig-Liberal matrix, and thereby creating alternative visions of the non-Tory agenda through which, one or the other might gain a personal as well as political ascendancy.

Palmerston's jaunty image belied a more sophisticated political outlook. Personal ambition did play a part, but through the 1850s, Palmerston was able to work out and present to the public as well as parliamentary associates, the contours of a more rounded Palmerstonian liberalism. Twice in the early 1850s Palmerston's position came under particular attack, in 1850 and 1851, and in successfully resisting calls for his dismissal in the former, and succumbing to them in the latter, much is revealed about the nature of Palmerston's political philosophy.

The most important challenge to Palmerston's position in the Russell government prior to his eventual dismissal in December 1851 came in the summer of 1850 when he was obliged to defend his conduct over the handling of the case of Don Pacifico.[6] In the House of Lords, Stanley and Aberdeen carried a motion censuring Palmerston's heavy-handed gunboat diplomacy in the affair. When the issue moved to the Commons, the government felt obliged to defend the Foreign Secretary and made the question effectively one of confidence in the ministry, securing a negation of the Lords' verdict by a vote of 310 to 264. Palmerston, however, was determined to turn the situation to his advantage and used the parliamentary platform as an opportunity to appeal to patriotic feeling above the petty feeble-mindedness of his opponents. He declared triumphantly that as in the days of the Roman empire when a citizen could claim protection by virtue of Roman citizenship, so too could a citizen of the British empire expect the same support. He won a resounding popular endorsement and this '*civis Romanus sum*' speech rescued Palmerston's ailing fortunes and his perceived renewed importance, indeed indispensability, now served to defend him against continued royal attacks.[7] As Palmerston remembered: 'Towards the End of the Session Ld John again brought the subject [of removal from the Foreign Office] forward & proposed to me a change of office. I replied that after what had passed in the House of Commons ... and after the general and decided approbation of my Policy & Conduct which had been Expressed from one End of the Country to the other by all the Liberal Party it was quite impossible for me to consent to any such arrangement.'[8] Palmerston saw his success over the Don Pacifico question as a triumph for public opinion. His invocation of '*civis Romanus sum*' had brought the question down to the basic interests of every member of the public and out of the exclusive realm of high political debate. As the *Globe* observed, 'Lord PALMERSTON, the House of Commons, and the Nation, are henceforth at one', identifying Palmerston as a stalwart defender of the interests of the people, 'a Minister whose protecting arm was over every one of his countrymen' and who had thereby earned 'the national affection and respect'.[9] While *The Times*, the *Morning Chronicle* and other papers hostile to Palmerston regretted his success,[10] they made a faulty attack when they tried to turn what was effectively presented as a moral question into one of party political intrigue in arguing that the debate was simply a Peelite scheme to undermine the Whigs. Palmerston had won a popular victory, by charming extra-parliamentary opinion with his patriotic rhetoric. Even his sternest critics, in the press, at Court and in the Cabinet, were obliged in the end to acknowledge, however grudgingly, Palmerston's enhanced standing on the back of a popularly applauded, patriotic stand.[11]

Riding the wave of popular enthusiasm, Palmerston, whom the editor of the *Sun* described as 'one of the manliest intellects in England; one of the noblest statesmen in all Europe, perhaps the wisest and certainly the most accomplished diplomatist who ever directed the foreign affairs of our Country', did indeed appear to carry with him 'the hearty sympathies of the people'.[12] Thus it was that the Foreign Secretary did not find allies wanting. Declarations of support came in from all over the country, spanning the social spectrum.[13]

Critics of Palmerston's conduct, though making plausible

cases against him, failed to hit their target.[14] In the aftermath of the debate, Palmerston's victory was applauded widely and local newspapers from around the country, copies of which were often sent to Palmerston, confirmed his renewed popularity and connection with the people.[15] From other quarters, tributes to his manly conduct and 'noble generous and patriotic course' confirmed the impression that Palmerston had done much to consolidate, even enhance, his popular image of the masculine English minister.[16] Popularly, at least so it seemed, Palmerston had convinced large numbers of the British people that he was their ablest minister, a stout and determined defender of British interests. Significantly, this appeal cut across social boundaries, and Palmerston's determination to defend the interests of the Briton abroad appealed equally to the crude patriotism of the man in the street as it did to the commercial classes of industrial areas such as Manchester where support for Cobdenite free-trade pacifism rapidly lost ground to the strong-arm guardianship of Palmerstonian foreign policy.[17] He had shown himself to be unswerving in the pursuit of British interests and although a classic case of gunboat diplomacy, the Don Pacifico affair did not undermine Palmerston's reputation for a demonstrable sympathy towards liberalism across Europe.

In December 1851, when he was expelled from office, Palmerston's dismissal occasioned such outrage at the *Morning Post* that the subject was the main leader article every day from 25 December 1851 until 2 January 1852. In a private interview with Walewski, the French ambassador, Palmerston had intimated that he approved of Louis Napoleon's *coup d'état*. In fact, he was probably doing little more than pragmatically accepting a *fait accompli*, but nonetheless his views were reported to Paris as the official view of the British government. The Cabinet, however, had not given its approval for such an endorsement and Palmerston's breach of etiquette and policy was repaid with his enforced resignation from the ministry at the end of December. The loss, in the 'present critical state of European affairs', of the services of a minister whom, the *Post* believed, history would accord a place 'in the very highest ranks of statesmanship' was a setback at both the domestic and international level.[18] The *Post* was greatly troubled that the explanation for this loss was that, in effect, Palmerston was too unpopular abroad. 'Public opinion will not be satisfied with light explanations of so great a misfortune;' an article observed, 'still less with explanations which attribute the result to unworthy or discreditable causes', more especially since it was Palmerston above all others to whom the longevity of the Russell government ought to be attributed.[19] To remove a politician whose only fault was 'that he loves his country so well, and serves his SOVEREIGN so faithfully, that he prefers the independence of the one and the dignity of the other to the good or ill pleasure of certain foreign politicians', appeared unjust indeed.[20]

Significantly, it was not only the Palmerstonian papers that expressed such sentiments. Both *The Times* and the *Morning Chronicle* rued Palmerston's dismissal. In the article which first announced the Foreign Secretary's fall, *The Times* wrote of Palmerston (suspecting it had seen the last of him in office) commending his industry, courage and charm and steadfastly refrained from repeating the charges made against his foreign policy.[21] The *Morning Chronicle*, too, was sorry to lose the services of Palmerston. In an article on Christmas Day 1851, it chastised the Russell Cabinet for its inconsistency in dropping a minister whom the government had heretofore dutifully defended, and described his dismissal as a 'national humiliation'. Palmerston had not only been 'the keystone of the arch' for the last five and a half years, he was 'their only man of first-class ability; his policy, though dangerous always and injurious often, was at least bold, spirited, and not essentially un-English'.[22] With wide-ranging press support, it is not perhaps surprising to find that Palmerston's going was deeply regretted in the country at large. As with the national newspapers, in the provincial papers, his fall was widely seen in terms of a personal loss, the loss of 'the English minister'. Palmerston collected a variety of newspaper cuttings from this period and, not surprisingly, they are all from articles displaying a sympathy for his cause but it is interesting to note the diversity of their origins, and the uniformity of their sentiments.[23]

Letters of support sent from members of the public to Palmerston at this time emphasised three crucial reasons for deploring his removal: the threat to national honour, the ill-treatment of the people's hero, and the precarious state of European affairs. His claims to represent England were unquestionable, as a former Cambridge contemporary observed,[24] whilst the 'People's Minister' (as the Mayor of Southampton described him) was the one upon whom 'the people' relied above all others.[25] As far as Europe was concerned, such a veteran diplomat could ill be spared at this moment.[26] On this solid basis of confidence Palmerston could invert the traditional antagonism towards France — and in December 1851 with a Bonaparte at the head of the French government there was a good deal of suspicion and unease — and still be held up as the defender of liberty and peace. Having established himself, rhetorically, as the defender of these principles, public opinion could stoutly continue to believe that, however much the spectre of earlier Napoleonic menace might now be resurrected, Palmerston still stood as the defender of the national interest. The impression that Palmerston stood as the champion of liberal, constitutional government in Europe and as the fearless defender of British interests abroad not only confirmed his standing in the public eye as the truly 'national' minister, but also, as Russell was well aware, as the embodiment of 'English' values and honour.[27]

In playing on notions of a national mission, Palmerston had established his own primacy in British politics. His political force was clearly not spent by the end of 1851. As the *Morning Post* noted of his speech on the Militia Bill which heralded the downfall of his erstwhile colleagues in February 1852, he had shown 'at once that he had sagacity to comprehend, and ability to meet, what Parliament and the public felt to be the wish of the nation, and the necessity of the time'.[28] The Derby government which replaced that of Russell in February maintained a precarious balancing act for the following ten months, but it was unable ever to establish itself as a sound and secure ministry. Palmerston, meanwhile, consolidated his own position and a certain detachment from unquestioning party allegiance gave him an influential position in politics, at least a kingmaker, if not, indeed, a future leader-in-waiting himself.[29] Indeed, in the aftermath of Palmerston's split with Russell and the Whigs in 1851 and Russell's revival of the Reform question (of which Palmerston was never a very keen supporter), there was good reason to believe that Palmerston might be receptive to Conservative overtures.[30] With Palmerston wavering, apparently, and the Whigs under Russell floundering, Derby saw, firstly, no need or good reason to attack a possible valuable recruit and ally, and secondly, the imminent reward for his patient inactivity whereby internal divisions among the Whigs would kill the government more effectively than overt Conservative assaults. To Conservatives as well as Liberals, Palmerston's demonstrated strength with public opinion made him a figure to be reckoned with (ironically perhaps given Derby's own wariness of popular politics), and more than one overture was made to Palmerston by the Protectionists in 1852.[31] Indeed, there were good reasons to hope Palmerston might switch sides: he did at least adopt an attitude towards the ministry throughout 1852 of 'marked benevolence' and went out of his way to advise (or mentor) the new Foreign Secretary, Lord Malmesbury in private correspondence.[32] More than this, Palmerston gave serious consideration to the notion that he might bolster the position of the Derby government even as late as the autumn of 1852, when it was reported by Charles Greville that there 'is a strong conviction that it will end in P. joining Derby, provided the latter will give him a decent opportunity for so doing'.[33] Yet, the 'decent opportunity' Palmerston sought was not to join Derby, but to re-affirm his own claims to eminence within Whig ranks. A certain personal rivalry probably did get in the way: as George Cornewall Lewis observed, if Palmerston did join the Protectionists, 'Ld Derby would find not only that he had got a master, but a master who made him feel his servitude every day – & rode him with a sharp bit & a hard hand'.[34] And it is quite clear that

Derby would not have stood by and allowed Palmerston to steal his leadership.[35] But the rivalry between Palmerston and Russell for the leadership of the Whigs was more keenly felt and the decent opportunity which Palmerston awaited was not to join Derby, but to return to his former colleagues under a different leadership, but to do so by playing Derby off against Russell throughout 1852, threatening to take his popular following with him wherever he went.

II

As the Derby administration stumbled to its fall in the autumn of 1852, attention in the press turned to the question of its replacement. Russell was dismissed as unfit again to become Prime Minister by the *Morning Post*: between him and that station were now 'raised up obstructions permanent and insurmountable', primarily popular and parliamentary distrust.[36] Palmerston, however, held a very strong hand, as one who 'in his present independent position, enjoys a wider popularity, and exercises a larger and more wholesome influence on the European mind, than any other living man'. On this ground, the *Post* argued, he need 'make no approaches to any party in the State ... for to him *"Tout vient à propos"*, whether he wait or not'.[37] In such an apparently strong position, then, Palmerston had all before him. And yet, in December 1852, when he did return to ministerial office, it was not to the Foreign Office, but to the much humbler station of the Home Office. It may have been genuinely a case of fatigue, or perhaps a realisation that he had made too many enemies, both at home and abroad, ever to be able effectively to run British foreign policy again,[38] but Palmerston was resolute: at Lansdowne's urging, Palmerston had 'consented to take [the] Home Office', but he was adamant that 'Nothing sh[oul]d induce me to go back to [the] Foreign Office.'[39]

To many this was a curious backward step for Palmerston to take. The Duke of Argyll felt that Palmerston had made a great sacrifice 'of personal feeling to public duty'. Not only had the Foreign

Office been given to Russell ('the Minister who had summarily dismissed him from it'), but Palmerston now served 'under the leadership of a statesman whose arguments against his own policy he had described in the House of Commons as "antiquated imbecility"'.[40] Shaftesbury, too, confided in his diary at the time that Palmerston's acceptance of office, in direct contradiction of everything he had said previously, surprised him greatly, believing Palmerston had in some way been duped by Aberdeen and Russell, who had 'wanted to gag P.; and they have succeeded; they have bound the wild one between two tame elephants'.[41] Historians have often been just as surprised. David Roberts judged the Home Office 'one of the most humdrum of departments' and presented the appointment as a demotion, pointing out that the 'proud Foreign Secretary who had snubbed the crowned heads of Europe now haggled with vestrymen about their sewers'.[42] Jasper Ridley explained the move as motivated principally by pecuniary considerations: the Palmerstons, he observed, 'were beginning to feel the pinch without a ministerial salary', and the Home Office was simply the least objectionable post on offer.[43] And so Palmerston's tenure of the Home Office has often been treated as something of a curious aside in which biographers, obliged to include a chapter on the 'Home Office years', have tended to present a brief list of the measures overseen at that department between 1852 and 1855 before moving swiftly, and with some relief, on to more familiar Palmerstonian territory: Ridley even entitled his chapter: 'Home Secretary: the Eastern Question'.[44] Similarly, Donald Southgate's account of 'the policies and politics of Palmerston', ignored Palmerston's work at the Home Office and presented these years exclusively in terms of foreign affairs and disputes over foreign policy.[45]

Yet, as Roberts was obliged to concede, Palmerston's work at the Home Office was seen by many at the time as a test of his political character: was he a Liberal or a Tory ?[46] Palmerston himself, defending his decision to accept the post suggested that after twelve months of 'acting the part of a Rope Dancer & much astonishing the public by my individual Performances and Feats', now was the time, for practical reasons, to cease playing the part of 'a reckless Adventurer' and commit to the cause of 'the great Liberal Party, (not in the H[ouse] of C[om]m[on]s, nor at Brooks's nor at the Reform Club) but in the United Kingdom' and to fulfil his duty to his Tiverton constituents.[47] This professed commitment to 'the great Liberal Party' is important. Southgate is no doubt justified in claiming that it was 'the extravagances of his foreign policy' that most appealed to Liberal opinion,[48] but it was not all. It is important to weigh carefully Palmerston's contribution to domestic politics in these years for he demonstrated a far more sincere and dynamic interest in the work of the Home Secretary than has often been allowed and in so doing was able both to advance his own claims to eminence within Liberal circles but also, though he would not have know this in advance, take refuge in the Home Office when the fall-out from the ill-managed Crimean War showered down on Downing Street.

Far from seeing the Home Office as an unimportant political backwater, Palmerston addressed himself to the work of that department with as much energy as had characterised his work at the Foreign Office. His achievements there, however, speak of more than mere industry. Addressing his constituents in Tiverton in January 1853 Palmerston had insisted that not only did he have no interest in returning to the Foreign Office, but that he had accepted 'that office which I was most desirous to fill'.[49] This was not mere face-saving; Palmerston did have a genuine interest in the work he was now assigned. During the life of the government Palmerston oversaw the introduction of the Factory Act of 1853, which while not fulfilling all of the hopes of reformers such as Shaftesbury, did go some way towards improving industrial working conditions, especially for children. He also attempted to pass legislation which would have confirmed the rights of trade unions to combine for lawful purposes as laid down in an Act of 1825 (although he resisted trade union demands for the legalisation of peaceful picketing) and, more successfully, introduced the Truck Act under the terms of which workers were entitled to payment in money, rather than goods or tokens for employers' own shops. Palmerston also sought to improve the condition of society, both environmentally and morally. He pioneered legislation aimed at curbing pollution with the weak but well-intentioned Smoke Abatement Act in August 1853, and reform of the Board of Health in 1854, for example, and throughout was a firm friend of the temperance societies. Nor did he shy away from the thorny problems associated with prisons and their reform.[50]

Roberts judged Palmerston's reforming record, however, to have been only a 'partial success', though this is as much a verdict, in Roberts' view, on the 'weak coalition ministry of Lord Aberdeen' and the deep-rooted 'entrenched interests and widespread evils' of mid-Victorian society. It may or may not, therefore, be evidence of Palmerston's shortcomings that he did not achieve more at the Home Office; but what is both clear and important, is that in taking the seals of the Home Office, Palmerston had been obliged 'to define his basic social philosophy'. Roberts is vague on this, though, suggesting in the final analysis that Palmerston had a genuine sympathy for 'the masses' but distrusted them and that in the end his 'social outlook was paternalistic'.[51] This is fine so far as it goes, but we must read Palmerston's record a little more carefully.

In Jonathan Parry's narrative of the 'rise and fall' of Liberal government in the Victorian period, it is Palmerston's domestic record, both at the Home Office and subsequently at the head of government, as much as his popular ebullient foreign policy, that helped establish his claims to leadership of Liberal politics. With Liberal forces in the mid-1850s in need of a clear focus, Parry discerned three competing strategies: Russellite schemes for a Liberal-radical coalition based on constitutional and religious reform; a Peelite-inspired 'programme of economy and good administration'; or, the 'most successful' in the event, a Palmerstonian third way.[52] The race was essentially between Russell and Palmerston, but as Parry argues, Russell fell at three separate fences: he was not 'sufficiently Prime Minister', he continued to embody

Whiggish social exclusiveness and managed to alienate radical support through his perceived 'impulsiveness'.[53]

Palmerston seemed to offer a compelling alternative. His bombastic nationalism of the 1840s and early 1850s had endeared him to a broad cross-section of the population and his willingness to stand up to heads of state (including his own) suggested he had the spirit to provide compelling leadership. Yet until the 1850s he had little by way of a record in domestic politics beyond a general impression of moderate conservatism. Through his work at the Home Office and subsequently, however, he was able to elaborate on his view of society and government responsibility.

In the short term, there was another, striking, benefit to Palmerston in this attention to his domestic politics. With Britain fighting in the war in the Crimea from March 1854, arguments over foreign policy had given way to concern over how to manage the war itself. With unprecedented press coverage of the conflict, the conduct of the military campaigns was a matter of immediate concern and belief in Palmerston's ability to direct the war was recognised far and wide, from the Court to the popular press. Significantly, though, at this crucial juncture, Palmerston used his ability to manipulate the press to portray himself outside the bounds of government in quite a different light.[54] Though he was still held up as the most able minister for the direction of British foreign policy in the East, it is striking that most press attention in 1854 concerning Palmerston focused on his domestic politics and his work at the Home Office. The *Standard*, indeed, implied Palmerston should avoid speaking on foreign policy questions in Parliament.[55] The *Morning Post* was one of the few newspapers in this year, particularly once Britain had gone to war, to continue to peddle the line that a more determined and consistent Palmerstonian approach from the outset would have avoided this conflict.[56]

Whatever might have been the value of Palmerston's support for the government's foreign policy, it is notable that as soon as he had been re-admitted to the Cabinet, following his temporary resignation at the end of 1853, it was to his domestic reforms that the attention of the press was directed.[57] Newspaper coverage of Palmerston's political activities in 1854 was concerned primarily with issues such as the work of the Board of Health; the poor law; smoke abatement; the reforms of prisons, universities, and police; and town improvements such as sewage systems.[58] The absence of meaningful connections between Palmerston and foreign policy in newspaper articles during this year and a far greater preponderance of articles discussing his domestic undertakings is remarkable. In the summer, indeed, the *Standard* commented on Palmerston's 'ominous silence' in the principal debates of the parliamentary session (perceiving a bid for the premiership).[59] Towards the end of the year, *The Times* observed how Palmerston was no longer at the forefront of diplomatic debates, at least those before the public gaze, and wondered at his propensity to busy himself with other issues:

So now, if people have time to look back – and the long intervals of the intelligence give us time for almost anything – it is likely the question is now and then asked, 'What is Lord PALMERSTON doing? What does he think of the war? Would he have averted it? Would he have brought it earlier to a crisis? Is he gathering friends and concerting measures with a view to his old post?' We cannot undertake to answer all those questions, but the world may see at once one thing that Lord PALMERSTON is doing. Deep in the heart of the country, somewhere between the New Forest and Salisbury Plain, he is presiding over innocent rustic celebrities, delivering prizes to bucolic excellence, and teaching labourers how to be happy, and merry and wise.[60]

Meanwhile, the debate over the correct course in the war raged on at Westminster. Crucially, however, whereas it had been Palmerston as much as, if not more so than Russell, who had challenged Aberdeen's pacific approach to the crisis, the contest was now, in 1854, presented in the press as being between Russell and Aberdeen. In the *Morning Post*, for example, an article appeared in July highly critical of the leadership of the Prime Minister, though in discussing the merits of the Aberdonian versus the alternative policy, the *Post*, while accepting that many in the Cabinet were losing faith in the premier's approach (although these were not named), identified Lord John Russell and Lord Clarendon as the

leading lights among those 'expressing and acting on directly opposite opinions'. In the same edition Palmerston was mentioned in the
following leading article, but solely in connection with police
reform.[61]

In this way, Palmerston achieved many things at once. The
popular perception that Palmerston was the minister best equipped
to deal with the war was not directly challenged, yet in shielding
his criticisms of government policy from the public gaze he did not
appear disloyal or disruptive at a time when there was considerable
concern about the execution of the war itself. Meanwhile, the war,
as Olive Anderson among others makes clear,[62] was seen very much
as a test of Britain's institutions, of Britain's 'greatness', and it did
Palmerston no harm to be seen at this time as an active improver of
those institutions. Palmerston's developing domestic political
agenda, then, served his own political interests with regard to rivalries with fellow Whigs and Liberals, but also demonstrated to the
public that he was not a one-dimensional politician but had real
interests at home just as much as he had abroad.

III

Lord Palmerston consolidated his reformist record from the Home
Office as Prime Minister, championing, for example, education
reforms that would review school curricula and place greater
emphasis on science, modern languages and mathematics making
the education provided more useful and relevant to the needs of the
time; modest reform and opening up of the Civil Service through the
introduction of competitive entry and the establishment, for example, in 1855 of the Civil Service Commission; through the cultivation of an air of disinterested (even professional) government by
way of limited use of patronage, limited at least when compared
with his predecessors' use of such privilege; and through the
introduction to government of a body of more modern politicians,
professional and skilled rather than simply high-born, he weakened
the aristocracy's hitherto hegemonic grip on power. His was a

government 'ethos' of efficient administration rather than unchecked legislative innovation; contrary to popular perception the Palmerston governments were very active, but active in a careful manner: Palmerston guided the ship of state towards moderate change but he made sure statutes were lasting and permanent.[63] His 1864 quip to Goschen that the government 'cannot go on adding to the statute book *ad infinitum*',[64] was less a signal of his reactionary intent, rather a plain statement of his view that good government meant sound administration and not perpetual revolution.

Here, however, Palmerston's record has attracted consider-able debate. Earlier commentators such as Guedalla were content to take Palmerston at his word and characterise his attitudes to govern-ment at home as one of less is more.[65] More recently, however, closer examination of Palmerston's record as Prime Minister has prompted suggestions that he was not simply more progressive than historians such as Guedalla allowed, but positively encouraged a new, more modern (and democratic), era and supervised the pol-itical education of future Liberal heroes such as Gladstone.[66] Thus, *pace* W. L. Burn, Palmerston might be said not simply to have 'handled life at so many points' but to have moulded it. Historical fashion today, then, is to portray Palmerston as the quintessential mid-Victorian Liberal. As Parry concludes:

in administrative, financial and foreign policy, Palmerston squared the circle. He presided over far-reaching change in the image of the state. To a much greater ex-tent than before, its ministers seemed disinterested, its taxes justifiable, its fiscal stance neutral as between interests, its success in promoting liberal commercial, constitutional and religious values cheap at the price. The sting was drawn from radicalism; it sought increasingly to participate with dutiful aristocrats in sober administration. Liberalism came to look responsible. Again, much more than in the 1830s, the 'permanent interests' of the country could place trust in it. Where national and propertied interests were concerned, Palmerston seemed to have as safe a pair of hands as one could expect in a liberal age.[67]

Yet enthusiasm for Palmerston's 'liberal' successes should not obscure an essential conservatism that underlay his political philo-sophy. While Palmerston spoke confidently of 'progressive improvement' as the 'law of our moral nature', and while, in large part, he successfully won the battle for the hearts and minds of the working classes,[68] he maintained a clear idea about the proper leadership of that progress towards a better life. Palmerston's social reforming conscience was essentially that of the benevolent patrician. In this, his politics clearly echoed the lessons of his Edinburgh education during which the young Palmerston had listened to Dugald Stewart advocate a kind of virtual representation: 'the most perfect Democracy which can be realized,' Stewart had told his students, 'must admit of certain delegations of power to select councils, or to individual magistrates'.[69] The 'happiness of mankind depends,' Stewart had argued, 'not on the share which the people possess, directly or indirectly, in the enactment of laws, but on the equity and expedience of the laws that are enacted'.[70] Palmerston's view of the nature of society and his opinion of the proper relationship between governed and governing was derived from this Whig sense of social order and might be discerned in his attitudes to social and political reform.

On 10 October 1854, in his capacity as Home Secretary, Palmerston visited Parkhurst Prison on the Isle of Wight where he was appalled by the condition in which prisoners were kept: the cells, he judged, were not 'sufficiently ventilated' where he found the air felt 'very close & oppressive even when the door was open', while he learned too of poor sanitary conditions that were damaging the inmates' health and on his return to London he pressed for improvements to be made in these conditions. He also found boys held in the prison whose 'countenances were good and their conduct was said to be good also' whom Palmerston would have preferred to see sent to 'some Reformatory School' rather than detained in the prison. Yet, however concerned or even progressive he might have seemed on the matter of prison conditions, he concluded his report on this visit with the note: 'I think [the] Colonial Office should be asked whether a certain number of the Parkhurst boys might not at the end of their terms of confinement be sent to the Australian colonies. I fear that being discharged at home they are likely ... to fall back into a fresh system of offence.'[71]

Thus if it was Lord John Russell who appeared socially exclusive, Palmerston remained just as sceptical of the masses; indeed, more so, consistently opposing Russell's plans for franchise extension throughout his political career. He resisted strenuously plans for franchise extension proposed in 1854, for example, on the grounds that while a greater number of electors might in itself pose little or no risk to the security of the constitution, what Palmerston did 'think objectionable is the admission of a great number of electors of a lower class in regard to intelligence, property and independence.' He feared intimidation, manipulation and corruption would increase with the creation of a larger, and necessarily financially poorer and politically illiterate, electorate; but more seriously, he worried that the stability of the existing, responsible, system of representation, in which power was delegated to responsible ministers (what Dugald Stewart would have referred to as 'select councils'), would be jeopardised by the proposed reforms. 'A low class of electors may naturally be expected to chuse a low class of representatives;' he warned Russell, 'but even where men of a superior kind are chosen, these men insensibly and unavoidably adapt their language, their tone, and their votes, to the lowest class of electors, if that class is numerous; just as actors are led to neglect the boxes and the pit, and to play for the shilling gallery.'[72]

Far from making Palmerston a Regency throwback, however, this tends only to strengthen his claims to stand as symbol of the age. His Whiggish reserve reassured many traditionalists, and while he did not share Russell's mature tastes for electoral reform, and certainly fell short of radical demands for a more representative system of government, he was able to buy off such critics with a vicarious role in his popular (though not necessarily populist) foreign policy. And this had value beyond the Whig and Liberal ranks. Palmerston by the mid-1850s had just about shored up a rackety position among his own colleagues and political associates, but his modest reform agenda combined with a commitment to efficient administration won admiration across the floor of the House as well.

Even by the later 1850s, for example, when Palmerston's unwillingness to join the Protectionists could not have been clearer, Lord Derby resisted schemes to attack him in Parliament. During the Crimean War, Derby had seemed reluctant to press charges against the government's foreign policy, preferring to await the government's collapse over Reform and handed to Palmerston, on a plate, the patriotic card.[73] Again, in 1857 and 1858, as the Palmerston government struggled to cope with imperial revolt in India, and when Disraeli was clearly eager to have a go at Palmerstonian foreign policy, whether over its alleged inconsistencies and dishonourable secret treaties, or over the Indian Mutiny itself, Derby, as Angus Hawkins has pointed out, 'preached the merits of inaction'.[74] This, at a time when the breach between Russell and Palmerston seemed particularly wide, might well have been a good opportunity to press home the advantages of the erstwhile 'masterly inactivity'.

In large part it seems, this was because Derby recognised the points of similarity between himself and Palmerston and clung to an increasingly forlorn hope that he might succeed in persuading Palmerston, even when Palmerston was publicly identifying himself as a Liberal Prime Minister, that his true friends and allies were to be found among the Conservatives. For this, Derby has attracted much censure, largely from an historiographical tradition that privileges Disraelian Conservatism over other mid-Victorian varieties, though it should also be noted that, even so, Disraeli too found it difficult to attack Palmerston, supporting as he did much of what Palmerston stood for and was himself drawn to try to attack Palmerston's foreign policy whilst simultaneously absolving Palmerston for any of its shortcomings. Thus, might Parry argue that in the light of Tory weaknesses, Derby 'concluded that the best security for traditional interests lay with a strong Conservative opposition restraining a responsible Palmerstonian government.' More than this, indeed: 'The defining fact about Palmerston's rule is that he governed nearly throughout with parliaments elected under, and relatively sympathetic to, previous short-term Tory governments (those of 1852 and 1859). He preferred this to seeking a new mandate for Liberalism.'[75]

IV

The 1850s, for Palmerston, far from witnessing the end of his active public life, in fact saw the consolidation of his dominant position in British politics. These years represent a dynamic period in Palmerston's political career that in the end gave the lie to Disraeli's 1855 jibe that he was nothing but an 'old painted pantaloon' who was 'really an impostor, utterly exhausted, and at best only ginger-beer and not champagne'.[76] The champagne might have lost a little of its sparkle over the years, but Palmerston had by the end of the decade nonetheless ensured that he would leave behind something more than 'a second class reputation'.[77] He had, through his work at the Foreign Office in the 1840s and early 1850s established a rapport with a broad cross-section of the population based on a combination of a steadfast defence of national interests and championship of just, liberal government (even the notion that Britain might have had a Providential mission to spread such ideas of good government). Yet his position within Whig circles remained a somewhat precarious one, underpinned only by a general sense that, thanks largely to his popular foreign policy, he was capable of carrying important bodies of opinion with him and was therefore a force not to be dismissed lightly. Although his fortunes were arguably more closely tied to the Whigs than any other group, his political identity remained a negotiable one which demanded careful attention on Palmerston's part to presenting himself as a balanced, moderate and broad-based politician. Hence his interest in domestic reforms at the Home Office and subsequently while as premier: it allowed him to demonstrate a social conscience that would legitimise his claims to pre-eminence in Liberal politics. Yet this was not mere opportunism, nor was it a desperate search for position. Palmerstonian social reform was in many ways motivated by the very same impulses that informed Whig orthodoxy and allowed him to elaborate on his essentially paternalist, benevolent, but strictly hierarchical view of society. In all of this, the 1850s saw Palmerston develop and execute a more rounded political philosophy, one very much of moderation, but one which also allowed him once and for all to steal a march on his rivals such as Russell.

Palmerston, in the final analysis, dominated the political scene at mid-century. He was not the anachronistic symbol of an earlier age who had outlived his usefulness and relevance, but to present him as the conscious, self-styled harbinger of late Victorian democracy and even modernity is to make similarly exaggerated claims. In fact he was neither behind nor ahead of his times, but very much of them. His commitment to social reform and desire to address the 'condition of England question' on some level suggests that there was not quite a 'moral vacuum' at the bottom of him; his wariness of the masses and his limited conception of the nature and value of democratic politics, however, speaks of his innate Whiggish, and very mid-Victorian, conservatism. His were the politics of balance and moderation, of careful accommodation of change where necessary but essentially, as Paul Smith observed, 'of getting from Monday to Friday without conspicuous damage'.[78] Moderation did not mean inaction, but a commitment to stability and the preservation of a certain 'equipoise'.

References

[1] W. L. Burn *The age of equipoise: a study of the mid-Victorian generation* (London: Allen and Unwin, 1964) p. 18.

[2] P. Guedalla *Palmerston* [1926] (London: Hodder and Stoughton, 1937 edn.) p. 405; E.D. Steele *Palmerston and Liberalism, 1855-1865* (Cambridge: Cambridge University Press, 1991) p. 367.

[3] According to a popular doggerel in Germany *c.*1848, 'Hat der Teufel einen Sohn / so heißt er sicher Palmerston'. See F. L. Müller *Britain and the German*

question: perceptions of nationalism and political reform, 1830-63 (Basingstoke: Macmillan, 2002) p. 57.

[4] On Palmerston's education, see Kenneth Bourne *Palmerston: the early years, 1784-1841* (London: Allen Lane, 1982) pp. 11-47 (esp. pp. 11-30).

[5] See J. P. Parry *The rise and fall of Liberal government in Victorian Britain*, (New Haven and London: Yale University Press, 1993) esp. ch. 8.

[6] Don Pacifico was a Portuguese Jew who had lost personal property in anti-Semitic riots in Athens in 1847. Pacifico laid claim to British citizenship by virtue of having been born in Gibraltar and appealed to Palmerston for assistance in pressing for what were widely regarded to be exaggerated claims for compensation against the Greek government. Palmerston, glad of an opportunity to face down the Greek government, ordered a blockade of Athens by the British navy, much to the disgust of many politicians at home.

[7] The Prince Consort had long recognised Palmerston's abilities but doubted his integrity. See, for example, Albert to Russell, 2 Apr 1850, quoted in B. Connell (ed.) *Regina v. Palmerston: the correspondence between Queen Victoria and her Foreign and Prime Minister, 1837-1865* (London: Evans Bros, 1962) p. 115.

[8] From a minute, in Palmerston's hand, on a letter from Russell, 22 May 1850 BP, GC/RU/343/enc.1.

[9] *Globe* 29 Jun 1850, 26 Jun 1850.

[10] See, for example, *The Times* 22 Feb, 20 May, 22 Jun, 1 Jul 1850; *Morning Chronicle* 27, 29 Jun, 1 Jul 1850.

[11] See, for example, Greville's observations on this theme: 'But he [Palmerston] has achieved such a success, and has made himself so great in the Cabinet, and so popular in the country, and made the Government itself so strong, that if he turns over a new leaf, takes a lesson from all that has happened, and renounces his offensive manners and changes his mode of proceeding abroad, he may consider his tenure of office perfectly secure': C.C.F. Greville *The Greville memoirs (second part): a journal of the reign of Queen Victoria, from 1837 to 1852* ed. H. Reeve (3 vols., London: Longmans, 1885) iii, pp. 347-8: 1 Jul 1850.

[12] The editor of the *Sun* to Col. Freeston, 30 May 1850, BP, MM/GR/38.

[13] James Aspinall to Palmerston, 26 Jun 1850, BP, MM/GR/47 and MM/GR/47/enc.1. On public demonstrations of support for Palmerston on the day of the debate itself, see the *Illustrated London News* 29 Jun 1850.

[14] For one such challenge, see: *On the speech of Her Majesty's Foreign Secretary, delivered in the House of Commons June 25, 1850. A letter to the right hon. Viscount Palmerston, in reference to the Greek question, exclusive of His Lordship's general foreign policy. By a Greek gentleman* (London: Effingham Wilson, 1850).

[15] See, for example, John Henderson [editor of the *Renfrewshire Reformer and Glasgow Saturday Post*] to Palmerston, 30 Jun 1850, enclosing a copy of the

paper, BP, MM/GR/49. Also *Sligo Champion* June 1850, BP, MM/GR/50.

[16] R.O. Warwick [Pensioner of Greenwich Hospital] to Palmerston, 2 Jul 1850, BP, MM/GR/52, refers to the way Palmerston has 'manfully... like the Old Champions of old, stood forward for the Honour and Welfare, of the British nation, and the just rights of her subjects at Home and Abroad'; see also: Abraham Jones Le Gras [?] to Palmerston, 8 Jul 1850, BP, MM/GR/54.

[17] See V.A.C. Gatrell, 'The commercial middle class in Manchester, *c*.1820-1857', (unpublished PhD thesis, University of Cambridge, 1971) pp. 448-50, for discussion of this 'accord between Palmerston's view of the world and that of the anti-Cobdenite opposition in Manchester'. For contemporary accounts of Palmerston's popularity in these districts and constituencies, see also the *Manchester Guardian* 29 Jun, 3 Jul 1850.

[18] *Morning Post* 25 Dec 1851.

[19] *Morning Post* 26 Dec 1851.

[20] *Morning Post* 30 Dec 1851.

[21] *The Times* 24 Dec 1851.

[22] *Morning Chronicle* 25 Dec 1851.

[23] *Dundee Courier* Feb 1852; BP, GMC/54/1-2; *Warder* 26 Dec 1851, BP, GMC/50; *Morning Advertiser* 31 Dec 1851, BP, GMC/51; *Lincolnshire Times* Feb 1852, BP, GMC/53.

[24] R. Alston to Palmerston, 27 Dec 1851, BP, GMC/51.

[25] R. Andrews to Palmerston, 26 Jan 1852, BP, GMC/106. In a similar vein, also: Henry Berkeley [MP for Bristol] to Palmerston, 27 Dec 1851, BP, GMC/65; George Coles [of Tiverton] to Palmerston, 2 Jan 1852, GMC/73; Edward Dawes [MP for the Isle of Wight] to Palmerston, 13 Jan 1852, GMC/77.

[26] See J. Davidson *The fall of the pope, and the fate of the French President* (London and Aberdeen: J. C. Bishop, 1852), which concludes: 'But, whatever be the cause [of Palmerston's resignation], never could the queen's government less spare the veteran diplomatist than at this juncture in Foreign affairs. The continent of Europe is now in such a precarious condition, that the "war of opinion" predicted by Mr Canning, may suddenly burst forth — a conflict more terrific than any of the great battles fought from Marathon to Waterloo' (p. 7). Davidson sent this pamphlet to Palmerston on 17 Jan 1852, (BP, GMC/76; GMC/76/enc.1).

[27] These points are discussed further in D. Brown 'The power of public opinion: Palmerston and the crisis of December 1851' *Parliamentary History* 20 (2001) pp. 333-58.

[28] *Morning Post* 23 Feb 1852.

[29] As Algernon Borthwick wrote to his father at this time: 'Putting aside the ill-conduct question, the Russell Cabinet is evidently "done for". Stanley can't make a Cabinet and Graham can't make a Party. Coalition must be the order of the day. Now to say true, it seems to me that any Body may coalesce with any Body Else:

Stanley and Graham / Palmerston and Graham / Graham and the Radicals / Palmerston and the Radicals / Palmerston and the Protectionists: these may all join and interjoin if it suit them — I see no Principles that stand in the way, for the truth is that no one has any, except Lord P. I see no impediment to their *all* joining him': Algernon Borthwick to Peter Borthwick, 13 Dec 1852, Glenesk-Bathurst papers, Brotherton Library, Leeds, MS. Dep. 1990/1/1173.

[30] A. Hawkins 'Lord Derby and Victorian Conservatism: a reappraisal' *Parliamentary History* 6 (1987) p. 287.

[31] W.F. Monypenny and G.E. Buckle *The life of Benjamin Disraeli, Earl of Beaconsfield* (rev. edn., 2 vols., London: John Murray, 1929) i, p. 1196.

[32] H.C.F Bell *Lord Palmerston* (2 vols., London: Longmans, 1936) ii, p. 61; D. Southgate *'The most English minister...': the policies and politics of Palmerston* (London: Macmillan, 1966) p. 310.

[33] Charles Greville to Clarendon, 21 Oct 1852, quoted in H. Maxwell *The life and letters of George William Frederick Fourth Earl of Clarendon* (2 vols., London: E. Arnold, 1913) i, p. 350.

[34] G.C. Lewis to Graham, 8 Sep 1852, Sir James Graham papers, Bodleian Library, Oxford (microfilm), Ms Film 124, Bundle 112.

[35] See, for example, J.R. Vincent (ed.) *Disraeli, Derby and the Conservative party: journals and memoirs of Edward Henry, Lord Stanley, 1849-1869* (Hassocks: Harvester, 1978) p. xiv.

[36] *Morning Post* 4 Oct 1852.

[37] *Morning Post* 7 Oct 1852.

[38] M.E. Chamberlain *Lord Palmerston* (Cardiff: University of Wales Press, 1987) p. 80; J. Ridley *Lord Palmerston* (London: Constable, 1970) pp. 404-5.

[39] Entry in Palmerston's diary, 20 Dec 1852, BP, D/13.

[40] George Douglas Campbell, eighth Duke of Argyll *Autobiography and memoirs* ed. Dowager Duchess of Argyll (2 vols., London: John Murray, 1906) i, pp. 378-89.

[41] Shaftesbury's diary, 30 Dec 1852, BP, SHA/PD/6.

[42] D. Roberts 'Lord Palmerston at the Home Office' *The Historian* 31 (1958) p. 63.

[43] Ridley, *Palmerston* p. 405.

[44] Ridley, *Palmerston* pp. 406-24. See also Chamberlain, *Palmerston* pp. 77-90.

[45] Southgate, *'Most English Minister'* pp. 315-55.

[46] Roberts, 'Palmerston at the Home Office' p. 65: 'Was the new Home Secretary, as the *Manchester Guardian* insisted, a liberal who supported all good reforms, or, as *The Times* claimed, at heart a Tory ? His work at the Home Office would, in part, answer that question.'

[47] Palmerston to Sulivan, 31 Dec 1852, BP, GC/SU/34/2.

[48] Southgate, *'Most English Minister'* p. 315.

[49] *Daily News* 4 Jan 1853.

[50] On Palmerston's work at the Home Office, see Roberts, 'Palmerston at the Home Office'; Ridley, *Palmerston* pp. 406-12; Chamberlain, *Palmerston* pp. 80-3.

[51] Roberts, 'Palmerston at the Home Office' p. 80.

[52] Parry, *Liberal government* p. 170.

[53] Parry, *Liberal government* pp. 173-5.

[54] On Palmerston's ability to manipulate the press, see D. Brown 'Compelling but not controlling ?: Palmerston and the press, 1846-1855' *History* 86 (2001) pp. 41-61.

[55] *Standard* 21 Feb 1854.

[56] *Morning Post* 3 Apr 1854.

[57] See, for example, the *Globe* 2 Feb1854.

[58] See articles in: the *Globe* 10 Mar, 3 Apr, 11, 31 Jul, 5 Oct, 2 Nov 1854; *Morning Chronicle* 7, 11 Jan, 7 Feb, 17 Apr, 27 Jun, 8, 13, 20 Jul, 1, 3 Aug, 11 Sep 1854; *Daily News* 27 Jan, 24 Mar, 30 Aug, 18 Nov 1854; *Standard* 30, 31 Mar 1854.

[59] *Standard* 1 Aug 1854.

[60] *Times* 2 Nov 1854.

[61] *Morning Post* 21 Jun 1854.

[62] See O. Anderson *A Liberal state at war: English politics and economics during the Crimean War* (London: St. Martin's Press, 1967).

[63] Parry, *Liberal government* pp. 180-3.

[64] Quoted in Chamberlain, *Palmerston* p. 107.

[65] Guedalla, *Palmerston*.

[66] Steele, *Palmerston and Liberalism, passim* (though for a very brief summary of the main arguments, see pp. 1-22, 367).

[67] Parry, *Liberal government* p. 191.

[68] Parry, *Liberal government* pp. 168-9.

[69] D. Stewart *Lectures on political economy*, ed. Sir William Hamilton (2 vols., Edinburgh: Constable, 1855) ii, p. 359.

[70] Quoted in D. Winch 'The system of the north: Dugald Stewart and his pupils', in S. Collini, D. Winch and J. Burrow *That noble science of politics: a study in nineteenth-century intellectual history* (Cambridge: Cambridge University Press, 1983) p. 36.

[71] BP, HA/N/10/1-2, memorandum by Palmerston on 'Parkhurst Prisons', 10 Oct 1854.

[72] Palmerston to Russell, 22 Jan 1854, BP, CAB/60. In a similar vein, see also Palmerston to Russell, 29 Jan 1854, and to Aberdeen, 12 Feb 1854, BP, HA/G/9 and HA/G/10.

[73] Hawkins, 'Lord Derby and Victorian Conservatism' p. 289.

[74] A. Hawkins 'British parliamentary party alignment and the Indian issue, 1857-1858' *Journal of British Studies* 23 (1984) pp. 86-7.

[75] Parry, *Liberal government* pp. 178, 192.

[76] Disraeli to Lady Londonderry, 2 Feb 1855, quoted in Monypenny and Buckle, *Disraeli* i, p. 1383.

[77] In its obituary notice of 21 Oct 1865, *The Times* observed that: 'Had he died at seventy he would have left a second class reputation. It was his great and peculiar fortune to live to right himself.'

[78] P. Smith, review of Steele, *Palmerston and Liberalism*, in *English Historical Review* 108 (1993) p. 145.

CHAPTER 5

Palmerston, the Whigs and the Government of Ireland, 1855-1866[1]
Allen Warren

Of Queen Victoria's Prime Ministers only Palmerston and Derby had extensive landed interests in Ireland; in the case of Palmerston consisting of some 10,000 acres in county Sligo along with some Dublin properties. First visiting the country in 1808, he returned almost annually until the Famine and made his final trip in 1858 in his seventy-fifth year. Throughout his exceptionally long ministerial career Irish business was central to the political and party environment in which he worked; beginning in the late 1820s with the battles over Catholic Emancipation and its political outfall, during the decade of Whig reforms from 1830, as Foreign Secretary again during the Russell ministry from 1846, and finally for nearly a decade as Prime Minister almost continuously from 1855 until his death in October 1865.[2]

It is therefore surprising that historians and biographers have devoted little attention to the place of Ireland in Palmerston's career and how its politics and government influenced and were influenced by his own interests, ideas and policies whilst in government. This paper is devoted to the final decade of his life and looks at how his earlier Irish experiences informed and moulded the now elderly statesman's mindset in relation to the domestic politics of Britain from 1855. By using this particular lens, it is hoped to comment on the more general debate about Palmerston's career as it has evolved over the last twenty years. Its general conclusion is that the now emerging consensus among Palmerston scholars of a popular and

cautiously reforming statesman at home and a liberal constitutionalist abroad needs to be qualified in the case of Ireland. This is
not because the older tradition of Palmerston as liberal abroad and
conservative at home has a continuing vitality in relation to Ireland,
but rather is explained by the connections between Palmerston's
liberal policies abroad, especially in relation to Italy and the Papacy,
and his increasing belief that Ireland in the decade of the Risorgi-
mento was incapable of sharing the vision of domestic reform that
he had modestly supported throughout his career.[3]

I

As a preliminary it is worthwhile to summarise Palmerston's Irish
engagements as a landlord, as a Canningite and later Whig Cabinet
minister in the 1830s, and as an independently popular and patriotic
foreign minister from the late 1840s.

In managing his Irish estates, Palmerston was an active economical reformer committed to rationalising his Sligo holdings; by
ending the continuous sub-divisions of plots and the middleman
system, and by investing heavily in the local economic and social
infrastructure through the improvement of roads, land drainage,
school building and town development. Precise detail is difficult to
establish especially for the years after the Famine, but the late
Kenneth Bourne calculated that Palmerston's investments over forty
years had increased his rents by some £3000 per annum by 1858.
This achievement was an important influence on Palmerston's later
attitudes to Irish improvement. Most of the changes on his estates
and their financing had been undertaken personally with little state
involvement. Influenced by his Edinburgh education under Dugald
Stewart, Palmerston saw the need for economic reform in the west
of Ireland and that the responsibility was the landlord's in terms of
estate management and agricultural practice. He supported assisted
emigration from his estates both before and during the Famine.
Even though slow to start feeding his tenants directly in 1847, the

recent judgement of Tyler Anbinder is that Palmerston's overall treatment of his tenants was better than average.[4] After the immediate crisis of the Famine had passed, Palmerston thought that further agrarian improvement was needed, that the landlord had the main responsibility, and that any recognition of tenant right was likely to be a barrier to progress. Similarly, he saw little role for the state directly in the improvement of the economic and social infrastructure through funded schemes for drainage, roads, railways, etc. In his mind, Ireland was no different from any other part of the United Kingdom. In this respect he shared Gladstone's vision of the Union as Chancellor of the Exchequer in the Aberdeen coalition as he extended the income tax to Ireland for the first time and set about equalising the spirit duties between the two countries. A decade later Palmerston gave no support to his new Irish Viceroy, Wodehouse, as he battled unsuccessfully with Gladstone for greater state involvement in Irish economic development.

Turning to Palmerston's party political Irish concerns, he was a moderate and pragmatic reformer in the main after the passing of Catholic Emancipation in 1829, a cause to which he had been prominently committed from the mid-1820s. In the 1830s as Foreign Secretary, and a former Canningite, he was not closely involved in the complex redefining of Whig ideology, recently extensively analysed by Richard Brent, Peter Mandler, Boyd Hilton and others. He seems to have supported most of the institutional and other Irish reforms of the decade. He did not contemplate a return to the Tory party along with Stanley and Graham in 1834, and was able to live with the Lichfield House compact a year later. During the famine years, he tended as mentioned to adopt a stance as an improving and active landlord — hostile to changes in the land laws, firm on the need for clearances, sceptical about state-aided relief and clear about the need for agricultural improvement. Peter Gray also describes his approach as moderate. He showed little interest in Ireland as Home Secretary from 1852 in the Aberdeen coalition, despite having overall Cabinet responsibility for its government.[5]

Finally, how does Ireland fit into Palmerston's reputation as a popular, patriotic statesman with an independent domestic political voice ? Historians have recently identified important changes in his national image after 1846 as a result of his approach to Italian and papal politics following the election of Pius IX, events which were to cast a significant religious shadow over British and Anglo-Irish politics in the two decades following the Famine. We know relatively little about Palmerston's personal religious beliefs, Shaftesbury famously wondering in 1855 whether he knew the difference between Moses and Sydney Smith. A supporter of religious toleration towards Catholics and Dissenters, Palmerston had a reforming Erastian approach to church affairs with a tendency to evangelical sympathy. He played little part in the Whig religious debates of the 1830s, supporting Irish non-denominational schooling and Irish church reform, as well as Peel's later increases in the Maynooth grant and the foundation of the non-denominational Queen's Colleges. The spirit of moderate church co-operation that informed Dublin Castle and the Roman Catholic hierarchy in the 1830s seems to have been broadly to his taste. What he did not like was the Romanising atmosphere that began to inform the Church of England and religious society more generally from the late 1830s and which was reinforced strongly by events in Rome after 1846. As Saho Matsumoto-Best has shown, Palmerston was at first encouraged by the election of Pius IX and the prospect of reform in the Papal States, even entertaining hopes that it might lead to a papally-inspired process of Italian unification. The events of 1848-50 changed the situation totally as Pius IX moved in a much more conservative direction, making diplomatic relations with the Vatican increasingly problematic. This was especially the case in relation to Ireland, where Palmerston had hoped that papal influence would encourage responsible political and social leadership on the part of bishops and priests. The hopes of establishing formal relations with the Vatican receded rapidly, and the Papal Aggression and Russell's Durham letter of late 1850 gave Anglo-Irish relations their highly sectarian character for the rest of the decade. Palmerston's own opinions moved increasingly from being anti-papal to anti-Catholic more generally, changes that influenced significantly his approach to Ireland after 1855.[6]

II

How then did Palmerston approach the problems, policies and politics associated with the governing of Ireland after coming into office in February 1855, and for which he was to have overall responsibility for the next decade, with a short Derby interlude in 1858-9 ? For convenience, the period can be subdivided into three — the first ministry itself from 1855 until its defeat in the Commons in February 1858 following the Orsini bomb plot, the first half of the second ministry from 1859 to 1861 co-inciding with the Chief Secretaryship of the Edward Cardwell, and finally, the Chief Secretaryship of Sir Robert Peel from 1861 to 1866, which included Palmerston's own death in October 1865.

    Brought to power by the failure of the Aberdeen coalition in the Crimea, Ireland was hardly a priority in early 1855. Putting aside the successful prosecution of the war, Palmerston's concerns were largely about the security of his ministry and his own reputation in the country, particularly as he might be forced into an election. Ireland was largely quiet and recovering rapidly in economic terms from the trauma of the Famine. Politically, the independent Irish party was already in disarray with electoral politics becoming largely determined by local circumstances over which ministers and managers had little control. As Sir George Cornewall Lewis, Chancellor of the Exchequer, commented,

How small a portion of the time of Parliament Ireland now occupies, compared with what was the case a few sessions ago! It must be said that ... the legislation of the last twenty-five years is beginning at last to bear fruit.'[7]

Having said that, there were important questions in relation to Irish politics that would significantly affect Palmerston's parliamentary and popular survival. Two were particularly relevant. The first was the pattern of Irish constituency politics itself. Divided as the Irish members might be in party political terms, they had been elected since the 1850 Irish Franchise Act on a significantly extended electorate. How local constituency politics would develop was not clear, but with a small majority the attitudes of individual Irish members and the impact of by-elections would be important. The second question arose directly from the events surrounding the Papal Aggression and the subsequent Ecclesiastical Titles legislation. The religious and political furore that flowed from both affected parliamentary and popular politics in powerful ways. At the parliamentary level it gave scope for Tories, particularly Disraeli, to try to present themselves as the true friends of Catholic Ireland, and as Derby's first ministry had demonstrated during 1852. At the popular level on the other hand, the events of 1850 had so stirred Protestant zeal in Britain and Ireland that anything that hinted at Irish sympathy was likely to stimulate a pan-Protestant defensiveness in the House of Commons. Horsman, appointed as Chief Secretary in 1855, noted perceptively that Palmerston had no real strength in the Commons, only support in the country. He had to tread carefully.[8]

Palmerston's Irish appointments show that he understood the situation. As Viceroy, he appointed George, seventh Earl of Carlisle, a grandee, who as the Foxite Whig Morpeth in the 1830s had been Irish Chief Secretary during the heroic years of Irish reform between 1835 and 1841. Carlisle was a Whig politician with a great future behind him, but his appointment sent out a signal that Palmerston saw moderate judicious government as appropriate. As Chief Secretary, he appointed Edward Horsman, in 1855 regarded as a moderate Liberal of sharp intelligence with robust views about the pretensions of bishops. Carlisle, who had tended to drop in and out of Whig politics since 1841, saw his own appointment as the culmination of his political life as a Whig aristocrat, during which he might put the keystone to the arch of his Irish work of fifteen years before. Senior figures in Dublin Castle, particularly Sir Alexander Macdonnell, the long serving commissioner for education and confidant of Carlisle, thought in the same terms.[9]

What this meant in practice was vigorous support for the national non-denominational system of education, equality of treatment for Protestants and Catholics in as many areas of public life as possible, and a sort of benign sweetness and light in the style of the viceregal court and in its public, social and philanthropic activities. None of this required much executive activity on Carlisle's part. The national education system was non-negotiable despite its weaknesses and the increasing sectarian atmosphere surrounding education generally in both the north and south. On law and order, the familiar threats as represented by Ribbonism or latter-day Young Ireland activity were seen as insubstantial, so much so that ministers allowed Smith O'Brien to return to Ireland in 1856, while agitation on the question of tenant right was largely confined to parliamentary debate at Westminster. Horsman humoured the Irish members led by Shee into the belief that the new government might consider a measure to compensate tenants retrospectively for their improvements, but only because both the earlier Derby and Aberdeen ministries had held out the same hope so as to retain the support of as many liberal and independent Irish members as possible. Where action was required was in respect of patronage, where Carlisle remained determinedly committed to equality of treatment for Catholics and Protestants. It was not an easy task as he found himself ground between the principles of religious equality, appointment on merit (as recently identified in the Northcote-Trevelyan report), administrative effectiveness particularly in the legal system, and a desire to reduce jobbery and waste, while keeping the wheels of government oiled and political support secure.[10]

If this approach suggested that the spirit of the 1830s without the poverty could be restored, then Carlisle, and by implication Palmerston, were both mistaken, and the difference lay in the increased sectarian divisions emerging in Irish society. In education, Dublin Castle found church leaders increasingly strident in their assertions and conciliation more difficult to achieve, conflicts which spilled over into the periodic parliamentary debates on national education and the Maynooth grant. At the popular level, ritual burning of bibles by Catholics did little to encourage Protestant sympathies and even Carlisle's benign presence was charged with sectarian electricity on occasion. His support for a Ragged School Union Bazaar in May 1856, for instance, produced a major public row with Archbishop Cullen and the hierarchy that rumbled on for weeks, eventually requiring his attendance at a St Vincent de Paul Society Bazaar as penance. But most ominous as far as Dublin Castle was concerned was the increasing sectarian disorder in the north of Ireland, culminating in major rioting in Belfast in July 1857 and the subsequent proclamation of the town. Not only did such developments make sectarian reconciliation more difficult, it also constituted a serious threat to law and order, especially when linked to the street preaching of Hugh Hanna. Carlisle, after meeting the resident magistrate described Belfast as the most 'wicked' place he knew and decided to prohibit magistrates from membership of the Orange Association, a move prompting vigorous protests from the governing classes in the north. Irish members protested directly to Palmerston and threatened a disruptive parliamentary debate in the new year. Some saw Carlisle as over-reacting, while others thought the move simply provided the Association with free publicity. The government vacillated, with no decision being made before its parliamentary defeat and replacement by the second Derby ministry in February 1858.[11]

Palmerston's attitude to Carlisle's ambitions during this period was to be politically pragmatic in public but more sceptical in private with the Viceroy commenting in his journal in December 1857: 'He [Palmerston] talked for some time: he set great store by the Militia, is very anti-Catholic; spoke of my being popular.'[12]

On national education, Palmerston held to the party line

without difficulty although clearly suspicious of Cullen's motives, and the scope that the education question gave for constant Westminster scheming among the Tories, Irish members and Peel-ites. On tenant compensation and the retrospective clause in partic-ular, he remained quiet in the attempt to protect Irish Liberal members in the ministry's reply to Shee's bill in 1855, but in private vigorously declared against it and made it clear that he would do 'absolutely nothing' on the subject the following year. On Orange magistrates, he thought that Carlisle had made an error, commenting to the Home Secretary, Sir George Grey:

Carlisle should recollect that such an announcement … was sure to put up the backs of all the Protestant gentry whether belonging or not to the Orange association and the probable effect would be, not to dissolve the Orange associ-ation but to exclude from the Bench many of the persons whom the Irish govern-ment would wish to see forming part of the magistracy.[13]

Not surprisingly, on his return to office in 1859 the order was never implemented. As a political strategy more generally, the Irish government's style in 1855-8 worked not too badly, although Hors-man felt that more should have been done to support sym-pathetic Irish members on the tenant right issue, but also acknow-ledging that almost inevitably the ministry's potential strength in England would be matched by weakness in Ireland.[14] When the gov-ernment was defeated on the China motion on 3 March 1857 only nine non-Tory Irish members voted in the majority. At the following general election the government maintained its numerical strength in Ireland but in Carlisle's view had improved its position in relation to the moderation of Irish members, both Tory and Independent.[15] The following month, on Horsman's resignation, Palmerston tried to reinforce his position by appointing the Irish Peelite, Henry Herbert of Muckross as his successor.[16] Now pre-occupied with the Indian mutiny, London was little exercised by affairs in Ireland other than by the potential impact on its support from those outraged by Carlisle's actions on Orange magistrates. While the debate on

the address following the election went well, the government
was surprisingly defeated on the Conspiracy to Murder Bill on
19 February 1858 and immediately resigned. Carlisle saw the defeat
as the Manchester men taking vengeance on Palmerston for truck-
ling to foreigners. His colleague, J. D. Fitzgerald (the Irish Attorney-
General) also saw the defeat as a largely self-inflicted wound by
the failure of Whigs and radicals to work together.[17] Even so,
Carlisle's brother was reporting opinion swinging back in favour of
Palmerston within a few days of the defeat, while Carlisle also
found Palmerston personally sanguine about a rapid return to
power.[18] As it turned out the Derby ministry survived the parliamentary session with Liberals increasingly fearing the introduction
of a radical Tory franchise bill in the New Year.[19] Not that the Derby
government was any more active. In London Disraeli continued to
trim to Catholic opinion whenever he could, while Eglinton and
Naas in Dublin tried to balance the sectarian divisions within Irish
political life.[20] Defeat of the government's reform proposals led immediately to a dissolution, which led to modest Conservative gains,
but not an overall majority.[21] Following the election, as Angus
Hawkins, Theodore Hoppen and others have shown, there was a
slow moving together among non-Conservative members over the
following weeks leading to the famous Willis' Rooms meeting on
6 June with Palmerston resuming his premiership.[22]

III

The formation of the second Palmerston government with its Whig,
Radical and Peelite components is often presented as the point at
which the disruption of 1846 was brought to an end. But, as again
Theodore Hoppen has stated, it was rather more a refashioning of
the Aberdeen coalition and there was no certainty that it would
prove any more durable. Certainly, Gladstone, Palmerston's biggest
ministerial catch, did not think so as he wrote to Samuel Wilberforce
on 17 June:

It is quite a mistake to suppose the formation of this Cabinet is the determining crisis of its political character. That must come in its development and may be there six or even nine months hence.[23]

As far as Ireland was concerned, the election had been a disappointment for the Liberals, with an overall loss of five seats as calculated by Fitzgerald, giving the Conservatives an Irish majority for the first time. As he wrote to Carlisle, 'We had most unfavourable circumstances to contend with and had to resist an unholy alliance of the Pope, the Cardinal and Lord Derby.'[24] What this lapidary summary meant was that sympathy among voters for the predicament of the Pope in the loss of the Papal Territories, Palmerston's public identification with the cause of Italian unification, Cardinal Wiseman's direct intervention the previous year through his much publicised tour of Ireland (with its echoes of the Papal Aggression), and skill of the Derby ministry not to offend moderate Catholic opinion had all worked in the Tories' favour.

As far as Palmerston was concerned, the general election results themselves did not alter significantly his dilemma in relation to the politics and governing of Ireland, it had simply increased the scale of potential Irish disruption. This was not simply as a result of the increased Tory numbers, but with a papal sympathy movement in full flood, it would be increasingly difficult for Liberal members to remain moderate in the House if they were to keep their seats in the future — a point made directly to Palmerston by the new Chief Secretary, following a pastoral letter from the Roman Catholic bishops, highly critical of the national education system in August.[25] More immediately important to Palmerston was the need to stabilise his ministry. Carlisle returned almost automatically to Dublin and was joined by the former Peelite, Edward Cardwell, as Chief Secretary. But this did not mean simply giving way to Irish Liberal demands. William Monsell, along with Thomas O'Hagan the leading moderate liberal ascendancy Catholic, expressed outrage that so few Irish Catholics were represented in the new government. Vigorous action, Monsell wrote, was needed if Liberals, as the

'natural' friends of Ireland, were to regain their rightful influence —
a properly drafted landlord and tenant bill, provision for Catholic
university education and an overhaul in the national education
system were all required urgently.[26]

Even so, Palmerston's government was not going to take its
orders either from bishops or Castle Catholics. Cardwell responded
robustly to Cullen's pastoral, refusing to receive it officially, Carlisle
re-affirmed the integrity of the national education system, and Gladstone set about vigorously scrutinising Irish expenditure on education and the costs of the legal establishment. At the same time the
Chancellor tackled directly the more unseemly side of Irish office
through holding an investigation into what had been authorised by
the outgoing government in respect of the Galway postal contract.[27]

Nevertheless in the highly charged international situation in
both Italy and in Anglo-French relations, Palmerston realised that
the fate of his government might depend on the votes of the Irish
members, themselves under pressure from bishops and priests. In
late October 1859 Cardwell brought forward a four point Irish plan
for the coming session — an Irish reform bill, a comprehensive law
of landlord and tenant, a response on education questions and minor
reforms in the treatment of lunatics and the poor.[28] By January 1860
Fitzgerald was already reporting plotting among Irish members to
secure the rejection of the anticipated French commercial treaty in
order to protect specialist trades in Ireland.[29] Similar rumours were
circulating about possibly defeating Gladstone's budget itself,
rumours that coincided with Cullen's call for a rate in aid for the
Pope.[30] In the event, Gladstone's budget speech in February was a
triumph, described by Palmerston as 'a masterpiece; I should say the
best speech he has ever made.'[31] Moderate Tories deserted Disraeli
in droves, even Derby not attending his party's meeting, all keen
not to defeat the government in what would seem to be a victory
for the Pope.[32] Much the same occurred later in the session in the
debates over the French commercial treaty. For his part Palmerston
showed a characteristic insouciance in this anxious atmosphere,

declining to moderate his endorsement of Garibaldi.[33] In fact, Cardwell's Irish programme did not add up to much in the end — the Irish reform bill was extremely modest in scale given that the Irish franchise had been reformed as recently as 1850 and was later withdrawn. Cardwell's land bill did allow compensation for improvements for the tenant but only if they had been undertaken with the landlord's prior consent, and an associated bill introduced by Deasy in fact embedded the contractual foundation of landed relations. As Collinson Black pointed out, taken together they made no real difference to the position of the typical tenant. Unsurprisingly, Palmerston, who studied the draft legislation in detail, was able to endorse it as entirely consistent with his own practice in Sligo. Cardwell's verdict was that it completed the work of the Encumbered Estates legislation and that Ireland now had a structure of land law that would encourage capital to flow into the country. On education, Carlisle unusually speaking himself in the Lords' debate re-affirmed the national education system despite current criticisms, a position vigorously repeated by Cardwell in the Commons. Greater balance was introduced among the Board of Education commissioners in line with Carlisle's ideals, but the government did not respond to the bishops' hostility to the model schools nor did it make any response on the university question.[34] What did concern the government was the continuing sectarian tensions in the north and Cardwell introduced supplementary provisions to restrict the inflammatory use of emblems, flags and music.[35] All in all the Irish government saw itself as doing quite well with Cardwell believing that their policy of not giving in to the aggressive party had been vindicated, and asking if there were any more sores remaining. Writing to Palmerston on 10 September he commented:

Everything here is as quiet as the grave. Dublin is deserted for the salt water. Papal recruiting, and Party Emblems, seem alike forgotten: and perhaps the excitement they occasioned may contribute to the present state of collapse. Foreign events too will not encourage dissatisfied persons here.[36]

While Palmerston and his Irish colleagues thought that their first eighteen months in office had been a success, both in restraining the aggressive religious parties in Ireland, and in preserving and stabilising the ministry at Westminster, Cardwell at least realised that the general position of the Liberal party in Ireland was insecure. Meeting Palmerston, whom he described as 'in excellent spirits and positively younger than ever', he continued to Carlisle:

Generally I said that our position in Ireland was that we had no reliable support: that there was a better feeling among Irish members towards us: but that the Italian question would continue to exercise an adverse influence: that our only enemy was O'F[errall]: that we stood well with moderate Catholics: and though not well with the Ultramontanes yet as well as possible: that the sorrows of the Pope greatly discouraged them.[37]

Writing to Palmerston a month later, he repeated that religious moderates on all sides were increasingly disgusted with the extremists, and that the government should do nothing provocative to stem that process.[38]

During the following session the Dublin government generally followed their own advice but the small nature of the government's overall majority and the unpredictable voting behaviour of the Irish Liberal members continued to threaten the ministry. In 1860 there had been anxiety over the Budget and the commercial treaty with the French, in 1861 concern centred more on the labyrinthine history of the Galway postal contract (the 'Bogtrotter question' as Palmerston called it) and the determination of Gladstone to cancel the agreement with the Atlantic Royal Mail Steam Company, a move seen by many Irish members as an explicitly anti-Irish decision to favour Liverpool. Irish members threatened Gladstone again with defeat of the budget unless the contract was retained. Gladstone demurred and Palmerston refused to meet an Irish delegation on the issue. But on this occasion, it was not so clear that the Tories would be unwilling to turn out the government. In the end the budget secured a better majority than expected with some Irish members standing up to what Chichester Fortescue called the 'ultra Papists' with some country Tories also refusing to endorse Disraeli's opportunistic scheming. In return Gladstone agreed that a Select Committee should investigate the whole Galway contract issue in order to clear the way to a properly negotiated agreement. The Committee reported rapidly with Palmerston announcing that a new properly drafted contract would be drawn up with Galway as the base.[39]

Since coming into office in 1855, Palmerston and his Irish colleagues had handled the affairs of Ireland with pragmatic caution. Until 1858 they had not wanted to ruffle the social calm that appeared to be settling over the island and which was reflected in the gradual breaking down of the Independent Irish party, and Carlisle in particular looked to completing the work of reconciliation which he had inaugurated in the 1830s. If they had a worry it was that the sectarianism of the north was creating problems of law and order and stimulating fears among the Catholic community more generally. From 1858 until 1861 threats to ministerial survival predominated in an atmosphere in which developments in Italy and the fate of the Pope directly affected the politics of Ireland in the constituencies and at Westminster. Irish Liberal members came under increased Ultramontane pressure threatening the security of the government. Palmerston as the leading champion of the Italian cause was permanently under suspicion, particularly as he did not always keep his anti-papal feelings entirely private.

IV

By the end of the 1861 parliamentary session, however, Palmerston seems to have felt more politically confident. The necessary development that Gladstone had predicted at the formation of the ministry seemed to have happened, with Palmerston establishing a modus vivendi with his energetic Chancellor. With the Italian question becoming acute, and a Conservative opposition unenthusiastic about removing the government, the disruptive potential of the Irish members diminished. This seems to have encouraged Palmerston to change direction. Prompted by the death of Sidney Herbert, he conducted a ministerial reshuffle in late July 1861 with Cardwell being moved to the Duchy of Lancaster. In his place, he appointed Sir Robert Peel, son of the former premier, and whom Palmerston had described in 1857 as having neither the 'temper, tact or discretion for the office' of Chief Secretary.[40] In a letter to an anxious Carlisle on 28 July, he made his intentions clear:

Now we the English government have heaped benefits and favours on the Irish Catholics. We have relieved them from all their civil and political disabilities, we have given them their full share, and in some cases more than their just and equal share of patronage and power and place. Dead to every proper sense of gratitude they turn against us as a body at the bidding of a foreign authority, thus to a certain degree verifying the foretellings of those who opposed Catholic Emancipation — we are now told that scarcely one supporter of the government would be returned at the present moment by any Irish constituency, among and over which the Catholic priesthood could exercise any deciding influence ... I do not mean that we ought to act unjustly by them, because they act hostilely to us ... It would at the same time be politic to draw a little closer to the Liberal Protestant gentry of Ireland upon whom alone we really can depend.[41]

A month later in a meeting with the former director of the All Hallows missionary college in Dublin, Palmerston reported that he had read the Catholic bishops a lecture on 'the absurd, ungrateful and childish course adopted by the Catholic priesthood in their hostility to the present government: a hostility founded simply on the ground that the Italian people do not choose to be subject to the temporal domination of the Pope'.[42]

The impact of Peel's appointment was immediate as he began a programme of what were regarded as Protestant speeches, particularly defending and enthusing upon the success of his father's non-denominational Queen's Colleges, which of course were an anathema to the bishops and had been previously condemned by them. Carlisle reported these 'Protestant harangues' as having the personal approval of both Palmerston and Russell. He found the Prime Minister in 'his usual radiance' in late November, and a few days later Palmerston made a personal donation as an Irish landowner to Peel's fund for additional scholarships for the colleges.[43] Reaction from established Irish opinion was mixed. For Dr Graves, Dean of the Chapel Royal and a regular Carlisle correspondent, all was well if the attacks were directed specifically towards the Ultramontanes, but Carlisle's own moderating influence was still required if Peel was not wholly to alienate moderate Catholic opinion, whose support was of such importance. Monsell, on other hand, was clear that by defending the Queen's Colleges particularly, Peel had alienated almost all Catholic opinion, with potentially disastrous electoral consequences. This was view endorsed by Henry Brand, the Liberal senior whip, who in his search for Irish constituencies for the parliamentary Irish legal office holders commented: 'Between those who cannot accept for fear of their seats, and those who won't for fear of the Pope and other reasons, there are scarcely any friends left to put in the place.'[44]

These electoral fears were quickly realised in County Longford, where the attempt to re-elect the sitting member, Colonel Luke White, on his appointment as a Lord of the Treasury, was completely overwhelmed by electoral disruption, corruption and what Peel called the 'hostility of a degraded priesthood' to secure the election of the commander of the former papal brigade, Major Myles O'Reilly. Peel's reaction was that little else could be expected as long as the government continued its 'wise and dignified' policy in Italy. He added that he also saw no reason to change the national education system and warned Palmerston against any dallying with liberal Catholic suggestions on the university question. More soberly, Brand commented that the Liberals would only save ten seats in the south of Ireland were an election to be held, and asking if anything could be done to break the Conservative control of the north.[45] A gap quickly opened up between Peel and Carlisle, particularly on the question of denominational balance in the distribution of patronage. The Viceroy stated that he would not retreat from the policy of equality that he had consistently pursued and that, if necessary, Palmerston could have his resignation. Similar sharp differences of opinion emerged about the attitudes and conduct of O'Hagan as Attorney-General, especially over the treatment of 'treasonable' priests like Father Lavelle. Palmerston warned Carlisle:

Don't allow yourself to be led by O'Hagan to shower patronage down upon Catholics. He is an agreeable clever man but an Ultramontane and the Catholics for some time past have been behaving so ill to us in Ireland that as I said to you some months ago we ought to draw off from them than draw on to them, and the turn of the scale should be given to the Protestants.[46]

All of this internal wrangling was happening while Ireland itself was experiencing the most distressed economic conditions since the Famine, and upon which Palmerston, described by Carlisle as 'infatuated' with Peel, could only comment, 'I see the Catholics are getting up a cry of distress in Ireland; I apprehend their real cause of distress is at Rome'.[47] Macdonnell, gloomily reflecting to Carlisle on all his years in Ireland, wondered whether there was future in the Whig enterprise for Ireland or whether it would have to be completed by a Liberal Conservative government.[48]

The following session of 1863 saw no change of direction. The government, rather perversely, saw its approach as vindicated by the successful placing of O'Hagan as member for Tralee on his appointment as Attorney-General through a defeat of the Tory/Ultramontane alliance in the constituency. It was decided that no government Irish bills were necessary, with Peel later reaffirming the finality of Cardwell's Land Act.[49] In the face of the economic distress of the previous two years, Irish members now turned their attention to the question of whether Ireland was unfairly taxed, which prompted a long defence by Gladstone of his 1853 Irish tax and excise equalisation measures.[50] Ten days later in one of his few parliamentary speeches on Ireland directly, Palmerston painted a sunny picture in which the continuing flow of emigrants represented Irish individual, family and social enterprise, with the remittances providing capital for agrarian improvement at home, and all within a system of land law, which since 1860 had encouraged new investment by landlords in their estates. The recent distress, he concluded, was simply the result of geology and climate.[51] The only obvious ministerial concession was in the endless saga of the Galway contract, on which Palmerston, in the face of back-bench radical opposition, re-affirmed the decision to grant the now properly drafted contract to operate from Galway.[52] Peel continued to have Palmerston's enthusiastic backing, and at the end of the year painted a picture of general political and economic progress with fewer priestly denunciations of the land system and in which traditional Ribbonism and the activity of Phoenix Societies and the Brotherhood of St Patrick were kept under close scrutiny.[53]

From early 1864 the general situation began to change. In Ireland, Carlisle suffered a succession of minor strokes, which required his resignation in August. In London as the prospect of a general election drew nearer, so the question of the shape and direction of any post-Palmerstonian political world became more intriguing. Baines' franchise motion and Gladstone's reply in particular showed that parliamentary reform generally was re-appearing on the political agenda. Not that Palmerston showed any signs of retiring. While his new false teeth might click rather disconcertingly, his other faculties seemed undiminished with De Grey reporting to Wodehouse (Carlisle's successor) in January 1865, '[o]ur chief is very well, shooting one day and killing sixty head to his own gun and hunting the next with all the glories of red coat and top boots'.[54]

As far as Ireland was concerned, Brand's earlier electoral anxieties were leading him to assess the Irish situation carefully and to urge conciliation especially after the Commons debate on the Schleswig-Holstein question in July 1864 in which large numbers of Irish Liberals deserted the government in its most critical division. Among ministers Gladstone most notably began changing his position in Parliament. Under further pressure from Irish members, he agreed to a Select Committee on the taxation question, he implicitly accepted that the Irish national education system had not worked wholly as intended, and he initiated a correspondence with O'Hagan and others on how to present the government in a more conciliatory light. More privately, he began to educate himself into the complexities of the Irish university question and how to meet the needs of the Catholic middle classes, and most famously indicated for the first time his preparedness to consider his position on the established church through his reply to Dillwyn's motion and by voting for the Roman Catholic Oaths Bill. Equally significantly, Gladstone also made clear the areas on which he was not prepared to make even cosmetic changes to the government's position. On taxation and the general question of economic development in Ireland, he was firmly opposed to any monetary policies that were based on principles other than equality of treatment for each kingdom, he resisted strongly the new Viceroy's enthusiasm for government led public works to improve the Irish socio-economic infrastructure and also reiterated that he saw little role for the state in the development of the Irish railway system. Finally, although supporting the establishing of a Select Committee on Irish land, he left it to Palmerston to repeat that the government had no intention of going beyond Cardwell's Act. Much of this can be represented as Gladstone simply trying to position the government more favourably in the months prior to the 1865 general election and his political postures are capable of more than one interpretation. As such they are outside the scope of this essay, but it is interesting that he was not anticipating any Irish work in 1866 except possibly in relation to railways, when composing a note for himself on 31 August 1865.[55]

On most of these questions Palmerston was much less flexible. In appointing Wodehouse, he selected a very different type of Viceroy. Wodehouse, a Tory by upbringing but Liberal in his own

opinions, had none of the finer sensibilities that had both characterised and limited Carlisle's Whig regime. On his retirement
Palmerston had first considered abolishing the Viceroyalty and the
Dublin Castle system altogether, integrating the government of the
United Kingdom as a whole with the appointment of a Secretaryship
of State. Wodehouse supported the idea, only accepting the posting
on the assumption that he might be the last Viceroy. But in the
circumstances of a pending election, it was eventually seen as
impolitic to suggest so radical a change.[56] On the university question, Palmerston privately continued vigorously to support Peel,
making it plain that he would do nothing to damage the Queen's
Colleges, and one interpretation of his appointing O'Hagan to a
vacant judgeship was to remove a pro-Catholic legal officer from
his Commons' front bench despite the political inconvenience of a
by-election.[57] He also discouraged Wodehouse's schemes of major
public works, which taken with Gladstone's opposition made them
stillborn. His approach remained what it had always had been —
that the economic future of Ireland would be determined by the
energy of the Irish landlord class operating within a framework of
land law that encouraged inward investment. Once that system of
law had been established by the legislation of 1860, the state had no
further role.[58] Where Palmerston did support Wodehouse was in his
preparations for dealing firmly with any Fenian rising or invasion.[59]

From early 1864, therefore, the government was sending out
very mixed messages. In Parliament, Gladstone in particular was
indicating some softening of line in contrast to the antagonistic
profile adopted by Peel over the previous two years. In Ireland, a
new Viceroy was spending large amounts of effort in trying to find
a possible common solution to the denominational dilemmas of the
university question, while at the same time indicating that it was
only through reforms in the social and economic infrastructure
that improvement could be secured, including the diminution of
sectarian conflict itself. At the same time, moderate Irish liberal
opinion — political and religious — was busying itself in attempted

rapprochements between the hierarchy and Queen's Colleges in order to try to improve the constituency position of their political allies.[60] In the background, however, there remained the Prime Minister supporting his Chief Secretary and not giving any ground on the position he had adopted since 1861.[61]

The general election in June 1865 went well for the government in Britain and Ireland with some 15 Irish seats gained. Admittedly, the government's position had been helped by a strongly anti-catholic speech by Derby on the Roman Catholics Oaths Bill, just before the election, but for his part, Palmerston believed that the approach of a firm hand tempered by electoral opportunism had been vindicated, 'The result of the elections is indeed highly satisfactory, not merely with reference to greater strength that we have acquired, but also with reference to the number of bores and troublesome men who have been thrown out.'[62]

Gladstone, of course, was more circumspect both in public and private, but as we have seen in his own note of August 1865 about parliamentary work to be done in 1866 there is little mention of Ireland.[63] For his part, Palmerston showed no sign of retiring, even though further parliamentary reform was likely to feature strongly during the coming session, and his increased majority meant that the ministry was now less dependent on Irish support.[64]

Palmerston died on 18 October before the Cabinet had given serious consideration to the coming session; that Ireland would feature was not in doubt as the country became infected with Fenian fever and cattle disease. Russell's succession seemed to indicate a change of approach almost immediately. In the first place, Peel was sacked as Chief Secretary, having refused to go gracefully.[65] He was replaced by Chichester Fortescue, an Irish liberal reformer, whose interests principally centred on the land question and the need for an acceptable system of tenant right. Wodehouse fully supported him in this.[66] Palmerston had been persuaded to allow a Select Committee prior to the election, but it is unlikely, given his earlier statements in private, that he would have allowed the introduction of a tenure reform bill as a ministerial measure had he lived. On the university question, the government had already announced that it would introduce a new charter for a national university, modelled on the lines of the federal University of London, but very little detail had been agreed before the election and Palmerston's death. It was a subject to which Wodehouse attached more importance than almost any other, continually trying to persuade his colleagues in London to move more in the direction of the Irish bishops.[67] He met persistent opposition from within the Cabinet from Sir George Grey and Clarendon in particular, and also increasingly in the Commons from Protestant discontents now led by the aggrieved Sir Robert Peel.[68] In Ireland, the government dug itself into a deeper and deeper hole as the prospect of legal action from Queen's Colleges and their alumni threatened to destroy the whole initiative. It was with some relief that ministers could escape from their commitments through their surprise defeat on parliamentary reform. Since 1864 university reform had been the main plank of reform among liberal Irish Catholics and their ministerial allies in Dublin and London. The experience had been chastening and it is no surprise that the future direction of Liberal/Irish reconciliation was to concentrate on church and land reform rather than education. It is unlikely that Palmerston would have allowed these negotiations with the hierarchy to continue as long as they did. Nor was the question of reform of the national education system any more attractive to ministers.

Palmerston and Carlisle had both resisted any attempt to modify the broad outlines of the system as established in the 1830s. Wodehouse was more sympathetic to amendment, but it was an issue also fraught with sectarian difficulties in both Britain and Ireland, particularly over the general regulations and the future direction of the model schools, which were almost as much of an anathema to the Roman Catholic bishops as the Queen's Colleges, concerned as they were in large part with the training of teachers for the national schools.[69]

Given the experience of 1865-6 it is not surprising that increasingly the church question came to be seen as the issue around which ministerial reconciliation with the hierarchy was to be sought. Wodehouse, as he struggled with the Fenian threat in late 1865 leading to the arrest and subsequent escape of James Stephens, the proclamation of Dublin, the distribution of troops and police on an emergency footing and ultimately in 1866 the suspension of Habeas Corpus, was convinced that some kind of settlement had to be reached with the bishops. If that were not possible around university education, then it would have to be found through a resolution of the constitutional position of the Church of Ireland, something that Gladstone was himself was also beginning to appreciate. Russell was sympathetic, Palmerston almost certainly would not have been. Having said that, there had been little ministerial discussion of the question before the fall of Russell's government. Gladstone's speech earlier in the session in reply to an Irish motion on the address was a marvellous exercise in ambiguity and gave no clue as to the government's intentions.[70]

For ministers in London both before and after Palmerston's death, Ireland was proving a worrying diversion — firstly, through the threat of major Fenian disorder and the risk of economic disaster if cattle disease could not be contained, and secondly, because they could not find a suitable issue on which political reconciliation might be built. Education in all aspects had proved too difficult, Gladstone had vetoed economic reform, the surface of the church question had hardly been scratched and the land question was likely to prove difficult. Henry Brand analysed the mood of ministers well on 3 May 1866 in writing to Wodehouse after what he thought had been a lucky ministerial escape on the first reading of Chichester Fortescue's Irish land bill. Parliamentary reform, not Ireland, was to be the key to ministerial survival, itself a reform initiative which was intended to have only the most marginal effect in Ireland. It would be a great thing he concluded if in one session the government could settle oaths, Church rates, reform and Irish land. The first were as good as settled to his mind, the last 'a long way off.' In fact, of course it was the third that brought down the ministry six weeks later and it would be left to Gladstone to refashion Liberal Irish policy for the post-Palmerstonian age.[71]

V

For E.D. Steele, the most distinguished of contemporary commentators, Palmerston's political career as a whole reflected 'a statesman who was not merely liberal but genuinely progressive by contemporary standards.'[72] This chapter has suggested a rather different interpretation of Palmerston's approach to the governing of Ireland. During the last ten years of his life the condition of Ireland paradoxically brought together Palmerston's liberal constitutionalism abroad and moderate reformism at home into an increasingly dogmatic resistance to the social and religious trends within Ireland itself. A moderate Irish reformer until the mid-1840s, Palmerston found the religiosity of Ireland and particularly its Ultramontane tone after 1850 increasingly unattractive. Conscious always of the need to be pragmatic on Irish affairs at Westminster if he was to retain his ministerial position, he would at times appear sympathetic to moderate Catholic opinion in Ireland. But once his second government was secure and in response to Catholic ingratitude as he saw it, he decided by appointing and supporting Sir Robert Peel to adopt an approach that tried to stiffen the Protestant landed classes. Such strategy might seem with the benefit of hindsight to have been profoundly mistaken, but at the time of his death a few weeks after the 1865 election Palmerston might well have regarded that election as a vindication of policies that affirmed Protestant reformism at home and anti-papal liberal constitutionalism abroad.

References

[1] The author would like to thank the Warden and Fellows of New College,

Oxford, who kindly elected him to a Visiting Fellowship during the Michaelmas term 2001, during which much of the research for this article was completed. He would also like to thank the librarians and archivists for the help received when consulting the following collections and for permissions to quote from them: the British Library (the Gladstone and Palmerston papers), and the Bodleian Library, Oxford (the Kimberley and Samuel Wilberforce papers). He would like to thank especially the Hon. Simon Howard of Castle Howard Estates Ltd., North York-shire, for permission to consult and quote from the Castle Howard Mss. The work for this article has been made particularly pleasant as part of the activity stimulated by the Yorkshire Country House Partnership, a collaboration between the country houses of the county and the University of York of which Dr Christopher Ridgway, the Curator of Castle Howard, and the author are co-chairs. Christopher Ridgway has been particularly helpful and supportive as has his assistant, Alison Brisby.

[2] Kenneth Bourne *Palmerston: the early years, 1784-1841* (London: Allen Lane, 1982) pp. 256-60. The Derby estates in Tipperary were sold by the 15th Earl in 1871.

[3] For a rather different interpretation, see E.D. Steele *Palmerston and Liberalism, 1855-1865* (Cambridge: Cambridge University Press, 1991) esp. pp. 317-30; George L. Bernstein 'British liberal politics and Irish liberalism after O'Connell', in Stewart J. Brown and David W. Miller (eds.) *Piety and power in Ireland, 1760-1960: essays in honour of Emmet Larkin* (Bloomington: Indiana University Press, 2000) pp. 43-64.

[4] Tyler Anbinder 'Lord Palmerston and Irish famine emigration' *Historical Journal* 44 (2001) pp. 441-69; cf. Desmond Norton 'On Lord Palmerston's Irish estates in the 1840s', *English Historical Review* 119 (2004) pp. 1254-74.

[5] On Catholic Emancipation, see Bourne, *Palmerston* pp. 249-50, 295. For Whig politics of the 1830s more generally, Richard Brent *Liberal Anglican politics: Whiggery, religion and reform, 1830-1841* (Oxford: Clarendon Press, 1987); Peter Mandler *Aristocratic government in the age of reform: Whigs and Liberals, 1830-1852* (Oxford: Clarendon Press, 1990); Boyd Hilton 'Whiggery, religion and social reform: the case of Lord Morpeth' *Historical Journal* 37 (1994) pp. 829-59. For the famine years, see: Peter Gray *Famine, land and politics: British government and Irish society, 1843-50,* (Dublin: Irish Academic Press, 1999) especially p. 53; and Donal Kerr *'A nation of beggars'?: priests, people, and politics in Famine Ireland, 1846-1852* (Oxford: Clarendon Press, 1994). On Palmerston at the Home Office, see: Jasper Ridley *Lord Palmerston* (London: Constable, 1970) pp. 406-10.

[6] See particularly, Saho Matsumoto-Best *Britain and the Papacy in the age of revolution, 1846-51* (Woodbridge: Boydell and Brewer/Royal Historical Society, 2003); David Brown *Palmerston and the politics of foreign policy, 1846-55*

(Manchester: Manchester University Press, 2002); John Wolffe *The Protestant crusade in Great Britain, 1829-1860* (Oxford: Clarendon Press, 1991); D. G. Paz *Popular anti-Catholicism in mid-Victorian England* (Stanford: Stanford University Press, 1992). For Shaftesbury's remark, see: Ridley, *Palmerston* p. 499. For Palmerston's pragmatic approach to the prosecution of Roman Catholic priests as in the Six Mile Bridge affair in 1853, Ridley, *Palmerston* pp. 501-2.

[7] Cornewall Lewis to Carlisle, 25 Mar 1856, Castle Howard [hereafter CH] J19/1/63/105. For the Irish political background, see: J.H. Whyte *The Independent Irish Party, 1851-9* (London: Oxford University Press, 1958), K.T. Hoppen *Elections, politics and society in Ireland, 1832-1885* (Oxford: Clarendon Press, 1984). For ministerial politics, see: Angus Hawkins *Parliament, party and the art of politics in Britain, 1855-59* (London: Macmillan Press, 1987).

[8] Horsman to Carlisle, 21 Nov 1855, CH J19/1/61/106. For the Conservatives and Ireland see Allen Warren 'Disraeli, the Conservatives and the government of Ireland: Part 1, 1837-1868' *Parliamentary History* 18 (1999) pp. 45-64; Wolffe, *Protestant crusade, passim.*

[9] For Carlisle's career see Diana Davids Olien *Morpeth: a Victorian public career* (Washington: University Press of America, 1983). At first, Carlisle was not offered a post in the government, probably because he had vacillated about the necessity for the Crimean War. He then declined a seat in the Cabinet as Chancellor of the Duchy of Lancaster, but on St Germains' resignation immediately accepted the offer of the Viceroyalty: Carlisle Journal 9 Feb - 3 Mar 1855, CH J19/8/32; Macdonnell to Carlisle, 12 Mar 1855, CH J19/1/56/57.

[10] For Macdonnell's assessment of the country: Macdonnell to Carlisle, 1 Jan 1855, CH J19/1/55/53; on patronage, which occupies a large element in Carlisle's correspondence: Horsman to Carlisle 17 Mar 1855, CH J19/56/76; on equality in educational treatment: Carlisle to Palmerston, 20 May 1856, BP GC/CA/474; on tenant right and the welcome defeat of Shee's bill: Horsman to Carlisle, 20 Mar, 6 Jul, 24 Jul 1855, CH J19/1/57/27, J19/1/58/66, J19/1/59/16; for Palmerston on Smith O'Brien: Palmerston to Carlisle, 26 Aug 1855, 16 Mar 1856, CH J19/1/59/57, J19/1/63/87.

[11] On the burning bibles incident: Horsman to Carlisle, 12 Nov, 26 Nov, 8 Dec 1855, CH J19/1/61/87, 115, CH J19/1/62/22; for the Ragged Schools incident: Macdonnell to Carlisle 3 May 1856, Granville to Carlisle, 5 May 1856, CH J19/1/64/84, 90, Horsman to Carlisle, 7 May 1856, CH J19/1/64/99, Carlisle Journal, 12 May 1856, CH J19/8/34; for Belfast rioting: Carlisle Journal, 20 Jul, 20 Sep, 21 Sep, 25 Sep 1857, CH J19/8/34; on banning of Orange magistrates: Grey to Carlisle, 15 Feb 1858, CH J19/1/78/28.

[12] Carlisle Journal, 14 Dec 1857, CH J19/8/35.

[13] For Palmerston's support for the non-denominational principles of the national

education system: *Parliamentary Debates*, 3rd ser. cxlii, 1884 (23 Jun 1856). For an extended treatment on Palmerston's approach to Shee's land bill and tenant right more generally: Horsman to James Wilson, 4 Dec 1855, CH J19/1/62/14; and on his determination not to touch the question in 1856: Horsman to Carlisle, 1 Feb 1856, CH J19/1/63/1; on Orange magistrates: Palmerston to Grey, 18 Feb 1858, CH J19/1/78/35.

[14] Horsman to Carlisle, 21 Nov 1855, CH J19/1/61/106.

[15] On the government's defeat in the Commons: Horsman to Carlisle, 4 Mar 1857, CH J19/1/71/19; on the general election results: Carlisle to Palmerston, 15 Apr 1857, BP GC/CA/491.

[16] In finding a successor to the temperamental Horsman, Palmerston was not overwhelmed by suitable candidates, initially offering the Chief Secretaryship to Villiers, who refused, and eventually settling on Herbert as the least problematic: Grey to Carlisle, 24 Apr 1857, 22 May 1857, CH J19/1/73/17, 54; Palmerston to Carlisle, 26 Apr 1857, 14 May 1857, CH J19/1/73/20, 42.

[17] On the address: Fitzgerald to Carlisle, 12 Feb 1858, 13 Feb 1858, CH J19/1/7812, 13; on the Commons defeat: Charles Howard to Carlisle, 20 Feb 1858, CH J19/1/78/34 (Charles Howard was Carlisle's brother and MP for Cumberland East), Carlisle Journal, 22 Feb 1858, CH J19/8/36.

[18] Howard to Carlisle, 23 Feb1858, CH J19/1/79/6, Carlisle Journal, 13 Mar 1858, J19/8/36.

[19] For Whig fears about a Tory reform bill: Grey to Carlisle, 2 Aug 1858, 7 Aug 1858, CH J19/1/81/74, 80.

[20] For the Derby ministry and Ireland, see: Warren, 'Disraeli, the Conservatives and the government of Ireland'.

[21] For the general election in Ireland generally, see: K.T. Hoppen 'Tories, Catholics and the general election of 1859' *Historical Journal* 13 (1970) pp. 48-67.

[22] Hawkins, *Parliament, party and the art of politics* pp. 240-64; K. T. Hoppen *The mid-Victorian generation, 1846-1886* (Oxford: Clarendon Press, 1998) pp. 207-9.

[23] Gladstone to Samuel Wilberforce, 17 Jun 1859, cited in H.C.G. Matthew (ed.), *The Gladstone diaries, volume V, 1855-1860* (Oxford: Clarendon Press, 1978) p. 401n.

[24] Fitzgerald to Carlisle, 17 May 1859, CH J19/1/83/35.

[25] Cardwell to Palmerston, 6 Sep 1859, BP GC/CA/378. For Irish episcopal politics see: Emmet Larkin *The consolidation of the Roman Catholic Church in Ireland, 1860-1870* (Chapel Hill: University of North Carolina Press, 1987) pp. 3-50; E. R. Norman *The Catholic Church in the age of rebellion, 1859-1873* (London: Longmans, 1965) pp. 1-85.

[26] Monsell to Carlisle, [n.d.] Jun 1859, CH J19/1/83/76.

[27] Cardwell to Cullen, 7 Sep 1859, BP GC/CA/379; Gladstone to Cardwell, 23 Sep 1859, Gladstone papers, BL, Add Ms. 44,530 fol. 82; Carlisle Journal, 22 Aug 1859, CH J19/8/37; Glyn to Gladstone, 29 Sep 1859, Gladstone papers, BL, Add. Ms. 44,392, fol. 180; Gladstone to Cardwell, 29 Sep 1859, Gladstone papers, BL, Add. Ms. 44,530 fol. 82; Gladstone, diary entry for 13 Sep 1859, Matthew (ed.), *Gladstone diaries* p. 424.

[28] Cardwell to Carlisle, 26 Oct 1859, CH J19/1/85/35.

[29] Fitzgerald to Carlisle, 30 Jan 1860, CH J19/1/86/74.

[30] For ministerial jumpiness: Cardwell to Carlisle, 1 Feb 1860, 7 Feb 1860, CH J19/1/86/73, 98; J. D. Fitzgerald to Carlisle, 2 Feb 1860, 3 Feb 1860, 8 Feb 1860, CH J19/1/86/75, 76, 93; Argyll to Carlisle, 3 Feb 1860, CH J19/1/86/81; Ellice to Carlisle, 8 Feb 1860, CH J19/1/86/105.

[31] See Palmerston to Carlisle, 11 Feb 1860, CH J19/1/86/116.

[32] Felton Hervey to Carlisle, 15 Feb 1860, 20 Feb 1860, 25 Feb 1860, CH J19/1/87/1, 12, 42.

[33] Argyll to Carlisle, 3 Aug 1860, CH J19/1/89/132; Agar-Ellis to Carlisle, 7 Aug 1860, CH J19/1/89/123; Howard to Carlisle, 7 Aug 1860, CH J19/1/89/126.

[34] For the Irish Reform Bill: Cardwell, *Parliamentary Debates* 3rd ser. clvi, 2073 (1 Mar 1860). The bill was withdrawn on 8 June. For land measures: Cardwell, *ibid.*, clvii, 1553 (29 Mar 1860); Cardwell to Carlisle, 30 Mar, 19 Jul 1860, 25 Aug 1860, CH J19/1/87/140, CH J19/1/89/77-78, CH J19/1/90/11; R.D. Collinson Black *Economic thought and the Irish question, 1817-1870* (Cambridge: Cambridge University Press, 1960) pp. 45-6; on education, Carlisle, *Parliamentary Debates*, 3rd ser. clviii, 321 (30 Apr 1860), Cardwell, *ibid.* clix, 2155 (17 Jul 1860).

[35] Cardwell, *Parliamentary Debates*, 3rd ser. clx, 1153 (10 Aug 1860).

[36] See Cardwell to Palmerston, 10 Sep 1860, BP, GC/CA/383.

[37] See Cardwell to Carlisle, 11 Nov 1860, CH J19/1/91/1.

[38] See Cardwell to Palmerston, [n. d.] Dec 1860, BP GC/CA/384.

[39] For Cardwell's analysis of the overall political situation in Ireland and at Westminster: Cardwell to Carlisle, 13 Feb, 6 Mar 1861, CH J19/1/92/49, J19/1/93/54; for the difficulties over the Galway contract, Cardwell to Carlisle, 4 May 1861, 10 May 1861, 14 May 1861, 21 May 1861, 4 Jun 1861, CH J19/1/93/42, 46, 48, 52, 111; John Hatchell to Carlisle 27 May 1861, 31 May 1861, 1 Jun 1861, CH J/19/1/93/98-9, 101, 102 (Hatchell was Carlisle's private secretary); Fortescue to Carlisle, 29 May 1861, CH J19/1/93/97; for the details of the row over the Galway contract, Gladstone, Disraeli and Palmerston, *Parliamentary Debates*, 3rd ser. clxiii, 1106, 1142, 1149 (14 Jun 1861); Stanley of Alderley to Carlisle, 12 Jun 1861, CH J19/1/93/135; and for Report of the Select Committee, *Parl. Papers* (1861) x; for Palmerston's announcement, *Parliamentary Debates*, 3rd ser. clxiv, 1735 (29 Jul 1861). For 'Bogtrotter

question', Palmerston to Sir James Graham, 20 Jun 1861, Palmerston papers, BL, Add. Ms. 48,582, fol. 64.

[40] Palmerston to Carlisle, 11 Apr 1857, CH J19/1/72/85.

[41] Palmerston to Carlisle, 28 Jul 1861, CH J19/1/94/49. Palmerston later repeated the instruction: Palmerston to Carlisle, 7 Jan 1862, CH J19/1/96/111.

[42] Palmerston to Carlisle, 21 Aug 1861, CH J19/1/94/107.

[43] Carlisle Journal, 22 Nov 1861, 27 Nov 1861, CH J19/8/39; Peel to Palmerston, 26 Nov 1861, 6 Dec 1861, BP GC/PE/18, 19.

[44] Graves to Carlisle, 19 Nov 1861, CH J19/1/95/107; Monsell to Carlisle, 21 Dec 1861, CH J19/1/96/122; Brand to Carlisle, 23 Nov 1861, CH J19/1/95/113.

[45] For Longford by-election and reactions: Peel to Carlisle, 27 Feb 1862, 5 Mar 1862, CH J19/1/97/59, 60; Brand to Carlisle, 24 May 1862, CH J19/1/106/18; for Peel's defence of national system of education and the Queen's Colleges, *Parliamentary Debates*, 3rd ser. clxvi, 2039 (22 May 1862).

[46] For Carlisle's differences with Peel on patronage: Carlisle to Peel, [n.d.], Oct 1862, CH J19/1/100/66; on O'Hagan: Palmerston to Carlisle, 9 Feb 1863, BP LB/1 (by way of contrast, Palmerston had thought O'Hagan the fittest man for the post of Solicitor-General: Palmerston to Carlisle, 17 Feb 1860, Palmerston papers, BL, Add. Ms. 48,581, fol. 50).

[47] For Palmerston's enthusiasm for Peel: Agar-Ellis to Carlisle, 5 Jun 1862, CH J19/1/98/115; and on Irish distress, Palmerston to Carlisle, 24 Apr 1862, CH J19/1/98/56.

[48] Macdonnell to Carlisle, 25 Mar 1862, CH J19/1/98/7.

[49] Peel, *Parliamentary Debates,* 3rd ser. clxix, 308 (13 Feb 1863).

[50] Gladstone, *ibid.*, 3rd ser. clxxi, 825 (12 Jun 1863).

[51] Palmerston, *ibid.* 1371 (23 Jun 1863).

[52] Palmerston, *ibid.* 1688 (20 Mar 1863).

[53] Palmerston to Peel, 17 Oct 1863, BP GC/PE/39; Peel to Palmerston, 5 Dec 1863, BP GC/PE/29.

[54] On Palmerston's teeth, Carlisle Journal, 29 Nov 1863, CH J19/8/39; for general health: De Grey to Wodehouse, 29 Jan 1865, Kimberley papers, Bodleian Library, Oxford, Ms. Eng. c. 4018, fol. 93.

[55] For Gladstone's increasing Irish engagements: *Parliamentary Debates*, 3rd ser. clxxiii, 1213, 1218 (26 Feb 1864); on national education, *ibid.*, clxxvi, 219 (23 Jun 1864); on general relations, Gladstone to O'Hagan, 1 Aug 1864, 27 Aug 1864, Gladstone papers, BL Add. Ms. 44,534, fols. 109, 120; on public finance, Gladstone to Grey, 13 Dec 1864, Gladstone papers, BL Add. Ms. 43,534, fol. 168; Gladstone to Wodehouse, 17 Dec 1864, in John Powell (ed.) *Liberal by principle: the politics of John Wodehouse, first Earl of Kimberley, 1843-1902* (London: Historians' Press, 1996) p. 102; Gladstone to Stafford Northcote, 13 Mar 1865, Gladstone papers, BL Add. Ms. 44,754, fol. 61; Gladstone, *Parliamentary*

Debates, 3rd ser. clxxvii, 674 (24 Feb 1865); on land: Gladstone to Maguire, 27 Mar 1865, Gladstone papers, BL Add. Ms. 44,535 fol. 38; on the Irish church in the Commons (Dillwyn's motion), *Parliamentary Debates*, 3rd ser. clxxviii, 430 (28 Mar 1865); on economic development in the Commons: *ibid.* clxxviii, 917 (7 Apr 1865); on university question: Gladstone Memo., 8 Jun 1865, Gladstone Ms, BL Add. Ms. 44,754 fol. 83; on Gladstone's work plan for 1866: Matthew (ed.), *Gladstone diaries*, p. 381.

[56] Palmerston to Grey, 22 Aug 1864, 28 Aug 1864, BP LB/1; Wodehouse to Palmerston, 27 Sep 1864, BP GC/WO/2; Wodehouse Journal, 1 Nov 1864 in Angus Hawkins and John Powell (eds.) *The Journal of John Wodehouse, first Earl of Kimberley for 1862-1902* (London: Royal Historical Society, Camden, 5th series, 9; 1997) p. 144 .

[57] On Palmerston and Peel on the Irish university question: Clarendon to Wodehouse, 4 Feb 1865, 17 Jun 1865, Kimberley papers, Bodleian Library, Eng. Ms. c 4018, fol. 130, c. 4027 fol. 46; Peel to Grey, 16 Jun 1865, ibid., c 4061 fol. 138; Palmerston to Wodehouse, 28 Jul 1865, ibid., c 4029 fol. 53; on O'Hagan's appointment, Brand to Wodehouse, 15 Jan 1865, *ibid.*, c 4017 fol.16.

[58] For Peel on public works: Peel to Wodehouse, 23 Dec 1864, Kimberley papers, Bodleian Library, Ms. Eng. c 4016 fol.158.

[59] Palmerston to Wodehouse, 18 Mar 1865, 17 Sep 1865, 3 Oct 1865, 9 Oct 1865, Kimberley papers, Bodleian Library, Ms. Eng. c 4023 fol. 74, c 4032 fol.37, c 4033 fol. 148, c 4034 fol. 46.

[60] Wodehouse's arrival in Dublin stimulated a great deal of activity and correspondence. He identified quickly with agricultural improvement and public works through his speech at the Lord Mayor of Dublin's banquet and with Irish university reform. A complex ecclesiastical and political diplomacy followed with H. A. Bruce coming to Dublin to try and fashion an agreement between the bishops and Dublin Castle that was acceptable to London. For his part Peel supported Wodehouse on agrarian reform but vehemently opposed any undermining of the Queen's Colleges. No firm decisions had been reached on legislation at the time of Palmerston's death: Wodehouse speech, 24 Nov 1864 in Powell, *Liberal by principle* p. 97; Sir Richard Griffiths to Wodehouse, 18 Nov 1864, Kimberley papers, Bodleian Library, Ms. Eng. c 4060 fol. 65; Wodehouse to De Grey, 7 Dec 1864 in Powell, *Liberal by principle*, pp. 1-6; Wodehouse to Grey, 27 Aug 1865, Kimberley papers, Bodleian Library, Ms. Eng. c 4061 fol. 38.

[61] For Palmerston's continuing anti-Catholic stance, expressed in almost identical language to that used on the appointment of Peel in 1861: Palmerston to Chichester Fortescue, 10 Sep 1864, 12 Sep 1864, BP LB/1.

[62] Palmerston to Woodhouse, 28 Jul 1865, Kimberley papers, Bodleian Library, Ms. Eng. c 4029 fol. 50.

[63] See above, n.55.

[64] For election analysis and comment: Grey to Wodehouse, 20 Jul 1865, Kimberley papers, Bodleian Library, Ms. Eng. c 4028 fol. 135; Wodehouse to Grey, 25 Jul 1865, ibid., c 4029 fol. 7. For detailed election analysis including assessments of the religious temper of the successful Catholic members: Grey to Wodehouse, 20, 25 Jul 1865, Kimberley papers, Bodleian Library, Ms. Eng. c 4028, fol. 135, c 4029, fol. 7. Gladstone's comment is characteristic: 'At present we are all in great glee. But by and by we shall perceive that a majority of 65 or 70 involves greater responsibilities from a majority of 15': Gladstone to Fortescue, 29 Jul 1865, Gladstone papers, BL, Add. Ms. 44,535 fol. 98.

[65] Peel to Russell, 19 Nov 1865, BP GC/PE/34.

[66] Wodehouse to Gladstone, 12 Feb 1866 in Powell, *Liberal by principle*, p. 109.

[67] Wodehouse to Grey, 20 Nov 1865, 21 Dec 1865, 26 Jan 1866, 25 Feb 1866, Kimberley papers, Bodleian Library, Ms. Eng. c 4036 fol. 38, c 4038 fol.122, c 4040 fol. 142, c 4043 fol. 38; Grey to Wodehouse, 5 Dec 1865, 15 Jan 1866, 23 Jan 1866, 1 Feb 1866, 9 Mar 1866, 26 Mar 1866, Kimberley papers, Bodleian Library, Ms. Eng. c 4037 fol. 73, c 4039 fol. 175, c 4040 fol. 82, c 4041 fol. 1, c 4043 fol.137, c 4044 fol.124; Grey to Archbishop Cullen, 30 Jan 1866, Kimberley papers, Bodleian Library, Ms. Eng. c 4040 fol. 205; Fortescue, *Parliamentary Debates*, 3rd ser. clxxxiv, 719 (5 Jul 1866).

[68] Grey to Wodehouse, 21 Feb 1866, Kimberley papers, Bodleian Library, Ms. Eng. c 4043 fol. 1.

[69] Wodehouse to Grey, 17 Jan 1866, 12 Feb 1866, 10 Apr 1866, Kimberley papers, Bodleian Library, Ms. Eng. c 4040 fol. 33; Powell, *Liberal by principle* p. 109; Kimberley papers, Bodleian Library, Ms. Eng. c 4045 fol. 98; Fortescue to Wodehouse, 2 Apr 1866, 16 Apr 1866, 28 Apr 1866, 29 Apr 1866, *ibid.*, c 4045 fol. 53, c 4046 fols. 27, 69, 73; Fortescue, *Parliamentary Debates,* 3rd ser. clxxxiii. 1002 (15 May 1866).

[70] Wodehouse to Gladstone, 12 Feb 1866 in Powell, *Liberal by principle*, p. 109.

[71] Brand to Wodehouse, 3 May 1866, Kimberley papers, Bodleian Library, Ms. Eng. c 4046 fol. 135.

[72] E. D. Steele entry on Lord Palmerston, *The Oxford dictionary of national biography* eds. H.C.G. Matthew and Brian Harrison (61 vols., Oxford: Oxford University Press, 2004) liv, p. 66.

CHAPTER 6

Prince Albert and Lord Palmerston: Battle Royal[1]
Karina Urbach

In memory of Jonathan Leiboff (1967-2003)

'Labour handed blueprint for a royal revolution.' So ran the headline of a conservative British tabloid on 16 July 2003: 'The vision of the 50,000-word "Future of the Monarchy" document is to bring the institution into the twenty-first century and thus ensure its survival. It is the product of a year's work by a ten strong commission set up by the Fabian Society, an influential think tank affiliated to the Labour Party.' The Society said the monarchy had to evolve to keep pace with public opinion, and that constitutional changes underway in the House of Lords and the judiciary heightened the urgency for royal reform. The proposals go to the heart of the monarchy's constitutional base.[2]

This is no exaggeration. According to the Fabian proposals the monarch would no longer be the Supreme Governor of the Church of England — a link that has existed since 1532. The Royal Marriages Act of 1772 would be repealed as well as male primogeniture abolished. The most populist demand made by the Fabian Society was that the Queen should pay 40 percent inheritance tax and that the subsidies of other royals should be cut. Of great political importance was the proposed Constitution Act, which would remove the monarch's right to dissolve or summon Parliament, the royal assent over legislation and the right to choose a Prime Minister in the event of a hung Parliament. That such an act was considered to be necessary was stressed by the Fabian Society general secretary Michael Jacobs: 'The Queen has behaved with exemplary impartiality. But if a future monarch were ever tempted to use their powers it would provoke a disastrous constitutional crisis'.[3] In other words, there seems to exist a certain uneasiness among politicians about Prince Charles who is known to interfere in politics and, if one thinks in a historical context, might develop into a modern day Prince Albert. Many other points in this memorandum look familiar to historians: the discussions over the monarch's income,[4] the restrictions of royal prerogatives and the subliminal criticism of members of the royal family. The following chapter will focus on similar clashes in the nineteenth century by looking at two key players: the 'interfering' Prince Albert, who tried to defend royal prerogatives and the national icon, Lord Palmerston, who did his best to undermine them.[5]

I

'If the devil has a son, his name is surely Palmerston.'[6] Prince Albert would have agreed wholeheartedly with this German saying of 1849. There was no love lost between the Prince and the politician: before Albert arrived on the scene, Palmerston and the Queen — both fun-loving and jingoistic by nature — got on swimmingly. However, when the Prince became the *spiritus rector* behind Victoria's decision making process, the tone of her letters changed considerably[7] — Palmerston was acutely aware of this development and felt threatened by it.

One does not have to believe in psycho-history to acknowledge that both men lived in different worlds. To Albert, Palmerston must have been John Bull at his worst: 'choleric, bold and of a very unconstant temper … unafraid of anyone but liable to quarrel with his neighbours, especially if they pretended to govern him … Also sneeringly disdainful of foreigners'.[8] Though Palmerston looked like a republican in disguise to the Prince and his monarchical cousins, this was far from the truth. Palmerston's domestic policy was by no means liberal: he was not a crusader for constitutionalism abroad and feared democracy as much as the majority of his fellow-politicians of the time.[9] Yet he combined this with a certain air of progressiveness that turned him into a 'genius for adaptation' as David Steele has described it.[10] Like Prince Albert, who occupied a minor position in the league of reigning houses, Palmerston was a social climber within the British aristocracy. His mother had been a commoner, his father an Irish peer, consequently Palmerston's background was closer to the world of the gentry than to the Whig aristocracy. But, like Albert, he married well and soon built up his network amongst the leading aristocratic families. Both Palmerston and Albert were driven men, working extremely hard, yet while Palmerston was rewarded and spurred on by public support, the Prince had to struggle in the shadows, an often frustrated one-man think tank whose ideas were — except for the Great Exhibition — rarely acknowledged.[11] He was more like an 'incorporated wife' with the Queen as his only channel of communication to the outside world: he had to make her express his fears, suggestions and warnings.[12]

A major drawback, which Palmerston would exploit in his fight against Albert, was of course his German background. The extent to which Prince Albert was torn between dynastic loyalties and the nationalism of his adopted country is shown in a hitherto neglected memorandum by Albert's brother, Duke Ernest II.[13] The document, which is now deposited at the Staatsarchiv Coburg, provides a glimpse of the ducal family's favourite pastime: networking. Today, the term network has many connotations, both positive and negative, and can have a sinister ring to it — indicating an air of conspiracy. Indeed, if this slim Coburg 'guide book' on networking had become public in the nineteenth century, it would have fuelled the British public's worst fears of a German conspiracy even further. It is an undated document, but Ernest II must have written it after he had become Duke of Coburg (i.e. after 1844). The 25 pages were intended for the family's eyes only and gave advice on how to act as a true Coburger at home and abroad. From the start Ernest calls the members of his family 'Glieder' (links) — the links in a chain often used as a metaphor in documents by German aristocrats.[14] It symbolises that one generation builds upon another and that a missing 'link' can destroy the family. Ancestors, current and future members of the family are one, they exist outside the conventions of space and time. The family and its glory have to be at the centre of the thinking of every 'link'. Though this was an ideal seldom achieved, it was easier to sustain it as long as the family stayed in one country or region, and it became more difficult when 'links' like Albert and Leopold lived in different countries.[15] To keep the widespread members close to the parent house, Duke Ernest II stressed the common interests and value system which would always connect them first and foremost with the 'entirety' of the Coburg house: 'Gegen Fremde stehe der eine für den Andern, und Alle für einen.'[16] All for one and one for all. This motto could have been taken from Dumas' *Three Musketeers*, published in 1844, a novel the bookish Ernest probably read.[17] The chivalry of Dumas' fictional aristocrats must have appealed to the self-conceit of the German aristocracy. All for one and one for all — is a sentence that would have certainly been relished by Albert's opponents. It had every potential for a Coburg conspiracy theory. The following pages of the memorandum even strengthen this impression:

da die Familie einem rein deutschen Haus entsprungen ist, [muß] sie ihr Haupt-augenmerk darauf richten, im allgemeinen eine rein deutsche zu bleiben. Möchten sich daher die Gesamtheit der Glieder ja immer in deutschen Elementen bewegen, und nie aufhören, zu Deutschlands Erhaltung und Wohlergehen beizutragen. Außer dem Chef des Hauses sind durch glückliche Umstände noch drei Glieder bestimmt worden, an der Regierung mächtiger Reiche directen oder indirecten Theil zu nehmen. Zwei sind durch Verheirathung und einer ist durch Wahl zu jenen Stellungen gelangt; die beiden Ersteren stehen der Natur ihrer Stellung nach ihrem Stammhause und deßen Intereßen noch beinahe ebenso nahe als denen jener Länder, in die sie so eigentlich hineingeheirathet haben. ... Im Gegentheil und im Gegensatz zu andern Häusern muß es den Gliedern unseres Hauses leichter werden, ein mächtiges Ganzes nach Außen hin zu bilden ... wenn wir das Bewußtsein in uns wach erhalten, daß wir isoliert wenig, in der Verbin-dung aller Glieder unendliches anstreben und erreichen können[18]

This concept of a strong international dynasty taking an active part in political affairs at home and abroad, clashed with the idea of

British nationalism. It also collided with the idea of the political impartiality of the Crown, which Walter Bagehot would later describe as one of the monarch's virtues.[19] David Cannadine has questioned whether Victoria and Albert did 'invent' the British constitutional monarchy in the way we understand it today.[20] He thinks that the Queen was — against her will — too Hanoverian in character (despite the change of name of the dynasty), and the Prince too close to a 'backward-looking concept of monarchical power'. In Cannadine's view, both were influenced by Stockmar's belief, 'that a monarch as the only disinterested part of the government, should reclaim supreme power, and reassert [himself] as the permanent premier who takes rank above the temporary head of the cabinet'.[21] Cannadine concludes that this form of constitutionalism hardly meant reduced monarchical power. On the contrary, Albert wanted to be 'a ruler who was emancipated from the politicians, rather than fettered by them; a crown that was influentially, not impotently, above the battle; a sovereign who governed as well as reigned'.[22] Palmerston would certainly have agreed with Cannadine's interpretation.[23] The main point of argument between him and the royal couple was the old feud of Parliament against monarchy: the stronger the state, the larger its bureaucracy and the more influential the electorate and public opinion became in the nineteenth century, the more the monarchy's role diminished.

Johannes Paulmann has measured the power European monarchies had on a scale from zero (no restrictions on the monarchy, as in authoritarian Russia) to one (greatest restrictions on the monarchy, as in England).[24] Prussia tottered somewhere in between at 0.5. The liberal — by German standards — duchies of Coburg and Gotha could therefore be positioned at 0.7 — halfway between the English and Prussian model, yet still a great mental leap for Albert to make.

While professional administrators and politicians 'usurped' one field after another, European monarchs tried to cling to two traditional spheres of influence: military and diplomatic. Albert was found guilty of meddling in both areas: 'the Queen and the Prince tended to regard the army almost as much as a private province as the Foreign Office', Connell wrote in the 1960s.[25] When Albert was asked in 1850 by the Duke of Wellington to become commander in chief, he refused claiming that: 'the Husband of the Queen has to be at her service, as secretary and advisor',[26] yet at the same time he made sure that his candidate, Lord Hardinge, got the position. Behind the scenes, Albert continued to interfere in military affairs and criticism of his conduct therefore simmered. Yet in the fight for control over foreign affairs, the Prince got into even more trouble.

Albert was of the opinion that Palmerston followed firstly a risky policy with which the Court could not identify and secondly dragged foreign policy issues into the public sphere for his own aggrandizement. Palmerston's 'recklessness' (Harold Nicolson)[27] clashed with Albert's idea of harmony between the states, which was in accord with Ernest's memorandum that had urged the family members to be 'Vermittler zwischen den großen Mächten und ... Schutzherr der kleineren'.[28] It also clashed with Albert's belief in the principle of an equality among the monarchs which he wanted to consolidate by corresponding with them in an unofficial manner.[29] The concept of a 'community of sovereigns' which had been invented at the Congress of Vienna was a strategy against the increasing social and political demands nationalism made on the monarchies. The new legal and moral community of 1814-15 was however not a real balance of power according to Paul Schroeder, but meant 'a balance of satisfaction, a balance of rights and obligations and a balance of performance and payoffs'.[30] Despite the pretence at 'equality' Britain and Russia emerged as the great powers — a situation Palmerston intended to use. He believed in English unilateralism based on his confidence 'in the superiority of the English constitution and economic system'.[31] With this strong foreign policy stance he won against the Prince on almost every issue: in the 1848 Schleswig-Holstein crisis, Albert backed the German nationalists who wanted to incorporate the duchies into a united Germany. Palmerston, who favoured Denmark, opposed a centralised, over-powerful Germany, and won.[32] While the Foreign Secretary supported — in the long run successfully — Italian nationalism, Albert wanted the Habsburg Empire to survive despite knowing its downsides. In France Palmerston happily welcomed Napoleon III,[33] while Albert still showed attachment to his relative Louis Philippe. The list seems endless, and the inference is clear: the monarchy could do little to hinder the Foreign Secretary's policies in the long run. Still, it could make his life more difficult. The royal couple's hatred of Palmerston drove them to use gossip about his libidinous lifestyle for political ends,[34] and made Albert correspond with Palmerston's colleagues behind his back. The Prince repeatedly put pressure on Lord John Russell to get rid of the obnoxious Foreign Secretary — and succeeded in 1851, when Palmerston expressed his satisfaction at Napoleon III's *coup d'état*.[35] Palmerston did not forgive the intrigue of 1851, though he put the main blame on Russell. Among his papers there is a special volume of letters entitled 'On my dismissal'. To his brother, Palmerston wrote about foreign intrigues and 'opposition in high places' that had brought him down. As revenge, he played psychological tricks on Albert via the media,[36] as well as by trying to break into his opponent's family network. Leopold, the King of the Belgians, owed his throne to a great extent to Palmerston's negotiating skills. It therefore made sense for Palmerston to contact his former 'protégé' when he was at loggerheads with the royal couple. A copy of one of his letters to the King of the Belgians dated January 1854 can be found in the Coburg archive — Leopold had passed it on to his Coburg network in no time: 'I cannot however refrain from availing myself of this opportunity', Palmerston wrote, 'to say how useful it would be if the just influence which your Majesty possessed at our court would be expected to soften at Windsor feelings towards the French Emperor … or at all events to prevent the manifestations and expression of feelings of an opposite kind'.[37]

II

How serious Albert's situation could become, when it pleased Lord

Palmerston, was shown in the events leading up to the Crimean War. Since 1853 a conflict between Russia and Turkey had been imminent. Aberdeen did not want to be drawn into it and his coalition Cabinet was consequently attacked for its weak policy towards Russian expansionism. On 16 December 1853 the then Home Secretary Lord Palmerston resigned. Though the main reason for his resignation was the new Reform bill,[38] the public assumed that the Eastern question was responsible. The 'Russian-friendly' Albert was accused of having pulled the strings.[39] Of course the Prince was used to being derided by the papers for his 'German notions'.[40] The nation — divided by social differences — seemed to need occasional foreigner-bashing or what Hans Ulrich Wehler once called 'negative integration' to achieve a bonding effect. Yet the criticisms of Albert in the winter of 1853-4 were unprecedented. There were three possible groups with an interest in inciting the anti-Albert campaign: Palmerston, the radicals and the Earl of Derby.[41] However, even they must have quickly realised it got out of their control.

It started with the *Daily News* on 19 December 1853 'reminding' its readers that Albert had been the principal agent in dismissing Lord Palmerston in 1851: 'some of [Lord Palmerston's] admirers may even go so far as to hint that courtly distastes and Coburg intrigues [were at work again].'[42] That opened the floodgates: 'When the enemies of England were closing around her and the national fortunes seemed at their lowest, Palmerston, the one Minister whom the people trusted, was again removed from his place.'[43] About the culprit, Albert, a critic wrote: 'It is too much that one man should be at once Foreign Secretary, Commander in Chief and Prime Minister under all administrations.'[44] Rumour soon had it that Albert, who had secretly built up an 'irresponsible dictatorship',[45] was already imprisoned in the Tower. This severe attack on the Prince made it blatantly obvious that the 1840 Act for the Naturalization of his Serene Highness Prince Albert of Saxe Coburg and Gotha had not turned him into an Englishman. Andreas Fahrmeir has shown that the rights of naturalised subjects already 'had been reduced in the course of the eighteenth century'.[46] Though Prince Albert had been naturalised without restrictions by Parliament, he was now in that very place called 'a foreign naturalized Prince'.[47] An anonymous writer argued: 'You may naturalize a man, but I will defy any human power to make an Englishman by any Act whatever.' It was thought natural that 'the Prince should be biased by the education of his fatherland.' The same argument would be used 50 years later by the Germans against one of Albert's grandsons.[48] The 14-year old Charles Edward, Duke of Albany,[49] would be considered unfit to become Duke of Coburg because of his Etonian upbringing. It was conceded eventually that he was not beyond hope and could be saved by a proper Prussian education. Carl Eduard would infamously exceed the target. Under his patronage, Coburg celebrated with the radical right a 'German Day' as early as 1922.[50] His grandfather's identification with England on the other hand was doubted all his life.

Though Palmerston joined the government again on 26 December 1853, the attacks on Albert did not cease. The Prince's main problem during this conflict was — as Paulmann has shown — that he could not defend himself publicly. Others had to do it for him. The Queen tried to put pressure on *The Times* and inspired pamphlets in defence of her husband. King Leopold, who was allegedly part of the 'Austro-Belgian-Coburg-Orleans clique', turned to Palmerston — complaining bitterly in his and his nephew's name against the attacks. Palmerston's cunning reply of 20 January 1854 aimed to divide the relatives — distinguishing between the 'good Coburger' Leopold and the 'unreasonable Coburger' Albert.[51] Eleven days later the 'Albert scandal' was discussed in Parliament. Here it became obvious that the position of a royal spouse was nowhere defined and that people's opinion on it differed considerably. In William Blackstone's *Commentaries on the Laws of England* (1765), the Queen's husband only gets a brief mention, and Aberdeen consequently tried to portray Albert as a sort of harmless private secretary: 'Is not the Queen the first sovereign in this country who for a long time has not had even the advantage of a private secretary ? Was there ever any objection to the private secretary of George IV or ... William IV ?'[52] Furthermore, the 'scheming' letter-writing of the Prince was far from the truth, as Lord John Russell stressed: 'There was one instance ... in which it happened that a Minister at a foreign Court wrote to [Prince Albert], and His Royal Highness immediately sent the letter to the Secretary of State for Foreign Affairs, and desired to know what answer he advised him to return.'[53]

The debate ended with clearing the Prince's name by giving the impression that he was completely powerless. Nothing could have pleased Palmerston more. Albert understood very well what this meant. Once Britain and France rushed to the help of the Sultan's government, the Prince, who wanted to bring the war to a swift end, loyally supported Palmerston's policy. This brought the royal couple some prestige and eventually a *modus vivendi* with the Prime Minister was achieved — they learnt to work together for a 'higher good'. Albert became — with great difficulties — Prince Consort while Palmerston was Prime Minister, a title that gave him some recognition but no actual power.[54]

III

The struggle between Palmerston and the Prince shows that it was not a caprice when 'the Queen bristled immediately there was the slightest sign of any infraction of her prerogatives',[55] but a last convulsion of a weakening monarchical body. Albert did not manage to get the monarchy's power back from its scale position at 1 to a slightly stronger 0.8 or 0.9. Furthermore, Palmerston's nationalistic-jingoistic language in a period of rising nationalism attracted the masses, while Albert, hindered by dynastic loyalties,[56] could not always agree with such concepts.[57] Ernest's memorandum with its appeal to a family network had simultaneously given the Prince personal strength and had made him personally vulnerable. After his death — as Keith Robbins has pointed out — the royal family would give up more and more of their prerogatives and though the widowed Queen Victoria occasionally interfered in foreign affairs and continued to bombard Prime Ministers with her letters, the height of her influence was long passed.[58]

Victoria and Albert would certainly have been shattered by the Fabian proposals of 2003 and could hardly have approved of the first comments made by Buckingham Palace on them: 'The report is a useful contribution to the debate on changes to the Monarchy. We will be interested in seeing public reaction.'[59]

References

[1] An earlier version of this chapter was published in Franz Bosbach and John Davis (eds.) *Prince Albert: Ein Wettiner in Großbritannien* (Munich: K. G. Saur, 2004). I would like to thank Professor Bosbach for his permission to reproduce this article here.

[2] *Daily Mail* 16 Jul 2003, p. 16.

[3] Quoted in *ibid*.

[4] In Prince Albert's case, see the controversy about his allowance when he became engaged to Queen Victoria in 1839: Dorothy Thompson *Queen Victoria: gender and power* (London: Virago, 1990) p. 36.

[5] The label 'most English Minister' for Palmerston was invented by his colleague, friend and rival, Lord John Russell. Donald Southgate used it for his monograph on Palmerston: Donald Southgate *'The most English minister': the policies and politics of Palmerston* (London: Macmillan, 1966). From the multitude of studies on Palmerston, see especially: Kenneth Bourne *Palmerston: the early years* (London: Allen Lane, 1982); Muriel Chamberlain *Lord Palmerston* (Cardiff: University of Wales Press, 1987); David Steele *Palmerston and Liberalism, 1855-65* (Cambridge: Cambridge University Press, 1991). For a recent evaluation see David Brown *Palmerston and the politics of foreign policy, 1846-55* (Manchester: Manchester University Press, 2002).

[6] Quoted in Frank Müller *Britain and the German question. Perceptions of nationalism and political reform 1830-1863* (London: Macmillan, 2002) p. 57.

[7] 'Another hand was starting to guide her pen': Brian Connell (ed.) *Regina vs. Palmerston. The correspondence between Queen Victoria and her Foreign and Prime Minister 1837-1865* (London: Evans, 1961) pp. 44, 47.

[8] John Arbuthnot, cited in Jeremy Paxman *The English. A portrait of a people* (London: Michael Joseph, 1998) p. 184.

[9] Palmerston's domestic policy has been neglected by historians for some time now. David Brown therefore warns that Palmerston should not be divided into two personalities, 'centre stage for Palmerston the Foreign Minister with a

walk-on part for the domestic politician': David Brown 'Lord Palmerston' *The Historian* 76 (2002) p. 36.

[10] Steele, *Palmerston and Liberalism*, p. 367.

[11] For a recent study of the Great Exhibition see Franz Bosbach and John Davis (eds.) *Die Weltausstellung von 1851 und ihre Folgen* (Munich, K.G. Saur, 2002).

[12] For the expression 'incorporated wife', see: Kim Reynolds *Aristocratic women and political society in Victorian Britain* (Oxford: Clarendon Press, 1998) pp. 6, 178-81.

[13] Nachlass Herzog Ernst II, Staatsarchiv Coburg, LA A 7206: 'Denkschrift seiner Hoheit über die politische Haltung welche seine Familie im inneren gegen ihre Glieder nach außen gegen die europäischen Mächte befolgen sollte'. Ernst II wrote an autobiography yet he had, typically for the genre, a rather selective memory: Herzog Ernst II *Aus meinem Leben und aus meiner Zeit* (3 vols., Berlin: W. Hertz, 1887-9).

[14] 'Du stehst, mein Kind, in einer langen Reihe, bist das Glied einer Kette, die Dich hält und die Du fortschmieden mußt': speech by Freiherr von Reitzenstein (1931), quoted in: Stephan Malinowski *Vom König zum Führer. Sozialer Niedergang und politische Radikalisierung im deutschen Adel zwischen Kaiserreich und NS-Staat* (Berlin: Akademie Verlag, 2003) p. 38.

[15] The family offered a textbook case for Bourdieu's theories on symbolic, cultural and social capital. The symbolic capital was the family's well respected 'trade name' (House of Coburg), the cultural capital meant the education, knowledge and taste the family instilled in its offspring, and the social capital consisted of excellent career networks offered to each member: Pierre Bourdieu, 'Der Habitus als Vermittlung zwischen Struktur und Praxis' (1970) in Bourdieu *Zur Soziologie der symbolischen Formen* (Frankfurt am Main: Suhrkamp, 1970); Pierre Bourdieu 'Ökonomisches Kapital, kulturelles Kapital, soziales Kapital' in Margarete Steinrücke (ed.) *Die Verborgenen Mechanismen der Macht* (Hamburg: VSA, 1992) 49-79. See also Hans-Ulrich Wehler 'Pierre Bourdieu: das Zentrum seines Werkes' in Wehler *Die Herausforderung der Kulturgeschichte* (Munich: C.H. Beck, 1998) pp. 27ff.

[16] 'Against foreigners we should stand up for one another': Nachlass Herzog Ernst II, Staatsarchiv Coburg, LA A 7206.

[17] The original *Les Trois mousquetaires* was translated into German within a year. For Ernest's interest in literature and politics, see: Rainer Hambrecht 'Herzog Ernst II und der Literarisch-politische Verein' in Harald Bachmann *et al.* (eds.) *Herzog Ernst II von Sachsen-Coburg und Gotha 1818-1893 und seine Zeit. Jubiläumsschrift im Auftrag der Städte Coburg und Gotha* (Coburg: Maro, 1993) pp. 73-90.

[18] 'Since the family comes from a pure German house, its main concern should be to remain, in general, purely German. So its members, as a whole, should

always move in German circles, and never cease to support the survival and well-being of Germany. Apart from the head of the house, another three members have been destined to be part, either directly or indirectly, of the government of important empires. Two have come to this by marriage, one by election. The first two, are by their nature, almost as close to their own house and its interests as they are to the countries into which they have actually married … Unlike, and contrary to other houses, it must be easier for the members of our house to present a powerful form to the outside … if we remain conscious of the fact that in isolation we can achieve little, but that if all our members are united our potential is unlimited': Nachlass Herzog Ernst II, Staatsarchiv Coburg, LA A 7206.

[19] Walter Bagehot *The English constitution* ed. R. H. S. Crossman (London: Watts, 1964).

[20] David Cannadine 'The Last Hanoverian sovereign ?: The Victorian monarchy in historical perspective, 1688-1988' in A. L. Beier et al (eds.) *The first modern society: essays in English history in honour of Lawrence Stone* (Cambridge: Cambridge University Press, 1989) pp. 127-65.

[21] *ibid.* p. 129

[22] *ibid.* pp. 140 ff.

[23] Small matters were quickly blown out of proportion. The Prince insisted that diplomatic despatches were seen first by the Queen before they were sent off. Palmerston differed. See Connell (ed.), *Regina vs. Palmerston* pp. 83 ff. Palmerston also felt bored at Albert's Court. Kim Reynolds has shown that under the Prince's regime, the Court withdrew from the engagement with aristocratic society: Kim Reynolds, 'The Victorian Court' in Wilfried Rogasch (ed.) *Victoria and Albert, Vicky and the Kaiser: a chapter of Anglo-German family relations* (Ostfildern-Ruit: Deutsches Historisches Museum/G. Hatje, 1997). Not being an attractive power centre for clever men and beautiful women but more like Nora's Doll's House, the bourgeois, almost square, Court could not compete with the salon of Palmerston's wife or the country seats of Whig aristocrats, and it is therefore no surprise that alternative courts opened up all over the country. This diminished Albert's English networking radius considerably.

[24] Johannes Paulmann *Pomp und Politik. Monarchenbegegnungen in Europa zwischen Ancien Régime und Erstem Weltkrieg* (Paderborn: F. Schöningh, 2000). For an appraisal of his arguments Karina Urbach 'Diplomatic history since the cultural turn' *Historical Journal* 46 (2003) pp. 991-7.

[25] Connell (ed.), *Regina vs. Palmerston* p. 198.

[26] Ernst Freiherr v. Stockmar (ed.) *Denkwürdigkeiten aus den Papieren des Freiherrn Christian Friedrich von Stockmar* (Braunschweig: F. Vieweg und Sohn,1872) p. 662.

[27] Quoted in Duncan Watts *Whigs, Radicals and Liberals 1815-1914* (London: Hodder and Stoughton, 2002) p. 63. There is no denying that Palmerston

revelled in a good crisis. See for example his handling of Anglo-Chinese affairs: J.Y. Wong *Deadly dreams: opium and the Arrow War (1856-1860)* (Cambridge: Cambridge University Press, 1998).

[28] The 'arbiter between the great powers and protector of the small states': Nachlass Herzog Ernst II, Staatsarchiv Coburg, LA A 7206.

[29] Cannadine sees here one of Albert's greatest faults: 'He conducted private correspondence with other crowned heads, independent of the Foreign Office, in which he did not hesitate to criticize his own government': Cannadine, 'Last Hanoverian sovereign' p. 143. Cannadine overlooks that this was the norm. All European ruling houses were also female 'news-agencies', run by the wives, daughters and mothers of monarchs. In this context Albert played the female part.

[30] Paul W. Schroeder 'International politics, peace and war, 1815-1914' in T.C.W. Blanning (ed.), *The nineteenth century: Europe 1789-1914* (Oxford: Oxford University Press, 2000) pp. 158ff.

[31] Eugenio Biagini 'Power politics, imperial strategies and local elites' *Historical Journal* 45 (2002) p. 682.

[32] Müller, *Britain and the German question*. See also Günther Gillesen *Lord Palmerston und die Einigung Deutschlands. Die englische Politik von der Paulskirche bis zu den Dresdner Konferenzen (1848-1851)* (Hamburg: Matthiesen, 1961); K. Kingston 'Gunboat liberalism ?: Palmerston, Europe and 1848' *History Today* 47 (1992) pp. 37-43.

[33] J.P. Parry, 'The impact of Napoleon III on British politics, 1851-1889', *Transactions of the Royal Historical Society* 6th series, 11 (2001) pp. 147-75. See also R. Golicz, 'Napoleon III, Lord Palmerston and the *entente cordiale*' *History Today* 50 (2000) pp. 10-17.

[34] The Foreign Secretary marched, late at night, into the bedroom of Mrs Brand — one of the Queen's Ladies of the Bedchamber — (he may have mixed up the room numbers, as another lady who usually occupied this room was — allegedly — waiting for him at the other end of the castle). The Prince described this event in great detail in a memorandum on Palmerston's 'worthless private character', and explained the wider implications to Lord John Russell: 'How could the Queen consent to take a man as her chief adviser and confidential counsellor in all matters of State, religion, society, Court, etc., etc., he who as her Secretary of State and guest under her roof at Windsor Castle had committed a brutal attack upon one of her ladies ? Had at night by stealth introduced himself into her apartment, barricaded afterwards the door and would have consummated his fiendish scheme by violence had not the miraculous efforts of his victim and such assistance attracted by her screams saved her ? Lord John said ... he unfortunately knew another lady in society upon whom he had tried the same thing !': quoted in Connell (ed.), *Regina vs. Palmerston* p. 147. Brian Connell rightly points out that Albert used here a 'questionable tactic', after all the incident had happened ten years

earlier. That the Prince did use the story shows, however, how desperate the royal couple was to get rid of Palmerston.

35 For this well known episode, see: M.E. Chamberlain *British foreign policy in the age of Palmerston* (London: Longman, 1980) p. 65.

36 The London papers, the *Morning Post* and the *Globe*, were 'inspired' by him. See: David Brown 'Compelling but not controlling ?: Palmerston and the press, 1846-1855' *History* 86, (2001) pp. 41-61. On a 'Palmerstonian' newspaper article that indicated Coburg family interests had influenced the Queen's decisions in foreign affairs, Albert commented: 'There was no interest of the House of Coburg involved in any questions upon which we quarrelled with Lord Palmerston, neither in Greece, nor Italy, Sicily, Holstein, Hungary, etc. Why are Princes alone to be denied the credit of having political opinions based on an anxiety for the national interests and honour of the country and the welfare of mankind ? Are they not more independently placed than any other politician of the State ?': Connell (ed.), *Regina vs. Palmerston* p. 167.

37 Nachlass Herzog Ernst II, LA A 7169, Politische Korrespondenz Januar bis Juli 1854, Staatsarchiv Coburg.

38 B. Kingsley Martin thinks that 'Palmerston threatened resignation on both questions [...] He told Aberdeen he could go no further with reform': B. Kingsley Martin *The triumph of Lord Palmerston: a study of public opinion in England before the Crimean War* (London: Allen and Unwin, 1924) p. 177.

39 Stockmar later wrote about the Prince's predicament: 'Er hätte am Liebsten den Krieg durch ein Zusammenziehen der vier Mächte abgewendet gesehen. [Albert kämpfte an zwei Fronten] gegen den vertrauensseligen pro-russischen Aberdeen ... auf der anderen Seite Palmerston [der mit Frankreich eine Allianz wollte]': Stockmar, *Denkwürdigkeiten* p. 654 ('he was fighting on two fronts. On the one hand campaigning against the naïve, pro-Russian Aberdeen, and on the other against Palmerston').

40 It was held against him 'daß er sich nicht ganz orthodox englisch kleidete, nicht ganz orthodox englisch zu Pferde saß, den shake hands nicht ganz orthodox vollzog': *ibid.* p. 658 ('that he did not dress, ride a horse or shake a hand in an orthodox English way').

41 Derby was an opponent of the Peelites, who were thought to be close to Albert.

42 Martin, *Triumph of Lord Palmerston*, p. 199.

43 *ibid.* p. 204.

44 *ibid.* p. 181.

45 William Coningham *Lord Palmerston and Prince Albert: letters by William Coningham Esq. together with the 'suppressed pamphlet, entitled 'Palmerston: what has he done ?' by one of the People* (London: Effingham Wilson, 1854) pp. 19-30.

[46] Andreas Fahrmeir *Citizens and aliens. Foreigners and the law in Britain and the German states, 1789-1870* (Oxford: Berghahn, 2000) p. 71. See also: Johannes Paulmann '"Germanismus" am englischen Hof, oder: Warum war Prinz Albert so unpopulär ?' in Peter Alter and Rudolf Muhs (eds.) *Exilanten und andere Deutsche in Fontanes London: Festschrift für Charlotte Jolls* (Stuttgart: Hans-Dieter Heinz, 1996) p. 392.

[47] Quoted in Paulmann, '"Germanismus"' p. 392.

[48] See *Kölnische Zeitung* 2 Jun 1899.

[49] It is not possible to get access to the private papers of Herzog Carl Eduard. Recently a student from the University of Bamberg has summarised the available material under great difficulties: A. Püschel 'Herzog Carl Eduard von Sachsen-Coburg and Gotha in der Zeit der Weimarer Republik und des National-sozialismus' (Zulassungsarbeit, Univeristät Bamberg, 2001). See also: Thomas Nicklas, *Das Haus Sachsen-Coburg: Europas späte Dynastie* (Munich: W. Kohl-Hammer, 2003). Lothar Machtan is planning to include Carl Eduard in his forth-coming study on the aristocracy and the Nazi movement.

[50] N. F. Hayward and D. S. Morris *The First Nazi Town* (Aldershot: Avebury, 1988); R. Hambrecht *Der Aufstieg der NSDAP in Mittel- und Oberfranken (1925-1933)* (Nürnberg: Korn u. Berg, 1976). Hector Bolitho dedicated his biography of Albert in 1932 to Herzog Carl Eduard, 'whose example has brought new honour and affection to the Coburg name': Hector Bolitho *Albert the Good* (London: Cobden-Sanderson, 1932).

[51] In his letter to Leopold, Palmerston did not offer to defend Albert. On the contrary, he indicated that there was some truth in Albert's Orleanist leanings and that he was far from acting as wisely as his uncle. Palmerston wrote to Leopold on 20 Jan 1854: 'I do not happen to have seen the attacks upon your Majesty [King Leopold] in the English newspapers to which you advert. Though I have seen and with great regret some of those which have been directed against H.R.H. the Prince Albert. But I would at all events have been ready even without your Majesty's authority, to have contradicted such charges against your Majesty if I had heard them made': Lord Palmerston to King Leopold, in Herzog Ernst II, LA A 7169 Politische Korrespondenz Januar bis Juli 1854, Staatsarchiv Coburg.

[52] 'The husband of a queen regnant, as Prince George of Denmark was to Queen Anne, is her subject and may be guilty of high treason against her': quoted in Paulmann, '"Germanismus"' p. 403.

[53] Russell in the House of Commons, 31 Jan. 1854, quoted in *ibid.* p. 414.

[54] An appropriate title had been debated since his arrival in England. Victoria had at first favoured 'King Consort' and there had been discussion about making him a peer. In the end he was styled His Royal Highness until June 1857 when the Queen by letters patent conferred 'upon His Royal Highness Prince Albert the title and dignity of Prince Consort', quoted in Connell (ed.), *Regina vs. Palmer-*

ston p. 284.

[55] *ibid*, p. 204.

[56] See: Rainer Hambrecht 'Eine Dynastie, zwei Namen: Haus Sachsen-Coburg und Gotha und Haus Windsor. Ein Beitrag zur Nationalisierung der Monarchien in Europa' in Wolfram Pyta and Ludwig Richter (eds.) *Gestaltungskraft des Politischen: Festschrift für Eberhard Kolb* (Berlin: Duncker and Humblot, 1998) p. 284; Manfred Hanisch 'Nationalisierung der Dynastien oder Modernisierung der Nation ?: Zum Verhältnis von Monarchie und Nation in Deutschland im 19. Jahrhundert' in Adolf Birke and Lothar Kettenacker (eds.) *Bürgertum, Adel und Monarchie* (Munich: K. G. Saur, 1989) pp. 71-91.

[57] Victoria did however become a national icon, something she could not have achieved as long as Albert was alive. Her descendants profited from this development. Queen Elizabeth's golden jubilee, celebrated in 2002 succeeded, as Gert Stratmann has shown, in putting the royal family symbolically at the centre of a multicultural, young national community. Jörg Neuheiser 'Conference report: Political Ritual in the United Kingdom, 1700-2000' *HSozKult*, 24 (Jul 2003). Albert's 'German-ness' was symbolically eradicated in 1917, and the last Coburg 'link' was finally broken: 'we for ourselves and for and on behalf of Our descendants and all other descendants of Our said Grandmother Queen Victoria ... relinquish and enjoin the discontinuance of the use of the degrees, styles, dignities, titles and honours of Dukes and Duchesses of Saxony and Prince and Princesses of Saxe-Coburg and Gotha'. Quoted in Johannes Paulmann 'Verwandtschaft, Vorbild und Rivalität: Britisch-deutsche Beziehungen von der Wiener Ordnung bis zum Imperialismus' *Westfälische Forschungen* 44 (1994) pp. 365 ff.

[58] Keith Robbins 'The monarch's concept of foreign policy: Victoria and Edward VII' in Adolf Birke *et al.* (eds.) *An Anglo-German dialogue: The Munich lectures on the history of international relations* (Munich: K. G. Saur, 2000) p. 123. Cf. David Cannadine: 'The growth of democracy and the party system, combined with her inability to work as hard and as intelligently on the papers as Albert had done, meant that during the last years of her reign, she was no longer performing the central, creative and controlling functions that Albert had sought and sometimes fulfilled. Personal monarchy, as the Prince Consort had understood and envisaged it, was no more': Cannadine, 'Last Hanoverian sovereign' p. 156.

[59] *Daily Mail*, 16 Jul 2003, p. 16.

CHAPTER 7

Palmerston and Russell
J.P. Parry

Between 1848 and 1859 Palmerston and Russell were rivals for the leadership of the Liberal forces in Parliament. Russell lost that battle, allowing Palmerston to dominate British politics from 1855 until his death a decade later. This essay is not a detailed discussion of the key events in that rivalry, but a much more general overview of the two men's inter-relationship over time — a subject which has been strangely neglected. It aims to do two things: first, to look at some of the major differences of approach between them, in the hope of illuminating their arguments; and second, to stress that they should not be seen just or even primarily as opponents. Their differences were significant, but can be exaggerated; their relationship was also a very successful partnership.

There were three particular areas of contrast between them, of which the most important concerned personality and temperament. Palmerston was very self-confident: sure of his own views and the logical base on which they rested, certain of his own judgement and its superiority to that of less rational or sensible people.[1] He had an unruffled executive temperament; he relied on hard work, superior intelligence and forcefulness to get his way in arguments. Because of this, he rarely over-analysed situations or plotted long-distance political strategies. He observed that politicians must 'take things as they find them, and deal with them as best they can'.[2] Russell, on the other hand, was insecure, restless and vain, partly because he underestimated the respect in which he was held and partly because he was schooled to believe that his destiny was to live up to a Whiggish ideal of heroic and progressive popular leadership. He maintained that the proper role of the statesman was to be bold and decisive. His worst mistakes were made when he felt frustrated by his inability to play that role, and tried to make amends by a lone initiative. The Durham letter was one, but the sacking of Palmerston in December 1851 was perhaps the greatest: he admitted later that it was 'hasty and precipitate'.[3] He had been ground down by taunts that he was not being sufficiently strong as Prime Minister, and by the weary task of arbitrating the incessant three-way dispute between Palmerston, the Court, and non-interventionist Cabinet Liberals. The dismissal was a crucial turning-point in the relationship between them because it released Palmerston from needing to accept Russell's leadership; he was genuinely offended, and after the defeat of 1852 he declined to attend a party meeting called by Russell. Moreover, Russell's vanity, sense of destiny and thirst for position ensured that tensions between them would continue through the 1850s. Out of office after 1855, he finished editing the correspondence of his hero Fox and began to write his biography. These occupations encouraged him to interpret the Canton, Reform and Orsini issues as re-runs of the great clashes between Fox and Pitt, with himself playing the virtuous patriot and Palmerston the unprincipled, warmongering foe.[4] And when previously in government, he had made several loose-cannon declarations, which he saw as homages to past Whig heroes and principles — such as when he proposed Reform in 1851 and 1853-4, supported Roebuck's motion in 1855, and made his statement on Vienna later that year. However his critics viewed them differently: as evidence that he was factional and selfish, uninterested in the pragmatic maintenance of government stability.

    In other words, most of the difficulty between them in the 1850s was caused by Russell's temperament and historical perspective. Because Palmerston attached enormous significance to the retention of office and the stability of governments, he was, on the whole, much more passive — which was often also a cleverer way to play the political game, as in late 1854.[5] This temperamental divergence also worked to intensify two other important differences of philosophy, which arose from the fact that Palmerston started his career as a liberal Tory and Russell as a Whig.

One concerned party. The Whigs in opposition to Pitt and Liverpool developed the idea of party, whereas the Pittite tradition was hostile to faction. Pitt and Liverpool both depended for their power on transcending party support to a greater or lesser degree, and Palmerston retained a willingness to serve the national interest with relatively little concern for the precise ideological make-up of his colleagues. By contrast, Russell's commitment to the idea of party made him much more of a legislative activist on key issues — Reform, education, Ireland — that could rally Liberal MPs. His Liberal Anglican moralism also made him anxious to galvanise the political machine out of its apparent complacency. But the fact that these issues were associated with a revival of party-based Liberalism, which would play into Russell's hands, made Palmerston all the more determined to direct politics on other lines, emphasising 'national' themes which suited his anti-factional stance.

Moreover, Russell's conception of party damaged his reputation after 1846. He upheld the traditional Whig notion that in opposition party was a virtuous bond protecting the honour of politicians from the temptation of place-hunting, while in government it prevented anarchy and feebleness. But the Whigs' ideas of an elite-led party required them to adhere to traditional patronage politics and to pack their Cabinets with members of their extended families: in 1846 Russell included eight peers (including his father-in-law), an Irish peer and an heir to an earldom in his Cabinet of sixteen. To many radicals, this approach seemed reminiscent of Walpole's *Venetian* factionalism rather than a patriotic defence of *English* taxpayers' rights, and Russell's Cabinet was mocked as a 'mere family party'.[6] Between 1848 and 1850 British politics were dominated by a drive to reject 'aristocratic' habits, values and policies. Liberal, radical and Peelite MPs tried to build a new image of the state based on free trade, hostility to vested interests, and British constitutional distinctness in relation to autocratic Europe. This strategy, which operated across a number of policy fields — economic, social, colonial and Irish — involved a deliberate rejection of old 'Whiggish' nostrums. In this context, it was easy to portray Russell as the leader of a self-interested clique, thirsting for power and place for his extensive cousinhood, irrespective of merit. Palmerston, on the other hand, appealed more effectively in this new climate, projecting a manlier and more disinterested patriotism on account of his straightforward open politics and cross-class appeal on foreign policy.[7] His perceived hostility to faction assisted his attractiveness to radicals.[8]

Connected with these contrasting approaches to party, finally, was a difference of constitutional perspective. Palmerston was at home in the pre-1832 world in which ministers prized their independence from parliamentary or popular pressure. He was an executive politician (one reason, incidentally, why in the 1820s he should not be seen as a Canningite).[9] Part of the attraction of foreign policy to him was that it gave him so much power of independent action; MPs and other ministers were much less likely to interfere in that area. For the same reason, as David Roberts showed, he was an efficient, active and energetic Home Secretary in the 1850s.[10] Though he became much more adept at managing publicity as his career developed, he remained wary of any politician who seemed willing to compromise his class and its values for popularity. In 1819, hearing of the Yorkshire Whigs' appearance at a large-scale meeting to demand an inquiry into the Peterloo massacre, he remarked: 'I cannot understand how people can submit to such degradation'.[11] Though Russell was no more of a mass orator than Palmerston, he needed to see himself as a popular leader, undertaking bold initiatives on behalf of the people and to protect their liberties. This accounts for his interest in parliamentary reform, both in the late 1820s and in the 1850s. He believed that it would improve the political and moral authority of government, strengthen the affections of the people towards the state, and restore the party dynamic and zeal of Liberalism. Palmerston valued the first, especially in 1830 (for his own reasons, as we shall see below), but he had a less idealistic vision of the second and disliked the third. Like Peel, he felt that a lot of the Whigs' rhetoric about their duty to protect popular liberties was bogus, disguising a partisan objective to rejig the electoral system in their favour. The liberal Tories were as willing to use the language of liberty as the Whigs, but they emphasised commercial and social themes more than constitutional ones. This was apparent from the first exchange between the two in Parliament. In 1816, as Secretary at War, Palmerston was responsible for the post-war army estimates. They were opposed by the young Russell in an invective about the danger of a standing army, which, together with massive levels of Crown influence, would 'erase even the vestiges' of 'departing liberty' and turn Britain from a 'mighty island ... into a petty continental state'. In turn, Palmerston went out of his way to ridicule Russell's claim that liberty was endangered by defence expenditure. The threat to it on the continent lay not in the fact of a large army — which in Britain was resolutely constitutional — but in deeper social values.[12] Palmerston took the enlightened Tory line, that in real terms liberty was already secure in Britain, was greater than anywhere else, and was growing generation by generation owing to commercial progress. He continued to feel that prosperity and good economic and political management would do more to win taxpayer loyalty to the state than bold constitutional gestures.

I

These differences were significant, and help to explain the tensions between the two men. Nonetheless there was also scope for reconciliation of them. First, Palmerston became more of a party Liberal than is sometimes recognised. This is not to deny that his relative flexibility as between parties was crucial to his success in the 1850s, when some sort of coalition government was inevitable and he became the indispensable man to the success of any of them, appealing to Liberals in some ways and Conservatives in others. However, we should also accept the argument of Paul Gurowich that, as Prime Minister, Palmerston was on the whole a Liberal resting on Liberal support.[13] Occasionally he relied on opposition backing to check radical initiatives from within his own party, but fundamentally he had made his decision about ideological bedfellows. In the context of the time, he was a genuine anti-Tory. It is not plausible that he could have worked for long in a Protectionist government in 1852, as some gossips thought he might. In December 1852 he expressed satisfaction to his old friend Laurence Sulivan that he had escaped 'the disagreeableness of finding oneself at the head of men with whom one has for 25 years differed'.[14] He was almost as cool towards the Peelites, and plainly feared that the Liberal party might be subsumed within Peelism. He was the only Cabinet minister who objected to Russell's request to them to join his government in 1846. And in 1849 he advised Russell against making the repeal of the Navigation Acts a matter of confidence, fearing that Peel would come back as Prime Minister and form a government, capturing many Liberals, so that the party would be handed over to him.[15] He disliked their approach to foreign policy; he also believed that a Whig-Liberal government must remain in power in order to avoid the two alarming alternatives of a reactionary Conservative administration, and then a radical ministry in reaction to that. Moreover, by this time Lady Palmerston had become in effect the party hostess for the Liberal party, fulfilling a function which Lady John Russell could not.[16] Admittedly her salon was not exclusively Liberal, and was for the personal benefit of her husband, but it still played a crucial patronage and entertainment role for the party. Once the Russells moved into Pembroke Lodge in 1847, they gave up all pretence of cultivating London society in favour of a quiet, intellectual, nature-loving existence.

Secondly, it is easy to exaggerate the extent of their differences on policy. Even in April 1857, when Russell was emotionally and tactically at odds with Palmerston, he acknowledged that 'on ballot and many other questions and even on general views of foreign policy I do not differ from him, and upon some, as church rates, I have shown myself less favourable to popular views'.[17] And there was less difference on parliamentary reform in practice than their tactical requirements made it appear. At the height of their struggle in the 1850s, it became a symbol of their divergence: Russell needed to identify with it in order to maintain support among Liberals and radicals, while Palmerston's coalition of support depended on him retaining the loyalty of many conservative-minded MPs. Nonetheless, since there was little popular enthusiasm for Reform at the time, this was a division without practical substance. Palmerston undoubtedly believed that it was just being agitated for various factional reasons and was not a pressing social necessity. But equally he resigned from the Cabinet temporarily on Reform in 1853 less because of any insuperable objection to the policy itself, than as a ploy to emphasise his independence from Russell when they were agreed on the question of the day (the East).[18] After Reform had failed to excite the Commons in 1860, Russell was very happy to drop it, and in a ritual Cabinet display of unity the only man who proposed reviving it in the 1861 session was Palmerston.[19] There had also been substantial agreement between them on Reform in practice in 1830-2. By then, as a result of the liberal Tory reforms of the 1820s, Russell had realised that his simplistic libertarian campaign against 'old corruption' was out of date. He, like Palmerston, accepted that the British constitution had in general defended liberties well. As I have argued elsewhere, he supported Reform primarily in order to strengthen popular confidence in the power of government to legislate responsibly for political, social and moral improvement.[20] Both men appreciated the enormous social power of evolving public opinion and saw that by harnessing that power to their purposes, ministers would gain more authority to provide enlightened national leadership.[21]

In 1830, both of them also believed that there was a crucial overseas dimension to this argument. Britain would gain in international strength by demonstrably founding her policy on the loyalty of the people. Her constitutionalism was a point of distinctness and a major asset in European diplomacy. A constitutional regime, backed by a united people, including willing taxpayers, could be more assertive against the continental autocracies. Indeed assertiveness was the only way forward for Britain in international affairs, because the power of the reactionaries was greater in Europe than it was at home, and potentially damaging to British interests. Though much less of an instinctive Reformer than Russell, it was not just desire for office in 1830 that made Palmerston accept the Reform bill. He felt that it was necessary to strengthen ministerial power at home and abroad, because in all departments of government, Tory complacency, feebleness and 'narrow-mindedness' were undermining British might. He claimed that Wellington's government lacked the vision, the 'energy and promptitude', the 'vigour and decision', to look after Britain's interests in Europe, which meant disciplining Miguel in Portugal and forcing Turkey to come to a fair settlement with Greece. This was because it had no respect for public opinion and foolishly believed that the continental powers' strategy of repressing constitutionalism could work.[22] Similarly, Palmerston argued that resorting to 'sword & bayonet' to govern Ireland in the late 1820s was fatally weakening Britain's foreign standing and prestige, by tying down her troops, revealing her disunity to other powers, and betraying the constitutional values on which her reputation rested.[23] And for both men, the foreign and Irish policy of Peel and Aberdeen in 1841-6 was an inglorious sequel to that of Wellington: a lack of 'energy and boldness' in Europe, which would cost money in the long run, and which was exacerbated by failure to pacify Ireland.[24] Fear of disorder across the Irish Sea weakened Britain's international prestige and preoccupied the army: in 1843 Russell complained that 'France and Russia may do as they please East and West, while O'Connell hangs on the rear of our forces'.[25] Both men agreed on the need for papal assistance in governing Ireland in the 1840s, with a view to pacifying the country and maintaining Britain's influence in Europe — hence the Minto mission to Italy of 1847.

This agreement introduces the main argument of the rest of the essay: that more attention needs to be paid to the areas of partnership and common ground between Palmerston and Russell, particularly on the vital question of England's duty to assert her position and values in international politics. The most persistently awkward dividing-line in elite Liberal politics between 1835 and 1865 was on this question. No Cabinet in this period contained a majority in favour of a policy of assertiveness: there was a preference for economy, caution, peace and not upsetting other powers, for a host of domestic and foreign reasons. Palmerston derisively called his economising Cabinet colleagues the 'Broadbrims', in a reference to Quaker pacifism.[26] It was the alliance of Palmerston and Russell that ensured that that majority was usually defeated — indeed Palmerston as Foreign Secretary in the late 1840s, and Russell as Foreign Secretary in the early 1860s, tried to ignore the Cabinet as much as possible. For this rough and ready alliance to work, it was crucial for Palmerston to talk the language of liberalism, and for Russell, as the ideological heir of Fox, to interpret Palmerston's policy in terms with which Whigs would identify.

II

The two men formed a highly effective alliance promoting the view that Britain had a constitutionalist mission in international politics. Of the two, Russell was the more prone to allow ideological and humanitarian considerations to shape his policy, as we shall see. Palmerston was more consistently concerned with the realities of British strategy and power — dealing with 'things as they are' — and he also saw the benefits of liberal rhetoric in getting domestic support for an activist policy which contained much pragmatism. He wanted to strengthen Britain's diplomatic and strategic position by making her an arbiter of European affairs in order to prevent continental domination by anyone else. He also had a psychological need to be the spider at the centre of world affairs, manipulating and manoeuvring all he surveyed from the Foreign Office. But it would be wrong to suggest that Palmerston's talk of promoting liberalism was just a rhetorical construct to hide his strategic objective. As befitted a child of the Enlightenment and an Edinburgh undergraduate, he perceived an ongoing world-historical struggle between Britain and Russia and the principles which each represented. He saw Europe divided into two camps, one relying on physical repression and the other gaining strength from the power of public opinion.[27] In 1836 he said that Britain could no longer work with the Eastern powers because 'their views and opinions are nowadays the reverse of ours'.[28] Constitutional states, meanwhile, were 'natural allies'.[29] Given the development of civilisation, constitutional values would almost certainly triumph in the end, but it was Britain's duty to join the struggle for them. World progress moved in fits and starts, always at risk in the short term from brute force or the eruption of passions; Britain's mission and interest was to promote it internationally, just as Whig government had a responsibility to intervene at home to promote social improvement.[30] To do so was in line with God's intentions for the progress of the world; it was military repression by the autocracies to prevent the natural spread of commerce and constitutionalism which was un-Christian. England's great advantage was that her power would grow with commercial and social evolution in the West. The establishment of stable constitutional governments elsewhere in Europe would help England's fundamental interests — peace and stability — because they would be followed by more liberal trading arrangements and a reluctance to make war for dynastic purposes.[31] England's rightful policy was to be 'the friend of liberty and civilization', because 'the selfish interests and political influence of England, were best promoted by [their] extension'.[32] Constitutional monarchy was England's trademark; its spread would assist her prestige and psychological dominance in Europe. Palmerston and Russell viewed the battle over European forms of government as the equivalent of military warfare. Every gain for autocracy was a gain for Austria, Russia or the 'Holy Alliance'; every republican regime might become a vehicle for propagating the ideas of the French Revolution.[33] Palmerston considered that 'large republics seem to be essentially and inherently aggressive'.[34] Either way, internal and external stability was unlikely. Victories for constitutional monarchies, on the other hand, demonstrated that Europe was following the Providential path to a higher civilisation.

So Britain's policy should not be 'non-intervention' — which in any case 'was not an English word'. It should only be 'non-interference' in the sense of not using force of arms to alter other countries' internal affairs.[35] It should be one of 'intermeddling in every way … short of actual military force' in places like Portugal where England's security was affected.[36] And elsewhere England's interest lay in 'interfering by friendly counsel and advice', to 'maintain the liberties and independence of all other nations', to 'throw her moral weight into the scale of any people who are spontaneously striving for … rational govt, and to extend as far and as fast as possible civilization all over the world'.[37] Russell, similarly, squared his support for 'intermeddling' with the old Foxite tradition of not interfering in the internal affairs of other countries, by arguing that it was Austria, not Britain, which was behaving irresponsibly in Italy, and should be opposed. In 1848 both men took the line that while England should not tear up the Treaty of Vienna, she should encourage Austria to abandon Lombardy and Venetia, because the political and intellectual awakening in northern Italy — the progressive movement of public opinion — was making it too difficult for her to govern them effectively any more.[38]

Of course some of this was rhetorical puff. In particular, it was all very well to say that the world was naturally moving

England's way, but in practice the combined weight of the continental autocracies was often stronger than this implied, particularly in the 1820s and 1840s. This justified activism, rather than passivity, all the more, but it also made it important to act selectively rather than to attempt to promote constitutionalism irrespective of circumstance. Focusing on specific foolish attempts by other powers to reach beyond their grasp, resisting the irresistible, especially in areas bordering the sea, was therefore a wise strategy which maximised chances of success. In general, Palmerston and Russell were in fact conservatives on the major issues of European politics. The British sought no territories there; British interest lay in peace and hence good trading conditions; the existing balance of power offered stability; good diplomatic relations had to be maintained with other powers. The number of occasions on which a naval power like Britain could give effective practical support to the development of liberal governments was small, and liberalism was always a relative term. British interests lay in the establishment of stable constitutional monarchies in Europe which were not in the pockets of France or Russia; they did not lie in destabilising Europe in pursuit of principle. Britain could not impose the liberal middle way prematurely. The example of France's political failure was ever-present. If change seemed likely to lead to the destruction of international order, to radical republican anarchy, or to a counter-revolution strengthening the grip of autocracy, then the status quo was the best solution. This can be seen by looking at Palmerston's attitude to Germany in the 1840s. In principle, he liked the notion of a consolidation of German regimes into a stronger unit, as long as this unit favoured constitutionalism and followed a liberal tariff policy. That would benefit British trade and would prevent instability in the region which France or Russia might exploit. On the other hand, most proposals for change looked likely to increase that instability, because they lacked substance. The subsequent reaction would either strengthen the hand of Austria and Russia in Germany or promote the cause of republicanism, which would be unacceptable both strategically (creating a Franco-German rapprochement) and ideologically. In 1848-9, therefore, he preferred to support the status quo.[39]

There were other domestic political benefits of a policy of selective strength which relied on naval power to project a powerful international image. One great merit of building up domestic confidence in Britain's global position was that it minimised the danger of popular panics about inadequate defence. The more vigour Britain showed in keeping continental illiberalism at bay, the less popular insecurity about defence there would be. This would allow government to justify necessary naval spending more easily, but also to keep it firmly under control and thus pacify the taxpayer. Canning had pulled off this trick in the 1820s, though as it happened the severe depressions of 1838-41 and 1847-8 made Palmerston's military expenditure controversial in any event. Secondly, it was easier to generate publicity and support at home for criticism of specific ill-deeds by other powers than to develop a consistent public interest in a European policy, which would always be difficult. And thirdly, emphasis on Britain's self-assertion against autocratic powers was very useful in domestic politics because it allowed opponents to be charged with a lack of patriotism. In 1849, for example, Liberal ministers criticised both wings of the Conservatives — particularly the Peelite Aberdeen, a friend of Metternich and the Tsar — for their Austrian sympathies.[40] Palmerston and Russell both insisted that a crucial component of British honour was the ability to make her own policy without foreign dictation. In Palmerston's famous speech on the Don Pacifico affair in June 1850, the passage which won him the loudest cheer was his scarcely-veiled rebuke to those who were engaged in a 'foreign conspiracy' against a minister upholding 'the dignity and interests of his own country'.[41] Russell made similar remarks, explicitly linking Aberdeen's 'unjust' attacks on his government's foreign policy to the promptings of 'foreigners'.[42] Palmerston's reference to conspiracy also clearly implicated the Court: Victoria and Albert loathed his policy and had constantly sought to tone down his despatches criticising other European crowned heads. When Palmerston resigned in 1851 and briefly in 1853, the popular press was full of stories that this was the result of pressure from foreign powers on the Germanic Albert. Russell's preoccupation with honour sometimes made him an even more strident defender of Britain's power of independent action than Palmerston. This is evident from his hostility to the papal bull of 1850 re-establishing the Catholic hierarchy, to the Conspiracy to Murder Bill in 1858, and to the idea of submitting America's *Alabama* claims against Britain to arbitration.

It is well known that in his later career the main benefit for Palmerston of this identification with the promotion of international liberalism was extra-parliamentary popularity, particularly among radicals. However, another great benefit, and in the 1830s and 1840s the major one, was that such a policy strengthened his hand in the Whig coalition by allying him with the Russellite tradition against the anti-interventionists. For a start, his high-profile attacks on Wellington's reactionary and feeble policy were politically shrewd because they helped to win him the Foreign Secretaryship in the Reform coalition of 1830. Once in post, he depended on support from the Russell interpretation of Fox's foreign policy legacy in order to defeat the pressures for economy and minimal continental intervention that were bound to intensify after the Reform Act. As leader of the Commons 1835-41, Prime Minister 1846-52, and Fox-ite moralist after 1852, Russell played a crucial role in making Palmerston's foreign policy possible.

III

Russell's approach to foreign policy reflected the ambivalence of Foxite Whiggism on the subject. He believed in a vigorous approach to promote the cause of liberty and to defend ideals of honour and responsibility. However the Whig party generally had a clear predisposition to a pacific and economical policy, and he saw some virtue in that stance too. Most Whigs had been extremely uneasy, most of the time, about the wars of 1776-1815. It was easy to present them as foolish crusades against national aspirations in America and France, whose principal domestic consequences had been the perpetuation of existing political abuses, increased jobbery, and the creation of a massive national debt. In reaction, the cry of military non-interference in the domestic affairs of other countries became a staple of progressive politics in the 1820s and 1830s. Defence expenditure and national debt interest payments made up the great bulk of the total national budget; the need for reductions to appease the taxpayer was obvious, before and especially after 1832. The tricky question, however, was how to square disapproval of military interference with the other great Foxite principle of 'the cause of civil and religious liberty all over the world'.[43] Napoleon had tried to crush liberty in the Iberian peninsula, prompting nationalist uprisings from 1808, encouraged by Britain; after 1815, the 'Holy Alliance' continued the attempt at suppression, in Spain and Italy. The question of whether Britain should assist these uprisings created a long-running tension within Whiggery between, on the one hand, Russell and his mentor Holland (Fox's nephew), and, on the other, the peace party led by Whitbread and Grenville. Russell later accused Grenville and the Whig leader, the second Earl Grey, of betraying the Foxite cause by failing to support the Spanish after 1808.[44] Such an allegation maligned Grey, but its real target was probably Grey's son, the third Earl.[45] At any rate, the ardently patriotic Russell visited the battlefields of Spain three times in 1810, 1812 and 1813, and was personally conducted along the lines of Torres Vedras by General Hill.[46] Puny Lord John was a soldier manqué; he loved military metaphors in his speeches and commanded a company of the Bedfordshire militia.[47] Indeed one cause of his restlessness in late 1854 was that he wished to take charge of the mismanaged war effort and save the situation in the Crimea.[48] Russell argued that nations, like individuals, displayed their honour by their disinterested defence of liberty, and that it was England's mission to act up to this ideal. He also believed that Britain's imperial commitments — for example in Canada — could only be defended by decisive vigour — explaining his policy as Colonial Secretary in 1839-41.[49]

Russell's Foxite inheritance made for some disagreements with Palmerston's gung-ho policy. He was more committed to the strategy of maintaining good relations with other powers in order to enhance prospects for peace, prosperity and progress. Despite his instinctive hostility to Austria's presence in Italy, he tried to rein in Palmerston's verbal attacks on her in 1849, fearing that they would drive her into Russia's hands and facilitate the latter's advance into 'the heart of Europe'.[50] Though he approved of Palmerston's assertiveness in Greece in 1850, he also believed in working with the French, whose attempts to mediate in the Don Pacifico affair his Foreign Secretary had ignored. He was particularly keen on maintaining an entente with France during the liberal Orleanist monarchy: he felt that the two powers could make an alliance for liberalism abroad, and that Britain's security interest lay in keeping such a benevolent regime in place in Paris. Conversely, he was more suspicious than Palmerston of Napoleon III and his imperial ambitions, partly because of ideology but especially from anxiety that his attempt to establish a monarchy in Mexico would alienate the United States.[51] And he was keener on mediation in the American Civil War. In general, he was very conscious of the responsibility to preserve peace, which he saw as one of the cardinal Foxite principles and the ideal of a true Christian and patriot. At several moments in his career he identified himself emotionally against bombastic warmongering. During the Near Eastern crisis of 1840 he took the responsibility of proposing a French peace plan to the British Cabinet, though Palmerston argued that to accept it would be to show that Britain was a dependency of France.[52] (He also felt that Russell over-estimated the risk that a constitutional regime in France would actually go to war over Egypt; French taxpayers would resist the idea.) In 1855, Russell was particularly anxious to try to find peace at Vienna, and made himself look unpatriotic and inconsistent by favouring it. After he resigned, he took to ruing the bloodshed involved in continuing the war, and saw himself as a Whig of the 1790s combating the nation's bloodthirsty spirit.[53] Similarly in 1857 he criticised the attack on Canton, believing it to be motivated by talk of 'prestige', a foreign word, instead of the character and honour of England on which her greatness was founded.[54]

Nonetheless, as noted earlier, a lot of these tensions in the 1850s — and indeed in 1840 — were exacerbated by Russell's personal insecurity in the face of Palmerston's willpower and success. They should not disguise the principles that they had in common. Russell, indeed, asserted that honour was more vital than peace: in September 1853 he sent the most famous phrase in diplomatic history echoing down the generations when he said in a speech that 'if peace cannot be maintained with honour, it is no longer peace'.[55] And he was not above talking of prestige himself.[56] Moreover, the most well-publicised differences between the two men on the French entente reflected their political situation at particular times rather than any divergence of strategic principle. Both of them knew that Britain usually needed to work with France to maximise her diplomatic and strategic influence, but it was politically awkward to admit this. It was very tempting to accuse a minister of lacking patriotism if he made too many compromises with constitutional illiberalism in order to pacify the French — as Russell suggested Palmerston had, in 1858.[57]

Most of the time, Palmerston and Russell took very similar views of Britain's international mission. Indeed, even when telling the Queen of his intention to move Palmerston from the Foreign Office in 1850, he made it clear to her that his object was to 'continue the same line of foreign policy without giving the same offence'.[58] The crucial dividing-line was between them and their opponents in and outside the Cabinet. To some extent their alliance

was already visible in the crisis of 1840, since, despite his vacillation in its later stages, Russell had been decisive in persuading the
Cabinet to accept the four-power alliance to uphold the integrity of
the Ottoman Empire against Mehemet Ali, against opposition from
Clarendon and Holland. Palmerston could not have achieved this
victory without Russell's support. After 1846 the two of them took
part in a long struggle against the 'broadbrims' in the Cabinet: the
Grey family party, led by Grey and Wood, combining adherence to
the Foxite tradition as they understood it with an ideological commitment to political economy; Clarendon, very keen on preserving
good relations abroad; and the more radical members keen to cut
costs. Outside the Cabinet, most of the leading Peelites were
quietists: Aberdeen told Russell that they had given their support to
his government expecting it to be 'a Ministry of Peace'.[59] And in the
aftermath of 1846, Cobdenism was a power to be reckoned with on
the backbenches and in the provinces, while MPs were insistent on
low taxes, given the unfavourable economic climate. In fact, had
Parliament been asked for more ships in 1840, it would probably
also have rejected the idea.[60] Finally, the Queen and Albert were
anxious to maintain the European status quo and not to rock any
diplomatic boats. Despite the internal disagreements between these
groups, they supplied a lot of pressure for what Russell's father-in-
law Minto disparagingly called a 'low and narrow policy', playing
into the hands of the autocrats.[61] It was largely for this reason that
Palmerston was particularly hostile to a Peelite takeover of the
Liberal party in the late 1840s.

Grey and Wood argued that peace and good relations with
France were vital if British finances were to cope with the severe
economic depressions of the 1840s. They also feared that Palmerston was too hostile to the United States. They became the most
forceful Liberal advocates of the French *entente*, the policy which
Peel and Aberdeen were also pursuing, and by 1845-6 wanted a
rapprochement of free traders in both parties, a Liberal-Peelite
coalition on *laissez-faire* and non-interventionist principles.[62] In

December 1845, Grey (without Wood) attempted to block Palmerston's return to the Foreign Office, thus preventing the formation of a Liberal ministry to repeal the corn laws. Russell would not give in, telling Grey that Palmerston was 'the person in the United Kingdom best fitted for that department'.[63] When Russell formed his government in 1846, not only did Palmerston go back to the Foreign Office, but he put supporters of assertiveness in key positions, particularly Auckland at the Admiralty. Palmerston immediately adopted a robust policy towards France over the Spanish Marriages affair, underlining his view that the Peel-Aberdeen policy had lowered the reputation of the country.

Moreover, in the late 1840s Palmerston and Russell fought together against three challenges from the low-tax wing of the party. The first concerned defence. The cooling of the French *entente*, and the aggressive remarks of Louis Philippe's son about the possibility that steam power could challenge British naval hegemony, had created a mini-invasion scare in 1845; Palmerston claimed that, because of steam, the Channel was 'no longer a barrier', merely 'a river passable by a steam bridge'.[64] He insisted that Britain must build up her defences, reassert her dominance and prestige, and see off the challenges posed by the insular parsimony of ascendant radicalism.[65] On four occasions in 1846 and 1847, Palmerston and Russell joined forces to ask the Cabinet to reconstitute the militia. Each time it demurred at the cost and unpopularity entailed.[66] Wood, as Chancellor of the Exchequer, led the opposition, arguing that enough was being done and that extra spending would further antagonise supporters in the provinces, already angered by its religious and educational policy.[67] Secondly, there were a series of radical challenges to the maintenance of the imperial connection, which the government (including Grey) was determined to resist. In 1849-52 it became embroiled in intra-party disputes, particularly over Australian self-government and the Cape. An important component of Whig colonial policy was the urgent sense of responsibility for colonial good government, as a Providential duty.[68] This was also evident, thirdly, in the resistance put up by Russell and Palmerston in 1850 to the radical-Peelite motion demanding the abolition of the African squadron, which attempted (without much success) to prevent the continuation of the West African slave trade. There was so much opposition within the Liberal coalition to funding the squadron, on grounds of economy and the Dissenting belief that an international crusade mounted by aroused religious opinion would kill the trade more effectively, that Russell made the issue a vote of confidence, to the fury of many MPs.[69] Russell and Palmerston shared a lifelong commitment to the idea of Britain's duty to attack the slave trade, as a symbol of her honour and the Christian beneficence of her naval power.[70] Palmerston in 1846 had described Britain as 'the main instrument in the Hands of Providence' for the accomplishment of Europe's destiny, the ending of the trade.[71] Russell now told the Commons that unless Britain continued to do her duty against slavery, she would be betraying her 'high ... moral, and ... Christian character', and would no longer have the right to expect the continuation of the divine blessing which had allowed her to escape revolution in 1848.[72] But this display of government force was a pyrrhic victory as the strength of the squadron was much reduced thereafter.

Naturally, this partnership increasingly came under strain between 1848 and 1851 because of the unpopularity of Russell's government, the attacks on his personal patriotism, and the attractiveness of Palmerston's foreign policy, which made him the strongest figure in a weak Cabinet. Russell's inability to use the Papal Aggression issue, or Reform, to sustain a base of support drew attention to Palmerston's superior appeal in the post-1848 climate. After 1851, despite Russell's formal position as Liberal leader, Palmerston and he were clearly in rivalry for power, and everything that took place between then and 1859 needs to be seen in that context — even the occasions on which they worked together. However, that is not to underestimate the significance of those occasions. One was in 1853-4, over the Eastern Mediterranean, when Palmerston and Russell, the two establishment politicians with the strongest parliamentary and popular following, almost single-handedly forced the divided Liberal-Peelite Cabinet to strengthen its resistance to the Russian advance towards Constantinople. They felt that this was necessary for Britain's honour, given her strong naval presence in the region, and in order to stop Napoleon III stealing a march on her. They believed that failure to act vigorously would demonstrate to domestic opinion the effeteness of propertied government, and undermine its legitimacy. And they each wanted to assert their own patriotism against their critics, both to avoid losing position against the other, and to enhance their standing *vis-à-vis* the large number of Peelites in the Cabinet.[73]

Similarly, in 1859, the two men, widely assumed to be heads of opposed factions in opposition during the Derby government, reached a pact to work together, leading to the famous meeting at Willis's Rooms which preceded the defeat of the Conservative government. They needed to come to an understanding on parliamentary reform, since it was the issue on which their supporters had differed the most. But the main reason for their agreement was foreign policy. However, it was not an agreement on the details of an Italian policy — since the scope for a successful strategy was not apparent until the Treaty of Villafranca the following month. It was, rather, a belief that, given the Italian crisis and invasion panic, Conservative feebleness must be rejected: Britain must have a majority (and therefore a Liberal) government and must assert a strong image abroad based on their personalities and approaches. It was not quite the old Whig notion of 'men not measures', but it came close to it. Russell lectured Wood: 'My conviction is that in the present state of foreign affairs, it is most desirable for the country that Palmerston should be in office'.[74] Russell himself took the Foreign Office to keep out Clarendon or Granville, either of whom would have adopted a very much less assertive policy in Italy.[75] Palmerston had written to Russell on 18 May that the Liberals must create a strong government so that 'this country and other countries should know in the present state of the world … the organ of Great Britain is a government … that … may have … weight … authority and … independence of action'.[76] Thus the 'two terrible old men' got in harness to pursue a didactic, over-confident foreign policy all the way up to the Schleswig-Holstein affair in 1864. At the Guildhall in November 1865, remembering Palmerston's life, Russell commented that 'his heart beat ever for England'. When Lecky expressed a different view, he retorted that Palmerston 'kept the honour of England very high; and I think that a great thing'.[77]

IV

So why did they usually work together in this way ? Three reasons suggest themselves.

Firstly, and most obviously, they believed in making Britain count in the world, as befitted her destiny as the world's greatest and most progressive power. It mattered to them — brought up in the shadow of Napoleon Bonaparte — that Britain should assert herself in this fashion, and that they should win fame and a place in the national pantheon for helping her. The British constitution was a great gift which had helped the nation to marry stability and progress and to develop powers of enterprise and energy, raising human potential nearer to God's intentions. It was reasonable to assume that the spread of similar values abroad — political values but also the religious, economic and social ones that supported them — would benefit the world. But this was not a utopian vision. The strategy was not concerned with the abstract promotion of these values, but with establishing accountable government, friendly to Britain and British trade, where her naval and diplomatic clout could do this successfully. There was also a religious aspect to the rhetoric, which should be neither ignored nor exaggerated. Their remarks suggested that Britain had a Providential duty to encourage the spread of civilisation and progress internationally against the deadweight of feudalism and autocracy and the inhumanity of the slave trade. This was a claim that British politicians had a *respon-sibility* to act vigorously abroad, just as at home. Irresponsible behaviour was a betrayal of the politician's task, to defend the security and power of his country, and, more indirectly, to promote the cause of humanity. Here there was a clear parallel with Whig interventionism in domestic policy. Materialism, *laissez-faire*, and apathy about constitutional reform corroded good relations between the classes; the politician who condoned them was failing in his patriotic and Christian duties. In foreign policy, the idea of respon-sibility to assert Britain's international power was particularly well suited to the period up to the mid-1850s, because it assumed that European politics could be understood in terms of the battle between virtuous progress and weakening but still vicious auto-cracy. From the mid-1850s, autocracy ceased to be such a threat, and so after the dismantling of Austrian and Bourbon power in Italy in 1859 the policy of Palmerston and Russell lost its focus. More-over, from around 1850, optimism in Britain about the *unguided* progress of the world became more exuberant, and British political culture was increasingly less constrained by anxiety that the contin-uing good fortune of the nation depended on particular Christian actions. The notion of upholding individual and national honour, a classic Whig concept, arguably also lost some of its purchase with the change in domestic political tone after 1848. For all these reasons, the Palmerston-Russell strategy became less politically potent by the 1860s.

Secondly, international assertiveness gave a crucial uplift to domestic Liberal politics. This was, firstly, because it emphasised libertarian constitutional and ethical themes that resonated with Whigs, liberal Tories and radicals, at a relatively abstract level, avoiding most of the divisions that necessarily arose in discussion of hard-edged domestic questions. The stress on Britain's identi-fication with constitutionalism was particularly important in making radicals accept propertied Liberal leadership. Indeed some historians argue that patriotic rhetoric was more attractive because of what it symbolised about liberties at home than because of its projection of national power abroad.[78] However, it should not be reduced to the former. The assertion of British power was important politically, not only for the obvious reason that in the 1850s, particularly, it allowed Britain to look very strong in Europe, but for three others too. First, important commercial and other interests valued it. Second, it was identified with attractive and inclusive values — manliness, vigour, energy — which Liberals like Palmerston and Russell used to contrast themselves with political opponents who were portrayed as aristocratic, spineless and effete. This was a constant and crucial but understudied theme in Liberal politics, from the late 1820s to its reincarnation by Hartington and Chamberlain for use against Granville and Derby in the 1880s. Thirdly, this vigour in turn validated propertied government. Concentration on 'national' issues offered the best chance of rallying Liberal forces, helping to keep centre-left governments in power against Conservative alternatives or the threat of radical ones at a time when the party system was in disarray. And these issues also emphasised ideas and myths that would help to bind together the national community and thus to realise in practice the ideal that their rhetoric sketched out: that the classes in Britain were united in a common identity and sense of purpose. Early- and mid-Victorian Liberals worried enormously about materialism, social division and chauvinism: a focus on vigour abroad was a way of bolstering pride in country and regime yet also introducing more altruistic themes to national discussion.

Finally, it was in the interests of both men to play the patriotic card. It was important for Russell not to cede ground on these issues to Palmerston, in order to prevent him developing too much of a personal advantage in their rivalry. Here there was a neat analogy with British diplomatic strategy towards France — that the best way of restraining her from asserting her power over Britain was to work with her, in Spain, Italy and the Near East, in order to ensure that any benefits from their activity were shared equally.

Indeed Russell's determination to keep close to Palmerston undoubtedly helps to explain why their joint pressure was usually able to defeat their opponents. Similarly Palmerston realised that he could only appeal effectively to Liberals if his language chimed with Russell's in important ways, even while trying to assert a separate identity in others.

Even at their moments of greatest rivalry, then, they realised that they needed each other for domestic political reasons and inter-national strategic ones. Like all great political rivalries, theirs was a complex relationship and it is important not to be too swayed by the gossip of the day which, like all political gossip, exaggerated the differences and difficulties between them. They were, after all, colleagues in Cabinet together for twenty-four years — an unrivalled record in the history of modern (post-1820s) Cabinet government. Palmerston felt betrayed by Russell's sacking of him in 1851, not least because he was an 'old friend'.[79] Afterwards, he said that, while he would never serve under him again, 'I love him and I always shall'.[80] For his part, Russell blamed Whigs like Wood and Clarendon rather than Palmerston for his eclipse in the mid-1850s.[81] Of course these sentiments do not give the whole picture: clashes of temperament and ambition also played a large part in their relationship. Despite that, they were not simply rivals, but one of the great double-acts of politics, and neither can adequately be understood in isolation from the other.

References

[1] Hence his problems with the less logical minds of monarchs. On his contempt for George IV's reasoning, see his letter, 19 Jan 1829, in K. Bourne (ed.) *The letters of the third Viscount Palmerston to Laurence and Elizabeth Sulivan 1804-1863*, (London: Royal Historical Society, Camden 4th series, 23; 1979) p. 228. For Lady Palmerston's view on his mishandling of Queen Victoria, see T. Lever *The letters of Lady Palmerston* (London: John Murray, 1957) p. 315.

[2] Bourne (ed.), *Letters to Sulivan*, p. 305 (31 Dec 1852).

[3] John, Earl Russell *Recollections and suggestions 1813-1873* (2nd edn., London: Longmans, 1875) p. 294.

[4] See J.P. Parry 'Past and future in the later career of Lord John Russell', in

History and biography: essays in honour of Derek Beales ed. T.C.W. Blanning and D. Cannadine (Cambridge: Cambridge University Press, 1996) p. 161.

[5] On Palmerston's refusal to help Russell unseat the government at this point, see J. Prest *Lord John Russell* (London: Macmillan, 1972) pp. 368-9 and D. Brown *Palmerston and the politics of foreign policy 1846-55* (Manchester: Manchester University Press, 2002) p. 203.

[6] For references, see Parry, 'Past and future', p. 143. See also Bernal Osborne, *Parliamentary Debates*, 3rd ser. c, 166 (6 Jul 1848): 'a snug family party'.

[7] This theme is very clear in *The two great statesmen, a Plutarchian parallel between Earl Russell and Viscount Palmerston, MP* (London, 1862).

[8] See A. Taylor 'Palmerston and radicalism, 1847-1865' *Journal of British Studies* 33 (1994) pp. 157-79 and M. Taylor *The decline of British radicalism, 1847-1860* (Oxford: Oxford University Press, 1995) pp. 149-57.

[9] See his comments on Canning, 19 Aug 1822, in Bourne (ed.), *Letters to Sulivan*, pp. 152-3.

[10] D. Roberts 'Lord Palmerston at the Home Office' *The Historian* 21 (1958) pp. 63-81.

[11] Bourne (ed.), *Letters to Sulivan*, p. 147 (21 Oct 1819).

[12] *Parliamentary Debates*, 1st ser. xxxii, 843-6 (26 Feb 1826), *ibid.*, xxxiii, 107-8 (8 Mar 1816).

[13] P.M. Gurowich 'The continuation of war by other means: party and politics, 1855-1865' *Historical Journal* 27 (1984) pp. 610-11, 629-30.

[14] Bourne (ed.), *Letters to Sulivan*, p. 305 (24 Dec 1852).

[15] Prest, *Russell*, pp. 223, 299.

[16] K.D. Reynolds *Aristocratic women and political society in Victorian Britain* (Oxford: Oxford University Press, 1998) pp. 173-4, 179.

[17] Russell to Dean Elliot, 23 Apr 1857, Russell Papers, TNA, PRO 30/22/13C, f. 264.

[18] Brown, *Palmerston and foreign policy*, pp. 186-8.

[19] E. D. Steele *Palmerston and Liberalism, 1855-1865* (Cambridge: Cambridge University Press, 1991) p. 104.

[20] Parry, 'Past and future', p. 151, and *idem, The rise and fall of Liberal government in Victorian Britain* (New Haven and London: Yale University Press, 1993) pp. 87-9.

[21] In 1829, Palmerston said of public opinion that 'he who can grasp this power, with it will subdue the fleshly arm of physical strength' (*Parliamentary Debates*, 2nd ser. xxi, 1668, 1 Jun 1829); and in 1833 that 'the province of a wise Govt. is to keep pace with the improved notions of the people' (quoted in K. Bourne *Palmerston: the early years, 1784-1841* (London: Allen Lane, 1982) p. 372).

[22] *Parliamentary Debates*, 2nd ser. xxi, 1659-60, 1663, 1667-8 (1 Jun 1829); and the letter of 14 Aug 1828, in Bourne (ed.), *Letters to Sulivan*, p. 213.

²³ See the various letters of Sep - Oct 1828 in Bourne (ed.), *Letters to Sulivan*, p. 217.

²⁴ On Europe, see Russell to Lady Holland, 7 Aug 1842, in G.P. Gooch (ed.) *The later correspondence of Lord John Russell 1840-1878* (2 vols., London: Longmans, 1925) i, p. 56.

²⁵ Prest, *Russell*, p. 193.

²⁶ D. Southgate *'The most English minister...': the policies and politics of Palmerston* (London: Macmillan, 1966) p. 243.

²⁷ *Parliamentary Debates*, 2nd ser. xxi, 1668 (1 Jun 1829).

²⁸ Southgate, *'Most English minister'*, p. 161.

²⁹ *Parliamentary Debates*, 3rd ser. xiv, 1045 (2 Aug 1832).

³⁰ I hope to develop the analogy between Whig domestic and foreign policy further in a forthcoming book, *The politics of patriotism*.

³¹ Constitutional states were 'less likely to go to war than despotic governments because money will not be voted lightly' by their parliaments: Bourne, *Palmerston*, p. 626.

³² *Parliamentary Debates*, 2nd ser. xxi, 1669 (1 Jun 1829).

³³ e.g. in Italy: Southgate, *'Most English minister'*, p. 214.

³⁴ Palmerston to Normanby, 28 Feb 1848, quoted in E. Ashley *The life of Henry John Temple, Viscount Palmerston: 1846-1865* (2 vols., London: Richard Bentley and Son, 1876) i, p. 81.

³⁵ *Parliamentary Debates*, 3rd ser. xiv, 1067 (2 Aug 1832).

³⁶ *Ibid.*, 2nd ser. xxi, 1646 (1 Jun 1829).

³⁷ *Ibid.*, 3rd ser. xiv, 1067, and (1838) Bourne, *Palmerston*, p. 627.

³⁸ Memorandum, 1 May 1848, in S. Walpole *The life of Lord John Russell* (2 vols., London: Longmans, 1889) ii, pp. 40-2.

³⁹ F.L. Müller *Britain and the German question: perceptions of nationalism and political reform, 1830-63* (Basingstoke: Palgrave, 2002) especially pp. 16-19, 24-5, 52-4, 72, 114.

⁴⁰ In July, Palmerston implicitly attacked Aberdeen, with other Austrian sympathisers, for defending her as a 'great symbol of the opinions which they entertained' about 'resistance to improvement': *Parliamentary Debates*, 3rd ser. cvii, 809 (21 Jul 1849).

⁴¹ *Ibid.*, 3rd ser. cxii, 422 (25 Jun 1850). See Southgate, *'Most English minister'*, p. 267.

⁴² *Parliamentary Debates*, 3rd ser. cxii, 697, 28 Jun 1850. See also Macaulay's worry, 3 Feb 1849, that Palmerston would become 'a sacrifice to the spite of foreign powers', in G.O. Trevelyan *The life and letters of Lord Macaulay* (Oxford: Oxford University Press, 1978 edn) ii, p. 186.

⁴³ See Russell's comments, 18 May 1874, in R. Russell (ed.) *Early correspondence of Lord John Russell, 1805-40* (2 vols., London: T. Fisher Unwin, 1913) i,

p. 317.

44 Russell, *Recollections*, pp. 5-9.

45 See E.A. Smith *Lord Grey 1764-1845* (Oxford: Oxford University Press, 1990) pp. 166-73.

46 Prest, *Russell*, pp. 12-14.

47 S.J. Reid *Lord John Russell* (London: Sampson, Low, Marston, 1895) p. 16.

48 *Ibid.*, p. 243; O.W. Hewett *'... and Mr. Fortescue': a selection from the diaries of Chichester Fortescue, Lord Carlingford, 1851-62* (London: John Murray, 1958) p. 68.

49 Parry, 'Past and future', p. 152.

50 Russell to Palmerston, 13 Apr. 1849, in Gooch, *Later correspondence*, i, p. 358.

51 P. Scherer *Lord John Russell: a biography* (Selinsgrove: Susquehanna University Press, 1999) pp. 282-4.

52 Prest, *Russell*, p. 166.

53 *Ibid.*, p. 377; Parry, 'Past and future', p. 161.

54 *Parliamentary Debates*, 3rd ser. cxliv, 1476 (26 Feb 1857).

55 At Greenock: Walpole, *Russell*, ii, p. 190.

56 *Parliamentary Debates*, 3rd ser. cxlviii, 1048 (9 Feb 1858), professing shock that, over the Conspiracy to Murder bill, Palmerston should think the favour of a foreign power of more value to England than 'the maintenance of her ancient prestige'.

57 A.L. Kennedy *'My Dear Duchess': social and political letters to the Duchess of Manchester, 1858-69* (London: John Murray, 1956) p. 32.

58 Walpole, *Russell*, ii, pp. 60-1.

59 Aberdeen to Russell, 17 Nov 1846, in Gooch, *Later correspondence*, i, p. 130.

60 Bourne, *Palmerston*, p. 617.

61 Minto to Russell, 3 Jan 1852, in Gooch, *Later correspondence*, ii, p. 95.

62 F. A. Dreyer 'The Whigs and the political crisis of 1845', *English Historical Review* 80 (1965) pp. 524-5, 536.

63 Russell to Grey, 21 Dec 1845, in Walpole, *Russell*, i, p. 416.

64 *Parliamentary Debates*, 3rd ser. lxxxii, 1224 (30 Jul 1845).

65 See Gooch, *Later correspondence*, i, pp. 117-19, 248-54.

66 M.S. Partridge *Military planning for the defense of the United Kingdom, 1814-1870* (London: Greenwood Press, 1989) pp. 128-31.

67 Gooch, *Later correspondence*, i, pp. 243-5. There was also a problem, as there was to be in 1851-2, about the most effective terms on which to organise it.

68 I discuss this at greater length in *The politics of patriotism*.

69 See H. Reeve (ed.) *The Greville memoirs: a journal of the reigns of King George IV, King William IV, and Queen Victoria* (8 vols., London: Longmans, 1896 edn.) vi, p. 332.

[70] In 1864 Palmerston wrote that 'there are no two men in England more determined enemies of the slave trade than Lord Russell and myself': Southgate, *'Most English minister'*, p. 151.

[71] D.B. Davis *Slavery and Human Progress* (New York: Oxford University Press, 1984) p. xviii.

[72] See Walpole, *Russell*, ii, pp. 106-7 for this and Palmerston's note of congratulation.

[73] This again will be discussed at more length elsewhere.

[74] Steele, *Palmerston and Liberalism*, p. 89.

[75] Scherer, *Russell*, p. 265.

[76] Steele, *Palmerston and Liberalism*, pp. 90-1. *The Times,* reporting on the Willis's Rooms meeting, observed that 'no consideration seems to have weighed more on the minds of the meeting than the obvious inability of our foreign minister to give effect to his propositions and remonstrances': *ibid.*, p. 93.

[77] Reid, *Russell*, p. 337.

[78] Taylor, *Decline of British radicalism*, p. 150.

[79] Lever, *Lady Palmerston*, p. 320. See also Palmerston, 17 May 1856, in Bourne (ed.), *Letters to Sulivan*, p. 311.

[80] G. Blakiston *Woburn and the Russells* (London: Constable, 1980) p. 215.

[81] Prest, *Russell*, p. 381.

CHAPTER 8

After Palmerston: the Mount Temples and 'Christian higher life' at Broadlands
James Gregory

Broadlands, as evocative of its master as Hawarden and Hughenden were for successors, was greatly transformed in tone and function following Palmerston's death. His heir was his stepson, William Francis Cowper, the second son of the fifth Earl Cowper, though his physical similarity gave credence to rumours that he was Palmerston's natural son.[1] He became Cowper-Temple when he inherited Broadlands under the terms of his stepfather's will after Lady Palmerston's death in 1869; in 1880 he was made Baron Mount Temple.[2] He and his second wife Georgina were involved in evangelical revival in the 1870s, supporters of temperance, animal protection and spiritualism. Their friends included John Ruskin, Lord Shaftesbury, Octavia Hill and Josephine Butler. As one newspaper reported at Lord Mount Temple's death in 1888, since death of Lord Palmerston the Mount Temples 'made Broadlands the centre of a social movement the influences of which will hardly be estimated in our day'.[3] This chapter examines their lives and careers as reformers.[4]

Biographers of Palmerston, if they have mentioned Lord Mount Temple, have used him to indicate a transition from Palmerston's alleged religious indifference and easy-going whiggishness to High-Victorian earnestness.[5] Despite contrasts in temperament and religious faith Cowper-Temple was devoted to Lord Palmerston, and Georgina recorded that her stepfather-in-law had loved him more than anyone after Lady Palmerston.[6] This intimacy, Cowper-Temple's place as a junior minister in Palmerston's government and

Cowper-Temple's possible influence on his ecclesiastical policies have been noted before.

If Palmerston has lacked a biographer for a generation, the Mount Temples have attracted only partial study. Brian Harrison noted Mount Temple as one of a number of prominent reformers 'appearing simultaneously in several moral reform organizations', and observed that there was 'no adequate biography'.[7] Van Akin Burd's meticulous research on their spiritualism and relationship with Ruskin is the only extended examination of the Mount Temples. Broadlands is seen as a 'haven for Utopian experiments and new religions', whose 'saintly master and mistress abstained from field-sports and wine, and thought of vegetarianism as one of the courses to the Kingdom of Heaven'.[8] But a comprehensive study, considering them as partners in diverse reform activity, is still required.

I

Lord Mount Temple's political career

After an inadequate education at Eton (followed by a few months at Edinburgh) and service in the Horse Guards, William Cowper was encouraged by friends such as the sixth Duke of Devonshire to turn to politics, the arena where he first became a public figure.[9] He was a Liberal MP for Hertford from 1835-1868, and South Hampshire from 1868-1880. He was the private secretary to his uncle, the Prime Minister Lord Melbourne, who treated him almost as a son.[10] He was a commissioner of Greenwich Hospital (1839), a junior Lord of the Treasury (1841), and Lord of the Admiralty (1846-March 1852; December 1852-February 1855), where his policy was to give cadetships to the sons of clergymen and poor gentlemen.[11] After a short period as under-secretary at the Home Office, he became President of the Board of Health (August 1855-February 1857, September 1857-March 1858), forming a close partnership with the Chief Medical Officer, Sir John Simon.[12] He was also Vice President of the new Education Committee of the Privy Council

(February 1857-1858), Vice President of the Board of Trade
(August 1859-1860) and first commissioner of the Board of Public
Works (February 1860-1866).[13] He turned down Gladstone's offer
of the chancellorship of the Duchy of Lancaster in 1868, for several
reasons including dislike of a sinecure and desire to stay in
the Commons as long as possible.[14] As one obituary put it, in the
Commons he was a lesser version of his brother-in-law, Lord
Shaftesbury.[15] As a peer he was less active, though interested in the
Criminal Law Amendment Act of 1887.

His political creed was summed up in 1885 as the belief that
'God has sent me into the world to do my best to improve it.' He
was a Liberal because 'I cannot rest satisfied with the defects and
deficiencies of the political and social conditions of my country.
My disposition is to hope and trust that legislative remedies may
be found for much of the suffering and error that now afflict the
people, and I do not share with the Conservatives their distrust of
the benefits of change, and their fear of failure in attempts at
improvements.'[16]

He supported factory reform.[17] A supporter of hygienic
reform, he was on the Health of Towns Association's central committee in 1844 and attempted to open the medical profession to
women in the mid-1870s.[18] He saw the position of Commissioner
of Works as an opportunity to 'minister to the good and happiness
of the people', and employed talented artists and architects to
improve the Palace of St James and London parks. The parks were
'to produce as much enjoyment as possible to all classes of the community', and he was 'anxious that every public space in London
which could afford a pleasant view or promote or provide for the
recreation of the public, should be turned to the best account'.[19]
Further environmental concern was represented by his role in the
Commons Preservation Society from 1865.[20] As chairman of the
Select Committee on the Enclosure Acts (1869) he helped preserve
many rural commons. In 1871 he led a backbench Liberal defence
of public access to Epping Forest (threatened by the Treasury),

becoming a public figurehead for the movement, in which Henry Fawcett played a prominent role.[21] Close to Broadlands, protection of the New Forest owed something to his efforts.[22] Safeguarding access to commons and parks has been seen as a contribution to a 'Palmerstonian' resistance by Whig-Liberals to Gladstonian 'grand maternal Government'.[23]

But Mount Temple had no ambition to be his stepfather's political heir. This was wise given the baiting he received as commissioner of the Board of Public Works, when one radical Liberal MP privately described him after one poor performance in the Commons as a warning to Ministers about 'putting weak men in a high Public office'.[24] He was realistic about his capacity, partly rejecting Gladstone's offer of office because 'he had not the power in debate, nor the eloquence in speech, that he thought necessary for that position (Cabinet); but he loved work'.[25] This love of work was manifested in his philanthropy.

II

Mount Temple's religion and philanthropy

In turning from the political to religious and philanthropic work it must be stressed that Mount Temple saw no division between public and private labours. An acquaintance described him as 'one of those men, who engaged in business or official life, are entirely dominated by an inner sense of religion'.[26] Another, receiving a report of the religious conferences he hosted from the mid-1870s, commented that it 'must be a wonderful help to live so much with the Earnest world'.[27]

Throughout his life he wished to be a 'reformer', which he understood to entail the subordination of politics to God and amelioration of 'the people'.[28] This position was by no means unusual, for Whig-Liberal politics in general was animated by religion.[29] The piety, humility and 'philanthropy on a massive scale', characteristic of Whig peers such as the Dukes of Devonshire, Sutherland and Cleveland, and the Earls Fitzwilliam and Zetland,

Jonathan Parry suggests, makes it 'in some senses irrelevant to treat them as culturally distinct from the mass of the Liberal party'.[30]

Georgina, in the memoir of her husband, refers to the 'low ebb' of religion when her husband was a child, and the neglect of 'maternal duty'. Rather like Shaftesbury, parental neglect of religious duties meant it was left to a maid to teach Cowper the Creed and Lord's Prayer. Christian instruction really began at a private school in Brighton following a desultory time at Eton, although Gladstone recalled that at Eton 'the stamp of purity, modesty, gentleness was upon him in a peculiar degree'.[31] Cowper considered an ecclesiastical career as an escape from the 'imminent dominion of sin'; but relatives persuaded him to join the Royal Horse Guards in 1827.[32]

Though a brief military career left him 'morally untainted', his close friend and mentor the Duke of Devonshire (himself an evangelical convert through Cowper's influence) regretted his worldliness and need for novelty. Devonshire criticised his 'spirit of justifying what you do when you are entangled by worldly intimacies and pursuits, your inconstancy in prayer and your want of method ... it is as if you required excitement from new preachers and new theories to keep your devotion awake'.[33] Given that the Panshanger circle was 'full of vice and agreeableness, foreigners and roués', this concern about worldliness was justifiable.[34] Cowper was attractive (earning the sobriquets 'Beautiful' and 'Fascinating Billy' from Lady Holland) and enjoyed the company of beautiful women.[35] His journal recorded his tension between spirituality and society.[36] Earnest friends found his flitting between mission hall and fancy ball disturbing.[37] As Groom-in-Waiting (1837-41) he was part of the most exclusive society, that surrounding the young Queen Victoria and was a dining companion in the period before Victoria's marriage,[38] and according to some Tory rumours even a prospective husband for the Queen himself.[39]

Lord Melbourne had to caution his romantic young nephew not to employ Pauline epistles as 'the instruments of flirtation'.[40]

When he did marry in June 1843, his bride was Harriet Gurney (daughter of the Quaker banker Daniel Gurney of North Runcton in Norfolk and a brother of Elizabeth Fry, who had married the daughter of the fifteenth Earl of Errol). On the engagement, Lady Palmerston had written to her friend, the Princess Lieven, about a match she 'thoroughly' approved of: 'my son William is engaged to a young, charming and very beautiful girl, a Miss Gurney, Lord Errol's niece, daughter of a *gentilhomme campagnard* as the Duke of Wellington used to say. She has lately spent several weeks in Paris, so it is possible you have heard of her, for her beauty is sensational.'[41]

It was a tragedy strongly felt by Lord Palmerston and his wife when Harriet died two months after the wedding.[42] But this calamity was not, as Peter Mandler believes, the factor in developing Cowper's religiosity,[43] as he had already been associating with 'extreme' and pre-millenarian evangelicals, and attending evangelical services and city missions. In 1845, when he gave his support to the Evangelical Alliance, he wrote defensively to his mother (with whom he had a close relationship) about what she saw as his 'exaggerated views of religion':

you have not been blessed with that conviction of the inspiration of Scripture, and with that knowledge of God and communion with Him in prayer, which has been given under the providence of God to others less good by nature than yourself, & apparently far more unworthy of such a blessing ...[44]

If his outlook became ecumenical by the 1850s, when a sister-in-law noted his charity towards high, low and broad church, and interest in other religions, his initial position was narrower.[45]

Later, corresponding with his friend Canon Basil Wilberforce, Mount Temple identified the several components of his religious experience and identity.[46] These were: infant assurance of the divine, an upbringing free from doctrinal bigotry, the influence of Henry Drummond's 'intensely spiritual High Churchism' (in fact Drummond was a leading figure in the Catholic Apostolic Church),

F. D. Maurice's 'broad instruction in unconventional real Christian facts' and 'deep Churchism' at his own Broadlands conferences.[47]

His private exploration of spirituality and religion continued throughout his life, as recorded in his notebooks and diaries. His public activity was shaped by a broad churchmanship developed under the influence of Maurice and Christian Socialism. Although he surprised John Bright by 'remarks on the subject of Church Establishment: he thought the time for them and for the need of them was passing',[48] Mount Temple was actually keen to reform the established church, in relation to patronage, Athanasian creed and lay activity in parochial government or preaching.[49] He eagerly supported efforts to build a greater sense of a Christian community. In the later 1850s he participated in evangelical conferences designed to regenerate Anglicanism.[50] Later in his life, Mount Temple continued to participate in metropolitan evangelical missions.[51] He was an early supporter of the Anglican Church Army founded in 1882.[52]

It is clear Shaftesbury feared his brother-in-law's 'liberal' influence on ecclesiastical patronage, worrying that 'Neology' would determine Palmerston's appointments,[53] yet it is Shaftesbury, not Mount Temple, who is remembered for his influence on episcopal patronage. In Church-State relations Mount Temple is commemorated as author of the 'Cowper-Temple' amendment to the Education Bill of 1870. This was an 'inspired' compromise which removed denominational instruction in order to safeguard teaching of the Bible in rate-paid schools from secularist or atheist attacks; though High Church Anglicanism was offended.[54] He joined the Anglican-dominated National Educational Union, established in 1869 to defend religious instruction and voluntary schools in the education system.

III

The Broadlands conferences
Apart from these national organisations and campaigns there

was the local arena of Hampshire which provided a location for important religious and philanthropic work. Cowper-Temple inherited Broadlands at Lady Palmerston's death, an inheritance for which he had been prepared for some time, following the death of Sir William Temple, Palmerston's brother, in 1856. Despite this expectation, the Cowper-Temples felt like intruders because of the place's strong associations with Palmerston's personality.[55] Cowper-Temple's estate management, which he assumed with pleasure, exhibits little to contrast him with Palmerston. Instead it was the evangelical work, including temperance lectures below the statue of Palmerston at Romsey, and religious lectures on carts or from cottage windows in the New Forest that advertised the differences between the two successive masters of Broadlands.[56] Above all, perhaps, it was the almost annual religious conferences from 1874 to 1888 he hosted at Broadlands, which represented bridge building between Christian denominations.[57] These also expressed a new spirituality, a 'holiness' or 'higher life' movement influenced by American religious developments.[58]

The conferences originated in conversation the Mount Temples had with the American Quakeress Hannah Smith when Lord Mount Temple suggested that Broadlands could host the meetings she had enthused about.[59] 'It was only earth,' one participant recalled of these conferences, 'however at its very best. Green trees, a flowing river, soft grass & God's saints walking about there talking of Him & dwelling in love.'[60] They were open to all, and participants came from across the Anglican spectrum, various nonconformist sects and the Salvation Army, Mount Temple being an early and generous patron of the organisation. Apart from Hannah Smith and her husband, participants included an artist protégé of the Mount Temples, Edward Clifford;[61] a former Plymouth Brother the Reverend Andrew Jukes; the religious novelist Catherine Marsh; the writer George MacDonald; the Reverend Wilson Carlile (founder of the Church Army), the African-American missionary Amanda Smith,[62] the missionaries Stanley Smith and

Ion Keith Falconer; the Peppers, early middle-class Salvation Army members; and Mrs Russell Gurney (Lady Mount Temple's friend, and a promoter of female higher education). The audience included the prominent Congregationalist the Reverend Newman Hall, mystics such as John Pulsford and the Reverend Rowland Corbet, aristocratic evangelicals such as Lady Ashburton, the Countess of Waterford and Lady Gainsborough. The literary critic, novelist and historian Julia Wedgwood attended at least one, as did the French Protestant pastor Theodore Monod. Other French and German pastors attended. Music was provided by the American singer Antoinette Sterling.

All were attempting 'this higher platform of faith', as Hannah Smith's husband Robert Pearsall Smith described them.[63] They saw the conferences as furthering a real Christian unity through understanding 'realities appertaining to the soul's communion with God', rather than glossing over doctrinal difference.[64] Mount Temple was also enthusiastic about participants' belief in *sanctification* rather than mere *justification* by faith.[65]

The Mount Temples provided hospitality and were fully involved in discussions, meetings and lectures. Mount Temple delivered 'intensely real' and 'trustful, reverent, soul-lifting prayers' and his influence helped maintain cordiality between the various groups. He was in his 'natural element',[66] the 'mainspring, their very heart', helping plan the programme of subjects and writing words of counsel to participants.[67] Guests were made to feel at home regardless of class, sect, or indeed race (the Mount Temples publicly embraced, and escorted to dinner, the African-American Amanda Smith in 1879). Some saw it as 'adventurous hospitality' given this diversity.[68] Although they did not arrange the actual conferences the Mount Temples' role in creating a 'delightful home feeling' was crucial. The beauty of the setting, like the similar Keswick conferences, helped create a sense that this was a 'foretaste of heaven'.

On the structure of the conferences, the following is a summary by the writer George W.E. Russell, who felt it 'almost impossible to avoid transcendentalism' in thinking of Broadlands and the company which gathered in it.'[69] The Mount Temples

> invited a large number of friends and acquaintances, male and female, who had this much in common — that they were interested in religious enquiry — and nothing more. A few weeks before the Conference began a syllabus of subjects for consideration was circulated among those who had accepted the invitation. On Monday evening the gathering assembled; the house at Broadlands filled to the attics, and many of the guests overflowed into the inns of Romsey. On Tuesday morning there was an early Celebration in Romsey Abbey. For those who preferred non-Sacramental religion, devotions were provided in the house. After breakfast we had Family Prayers and expositions. At eleven the whole company assembled in a glorious grove of beeches on the lawn, where a rostrum and seats had been arranged. Lord Mount-Temple presided with infinite grace and devoutness, and the Conference began …The debate was animated, amiable and desultory … we went on debating till teatime. In the evening there was a mission-service in the Park, and the day was wound up with Family Prayers and more expositions.[70]

The meetings were recalled with enthusiasm by participants like Anna Kingsford, qualified physician, vegetarian, anti-vivisectionist and mystic. She recorded 'spiritual things' as the sole topic of conversation whether 'wandering through the garden, or sitting on the sunlit lawns, or pacing the terraces under the beautiful stars at night'. But she also commented: 'It is indeed a convent life, only with all the beautiful surroundings of wealthy circumstances and the refined and cultured accessories which wealth procures.'[71]

This was echoed by some critical voices within the world of religious journalism. Russell notes that 'the luxurious appliances of the "Broadlands Retreat" made capital fun for people accustomed to the more austere regimen of Cowley or Keble'.[72] To some observers the conferences seemed amiable but ridiculous.[73]

IV

Spiritualism and utopianism
The most significant relationship the Mount Temples formed, given

his eminence and its consequences for ensuring their posthumous recognition, was with John Ruskin, who had been an admirer of Georgina at a distance, in Rome in 1842. Burd recounts her attempts to interest him in spiritualism, to which she had turned in her search for faith, and their spiritualism has recently been examined by Marlene Tromp. That she was a spiritualist was well-known in Anglo-American spiritualist circles. Spiritualism did not furnish her with insights of a 'higher kind' but showed there was 'something' and thus saved her from 'absolute infidelity', and she sought support for her spiritualist beliefs in Scripture.[74] Her husband, for her sake, became involved. His notes on lectures and the seances held at their town house from the 1860s offer insights into his spiritual and secular anxieties as refracted by mediums and spirit guides. His concern with the efficacy of prayer, for himself and as a comfort for the departed is clear. Spirits exhorted rest, and adjustments of diet and work habits. At least one seance brought communication with Palmerston, who offered thoughts on legislation and matters relating to the management of the Broadlands estate.[75]

For Mount Temple spiritualism was a Christian activity involving guardian angels and God's continuing revelation to man. As Georgina affirmed, he had no difficulty with spirit communication, believing in a 'great cloud of witness encircling the world'. Spiritualism had the possibility of elucidating aspects of the afterlife and could represent God's intervention in the present-day materialistic age. Spiritualism encouraged his sense that the world was merely a phase leading to a 'higher life'. Communication with spirits reinforced his sense of Christian duty and became an important activity. Yet his spiritualism, an interest that continued until his death, was not publicised in most of obituaries.[76]

The Cowper-Temples' more utopian connections, represented by their acquaintance with the American 'theo-socialist' Thomas Lake Harris who established a community at Santa Rosa, California, can only be outlined. There was some hope that the Mount Temples would join the community. Georgina recalled

Harris as 'a devoted servant of Christ and a man with open vision. He particularly interested us by his belief that the kingdom of Christ was soon to be set upon the earth and that we might all help in its unfolding.' This was disingenuous since by this time Georgina was fully aware of the bizarre, cruel, and sexually-dissident habits of the community. The Cowper-Temples were also friends of the brilliant writer Laurence Oliphant, who became a disciple of Harris. Having been seen off by the Cowper-Temples, Oliphant described them to his new associates as 'so true and loving and faithful'. In 1872, Oliphant, who was staying at the Cowper-Temples' house in Curzon Street in London, was married with them as witnesses.[77]

V

Lady Mount Temple
The Mount Temples' marriage was happy, her mother-in-law noting that Georgina 'evidently quite adores him, and he is evidently very proud of her' and that she shared 'all his feelings and notions',[78] although a colleague recalled that she 'always had her own way everywhere'.[79] Her closest friend, Emelia Gurney (Mrs Russell Gurney), spoke of a 'very near a perfect union'. Another recalled a remarkable 'partnership'.[80] But there were no children. Noting Ruskin's dedication of *Sesame and Lilies* to her, Girouard includes her in a group of 'queenly ladies' (like Emelia Gurney, Lady Waterford, Lady Canning, and Lady Marion Alford) who were 'noble by nature and usually noble by name as well, chatelaines of great houses, as good as they were beautiful and as artistic as they were good, sailing serene and splendid through Victorian drawing-rooms in a distinctive atmosphere of love, worship and deference'.[81] Naturally, her friends included 'queenly ladies' and the conferences attracted earnest aristocrats such as Lady Ashburton and the Countess of Waterford. Girouard notes that the marriages tended to be childless, and wonders whether some were unconsummated because of the elevation of spiritual over profane love. Yet the Mount Temples did have a ward, Juliet Latour Temple, 'the bright child of

Broadlands'.[82]

Lady Mount Temple's religiosity was manifested early. She was 'much addicted to hospitals' and her broad views, expressed in such actions as giving rosaries to Catholic patients, had agitated her elders.[83] Not surprisingly, Palmerston diagnosed her as a likely convert to Catholicism.[84] Kim Reynolds has cited her 'highly coloured religious correspondence' with Adine, the young wife of her husband's uncle, Lord Beauvale, in her examination of the generational trends in religiosity. The contrast of Georgina and her sister-in-law Emily Shaftesbury with Lady Palmerston's response to religious enthusiasm, typical of the Enlightenment, is clear.[85] Tending dying acquaintances was a recurrent activity: a friend who contracted smallpox noted with amazement that she immediately offered to nurse her.[86] If this 'tender sympathy for all who are in trouble' had elements of morbidity she was also inspired by the faith-sustained sorrows and deaths (of her beloved husband, sisters, nieces and nephews) that figure prominently in her *Mount Temple Memorials*, a volume which was, after all for private, family and sibling readership.

Unfairly, the editor of the Ruskin-Mount Temple correspondence distinguishes between her religiosity, which he characterizes as 'sanctimony', and her husband's 'more genuine kind' of Christianity.[87] Her brother distinguished between Mount Temple's placid temperament and her 'effervescence of temper', 'vehement indignation' against cruelty and dislike of ill-natured gossip.[88] She herself felt that she was 'only a seeker after truth, without the confidence and clear vision' of her husband.[89] As Burd notes, her earnestness was reinforced by her mother's death, which stimulated her interest in spiritualism. An unquiet temperament continued until the end of her life, when she raged against God during a sister-in-law's stroke in 1896.[90]

Georgina, born in 1821, was the sixth daughter and youngest child of the extremely wealthy Admiral John Tollemache.[91] Her childhood, if apparently happy, was isolated, particularly following her mother's withdrawal from society after her elder daughter's mis-alliance with the future Earl of Cardigan. Sisterly advice and the company of a 'good many devoted' evangelical-minded women friends led to doubts about the 'propriety of going out in the world'. Lady Holland wrote that Georgina's mother was frightened by the behaviour of her other daughters, and 'fell into great devotion, & has brought up the young lady in quiet very strictly. She does not go into society, or ever saw the inside of a theatre. These tastes are very consonant with those of William Cowper.'[92] Georgina saw him as a deliverance and expressed her sense of redemption by naming him the 'angel' of her life.[93] In 'the forty years of our happy companion-ship,' she recalled, 'he never varied in love and kindness to me'.[94] But at first, as a 'shy and shadowy woman, who had never before put the tip of her nose into the great world', she was a lonely addi-tion to the brilliant Cowper-Palmerston family.[95]

Georgina shared her husband's religiosity but not his untroubled faith. Her dominant concerns were the search for God and the lessening of cruelty and pain.[96] Her 'unfathomable and extraordinarily wide sympathy' made her a patron of social and moral reform nationally, in Romsey and at their other estates.[97] Dur-ing the Crimean War she helped organize nursing in a naval hospital in the Bosphorus.[98] With her husband's support she helped create and was variously the president, honorary secretary and a patroness of the Ladies' Sanitary Society, which lectured, published tracts and organised outings for poor children.[99] It was associated with the National Association for the Promotion of Social Science, and Georgina was listed as its president in the N.A.P.S.S.'s *Trans-actions*. Lord Mount Temple was an honorary auditor. She formed a temperance society in Mayfair and preceded her husband as a Blue Ribbonite. The 'Plumage League' for protection of birds was estab-lished with her patronage. The character 'Lady Mount Temple' in the film *Wilde*,[100] represents the 'prevailing attitudes of Society', and certainly in the mid-1880s the real Lady Mount Temple, with women such as the Duchess of Leeds, the Countesses of Aberdeen and Zetland, Lady Muncaster, Mrs Lowther and Mrs Reginald Talbot, opposed aristocratic immorality.[101] But it also echoes the close, relationship between Constance Wilde and Georgina, apparently a distant cousin.[102] She inspired many earnest people. Julia Wedgwood equated the presence of 'Desideria' with a 'bath of wondrous revival'.[103] The mystic Victoria Welby was a correspondent.[104] Emelia Gurney variously described her as 'Beatissima', 'My precious beloved one' and 'Ladye of Pity'.[105] She also dressed in an idiosyncratic, romantic way with a silver necklace of little cherubs climbing a tiny ladder or a habit-like garment of black and white with a silver chain that made her appear like a 'Sister of Mercy'.[106] Her costume and epithets are suitably Pre-Raphaelite, given the Mount Temples' patronage of D.G. Rossetti and William Morris. They also befriended the artists Edward Burne-Jones, George Frederick Watts, Edward Clifford, and Frederic Shields. They became very close friends and patrons of the writer George MacDonald and his family. Their cultural connections were also transatlantic in reach, for Lady Mount Temple corresponded with Walt Whitman.[107]

VI

Conclusion

This collection of essays reconsiders Palmerston across a range of fields; this paper has explored the theme of 'after Palmerston' and the differences in generations and personalities. The Mount Temples are worthy of further study on their own merits because of their interests and significance as prominent reformers of the period.

Born a Whig aristocrat, Mount Temple attained prominence through his connections with Melbourne and Palmerston; as Shaftesbury observed of himself, he was 'near the centre of all action in politics, the fountainhood of all information'.[108] But Mount Temple had little interest or talent in politics. Instead he was drawn to social and moral reform. He combined, according to a brother-in-law, 'the sacred with the social element ... it was possible to live in the world without being worldly'.[109] A sister thought him virtually the only man she knew 'who lived in the world quite unspoiled by it'.[110] Like Shaftesbury, he reacted against the perceived religious apathy of his parents' or grandparents' generation.[111] At Shaftesbury's death his brother-in-law's candidacy as the new 'leading philanthropist' was rejected as he was 'too open to impression', but at his own death Mount Temple was compared to Shaftesbury.[112]

The Mount Temples' spiritualism might support this verdict of impressionability, but in this they exemplified a wider tendency towards a personalized religion of sentiment which involved identification with fellow humans and animals. Charitable to all, 'cruelty was the only vice that they judged sternly'. For Georgina, philanthropy was a practical mission in a life of spiritual doubt. Propelled into a brilliant circle by marriage, she fashioned a role as a patron of moral reform and religious inquiry. George Russell described her as 'one of the most remarkable women of her time'.[113] Together these 'two blesseds' transformed Broadlands, already a rendezvous for the great and famous, into a centre for reform and a place 'impregnated with religion and with a passionate interest in religious questions'.[114]

References

[1] J.A.W. Gunn and J. Matthews (eds.) *The letters of Benjamin Disraeli: 1835-1837* (Toronto Press, 1982) p. 501, (25 Apr 1836). C. de L. Ryals and K. J. Fielding (eds.) *The collected letters of Thomas and Jane Welsh Carlyle* (Durham and London: Duke University Press, 1987) p. xxi, reprints Jane Carlyle's report (17 Feb 1847) of one lady's assumption that William was born during Lady Palmerston's second marriage.

[2] He is generally referred to as Mount Temple in the text of this essay. He became Palmerston's heir following Sir William Temple's death. He became, by royal licence from 1869, Cowper-Temple, and was made Baron Mount Temple of Mount Temple, Co. Sligo, on 25 May 1880. In 1932 the title was revived for Wilfrid Ashley, his heir's son. Lady Mount Temple's first name is spelt 'Georgina' here — which was the spelling that both she and her friends and relations used — as opposed to 'Georgiana', by which she is sometimes known.

[3] Newspaper clipping (probably *Liverpool Evening Express*) 16 Oct 1888, BP, BR 44/ 19/ 6.

4 A key source is Lady Mount Temple's privately published *Mount Temple Memorials* (London, 1890) [hereafter: *MTM*]. This reprints entries from her husband's journals and religious notebooks, and memorials from friends.

5 See, for example J. Ridley *Lord Palmerston* (London: Constable, 1970) p. 58; D. Southgate *'The most English minister…'. The policies and politics of Palmerston* (London: Macmillan, 1966) p. 411. K. Bourne *Palmerston: the early years. 1784-1841* (London: Allen Lane, 1982); and P. Guedalla *Palmerston* (London: E. Benn, 1926) have the most extensive references.

6 See *MTM*, p. 69.

7 B. Harrison 'State intervention and moral reform in nineteenth-century England' in P. Hollis (ed.) *Pressure from without in early Victorian England* (London: Edward Arnold, 1974) pp. 293-4.

8 Van Akin Burd *Ruskin, Lady Mount Temple and the spiritualists: an episode in Broadlands history* (London: Guild of St George/Brentham, 1982) and Van Akin Burd (ed.) *Christmas story. John Ruskin's Venetian letters of 1876-1877* (Newark: University of Delaware Press, 1990) chs. 2-3. See also J. L. Bradley (ed.) *Letters of John Ruskin to Lord and Lady Mount Temple* (Columbus: Ohio State University Press, 1964).

9 The role of William George Spencer Cavendish, a cousin of Melbourne's wife, in Cowper's political career is documented in P. Mandler *Aristocratic government in the age of reform: Whigs and Liberals 1830-1852* (Oxford: Oxford University Press, 1990) p. 48. See Georgina's letter in A. W. J. Clifford *A sketch of the life of the sixth Duke of Devonshire* (London: privately printed, 1870) p. 57. Politically, Mandler characterizes Cowper as a 'keen Foxite' in this period.

10 P. Ziegler *Melbourne: a biography of William Lamb second Viscount Melbourne* (London: Collins, 1976) pp. 234, 306; L. G. Mitchell *Lord Melbourne. 1779-1848* (Oxford: Oxford University Press, 1997) pp. 229-30, 263, 271. L.C. Sanders (ed.) *Lord Melbourne's papers* (London: Longmans, 1889) pp. 527-8 reprints exchanges between Lord John Russell and Melbourne in which the former offered a place in government for Cowper. Melbourne responded (3 Jul 1846): 'I do not think that he would mind being left out himself, but it would have been very unpalatable to his mother.'

11 *MTM*, p. 50.

12 R. Lambert *Sir John Simon, 1816-1904 and English social administration* (London: MacGibbon & Kee, 1963) p. 242.

13 D. Owen *The government of Victorian London. 1855-1889* (Cambridge, Massachusetts: Harvard University Press, 1982) pp. 78-9.

14 *MTM*, p. 71.

15 Shaftesbury married Emily Cowper, Mount Temple's sister.

16 G.W.E. Russell *Portraits of the seventies* (London: T. F. Unwin, 1916)

p. 276. An entry in Dod's *Parliamentary companion* of 1880, reprinted in M. Stenton (ed.) *Who's who of British Members of Parliament* (Hassocks: Harvester, 1976) i, p. 93, describes him as Liberal, 'in favour of local taxation being "relieved of its heavy burdens" also of tenant farmers being secured the value of their improvements'.

[17] J.T. Ward *The factory movement, 1830-1855* (London: Macmillan, 1962) pp. 243, 290, 304, 311, 324.

[18] A. Burton 'Contesting the zenana: the mission to make "lady doctors for India", 1874-1885' *Journal of British Studies* 35 (July 1996) p. 372.

[19] *Parliamentary Debates*, 2nd ser. clxiii, 630 (6 Jun 1861); *ibid.*, clxiv, 800 (12 Jul 1861).

[20] J. Ranlett ' "Checking nature's desecration": late Victorian environmental organisation' *Victorian Studies* 26 (1983) pp. 197-222.

[21] *The Times*, 1 May 1871.

[22] Robert Hunter's letter in *The Times*, 18 Oct 1888, summarizes his role in commons and open spaces campaigns.

[23] J.P. Parry *Democracy and religion. Gladstone and the Liberal party, 1867-1875* (Cambridge: Cambridge University Press, 1986) p. 116; J.P. Parry *The rise and fall of liberal government in Victorian Britain* (New Haven and London: Yale University Press, 1993) pp. 265, 271-2.

[24] T.A. Jenkins (ed.) *The parliamentary diaries of Sir John Trelawny, 1858-1865* (London: Royal Historical Society, Camden 4th series, 40; 1990) pp. 204, 215, 259. See also A. Hawkins and J. Powell (eds.) *The journal of John Wodehouse first Earl of Kimberley for 1862-1902* (Cambridge: Royal Historical Society, Camden 5th series, 9; 1997) pp. 69-70; P. Guedalla *Gladstone and Palmerston. Being the correspondence of Lord Palmerston with Mr Gladstone, 1851-1865* (London: Gollancz, 1928) pp. 175-76.

[25] *MTM*, p. 63.

[26] J. Tollemache *Some reminiscences of Georgina Lady Mount Temple, by her surviving brother, Baron Tollemache of Helmingham* (Helmingham, 1890) pp. 8-9.

[27] Letter dated 7 Sep 1875 from unidentified peer, BP, BR 57/54/5.

[28] *MTM*, p. 20, 19 Jan 1839: 'How I should welcome the scorn of the frivolous, the hatred of the selfish, the hostility of the worldly, which should prove to me that I was performing my duty.'

[29] *Ibid.*, p. 13. Parliamentary life also, by its routine and regulations, offered an antidote to the 'frivolous and dangerous companionship of Society' (*MTM*, p. 16).

[30] Parry, *Democracy and religion*, p. 62. Parry discusses Cowper-Temple at p. 59.

[31] Russell, *Portraits of the seventies*, p. 274. Gladstone recalled him in recollec-

tions of Dr Hawtrey, Cowper's housemaster at Eton: see J. Brooke and M. Sorensen (eds.) *The Prime Ministers' papers. W.E. Gladstone, I : Autobiographica* (London: HMSO, 1971) p. 25. Gladstone described him as 'perhaps the most' promising of the speakers in the Society, in a letter dated 26 Nov 1827, see p. 199.

[32] Russell *Portrait of the seventies*, p. 274, records that his relative Lord John Russell and others chose this career to divert Cowper from Holy Orders.

[33] BP, BR 43/17/1 (1 May 1837). For the religious influence Cowper exerted on Devonshire, see J. Lees-Milne *The bachelor duke. A life of William Spencer Cavendish, sixth Duke of Devonshire 1790-1858* (London: John Murray, 1991) pp. 108-15, 124-8.

[34] D. Cecil *Lord Melbourne* (London: Book Club Associates, 1972) p. 179.

[35] *MTM*, p. 18 (21 Apr 1837).

[36] *Ibid.*, p. 11.

[37] *Ibid.*, p. 18.

[38] Viscount Esher (ed.) *The girlhood of Queen Victoria* (2 vols., London: John Murray, 1912) i, pp. 218, 235, 247-8, 256, and ii, p. 296.

[39] D. Creston *The youthful Queen Victoria. A discursive narrative* (London: Macmillan, 1952), p. 441; p. 340 for Tory rumours: unfortunately there are no footnotes.

[40] Cecil *Lord Melbourne*, p. 527.

[41] Lord Sudley (ed.) *Lieven-Palmerston correspondence, 1828-1856* (London: John Murray, 1943) p. 246. Lady Holland wrote: 'William Cowper is going to marry a lovely girl, Miss Gurney. She is not of the Quaker branch, but most of her relations are of that persuasion. They will not be rich, but in love, & good qualities', see the Earl of Ilchester (ed.) *Lady Holland to her son, 1821-1845* (London: John Murray, 1946) p. 205, letter dated 9 May 1843.

[42] K. Bourne (ed.) *The letters of the third Viscount Palmerston to Laurence and Elizabeth Sulivan 1804-1863* (London: Royal Historical Society, Camden 4th series, 23; 1979) p. 278.

[43] Mandler, *Aristocratic Government*, p. 277; his description of Cowper's evangelical religion as 'gloomy' is wrong. He believed the devil hated mirth and *MTM* stresses his 'brightest temperament'. In 1833 epiphany took place at an inn in Killarney when he realized his belief that Divine law could be observed differently according to the different states of society was wrong, *MTM*, p. 12.

[44] Drafts of letter, dated subsequently 1 Nov 1845, BP, BR 43/16/1-2. Lady Palmerston said she 'always felt as if he was a contemporary' (*MTM*, p. 69).

[45] Burd, *Ruskin, Lady Mount Temple and the spiritualists* attributes this verdict to Lady Palmerston, but the observation is from the dowager Countess Cowper, widow of the sixth Earl, see her letter, 26 Apr 1876, printed in *Earl Cowper, K.G.: a memoir* (privately printed, 1913) p. 300.. On Cowper's evangelicalism, see also

B. Hilton, 'Whiggery, religion and social reform: the case of Lord Morpeth' *Historical Journal* 37 (1994) pp. 838-9.

[46] BP, BR 44/19/8: B. Wilberforce *In memoriam. William Francis Baron Mount Temple. A brief sketch* (Southampton, April 1889, supplement to the St Mary's Parish Magazine) and reprinted in *MTM* pp. 179-90. For the influence of the Conferences on Wilberforce and his friendship with the Mount Temples see G.W. E. Russell *Basil Wilberforce* (London: John Murray, 1917) ch. 4.

[47] *MTM*, pp. 103-5, records the Cowpers' interest in the Apostolic Church.

[48] R.A.J. Walling (ed.) *The diaries of John Bright* (London: Cassell, 1930) p. 341 (31 May 1869).

[49] See his letter to *The Times*, 25 Nov 1885, in which he supports the Church as a defence against atheism and for its duty to provide support, aid to all parishioners especially the poor, suffering and ignorant'. See also BP, BR 43/28/2, for a letter to his wife 5 Apr 1871, concerning the Church Reform Union, established by Mount Temple, the Reverend W.H. Fremantle and the Reverend John Llewelyn Davies in 1870.

[50] G. B.A.M. Finlayson *The seventh Earl of Shaftesbury* (London: Eyre Methuen, 1981) p. 528, n.88.

[51] Clifford, *Broadlands as it was*, p. 138; Tollemache, *Some reminiscences*, p. 8.

[52] The Mount Temples' friend Edward Clifford was active in the Church Army, see BP, BR 44/16/15, Church Army circular, Mar 1896. See Clifford, *Broadlands as it was*, pp. 138-52.

[53] Finlayson, *Shaftesbury*, pp. 378-79, n.43 and n.44, p. 381. See Chapter 3, above.

[54] *MTM*, p. 75; *Authorised report of the church congress* (Southampton: Gutch & Cox, 1870) p. 11. See his address to a National Association for the Promotion of Social Science conference, *Addresses of the Earl of Shaftesbury and the Honourable W.F. Cowper on Tuesday October 12th 1858 on the health, physical condition, moral habits, and education of the people* (London: Benson & Mallett, 1858) p. 15, for his earlier thoughts on rate-maintained schools and 'the sword of secularism'.

[55] *MTM*, p. 73.

[56] E.V. Jackson *The life that is life indeed: reminiscences of Broadlands conferences* (London: James Nisbet, 1910) p. 42.

[57] See E. M. Gurney (ed.) *Letters of Emelia Gurney* (London: J. Nisbet, 1902) pp. 142-50; Jackson, *The life that is life indeed*; 'E.C.' [Edward Clifford] *Broadlands as it was* (London: printed for private circulation, 1890); in abbreviated form in *MTM*, pp. 139-42) and *Fragments from a Broadlands conference. Love, faith, life* (Hereford, 1887). See *Hampshire Independent* 21 Jul 1888, on the final conference.

[58] The first Broadlands conference led to one in Oxford (1874) and Keswick in

the Lake District (1875); the latter became an internationally-renowned evangelical centre in the twentieth century, see D. W. Bebbington *Evangelicalism in modern Britain. A history from the 1830s to the 1890s* (London: Unwin Hyman, 1989) pp. 151-80. Bebbington (wrongly dating the first conference as 1873) emphasizes the affinity (though not identity) of Keswick and Broadlands (p. 171). See also M.E. Dieter *The holiness revival of the nineteenth century* (2nd edn., London: Scarecrow, 1996). Broadlands is identified as part of the 'deepening of Spiritual Life' in L.E. Elliott-Binns *Religion in the Victorian era* (2nd edn., London: Lutterworth Press, 1964) p. 225.

[59] Clifford, *Broadlands as it was*, p. 16. Clifford was present, and said it was Lady Mount Temple, but in *MTM*, p. 117 she said it was her husband's offer (another estate had been offered but had become unavailable).

[60] Recollections by Edward Clifford (dated 1875), BP, BR 44/14.

[61] Clifford, a poor student at the Royal Academy, became an enthusiastic imitator and collector of the work of Burne-Jones from *c*.1866. He received crucial patronage from the Mount Temples, for him they were moral exemplars.

[62] A. Smith *An autobiography. The story of the Lord's dealings with Mrs Amanda Smith the coloured evangelist* (Chicago: Meyer & Brother, 1893) pp. 260-61, 274.

[63] BP, BR 57/53/3.

[64] Wilberforce, in *Memoriam*.

[65] *MTM*, p. 117.

[66] Clifford, *Broadlands as it was*; Gurney (ed.), *Letters*, p. 145.

[67] Gurney (ed.), *Letters*, p. 148.

[68] Jackson, *The life that is life indeed*, p. 29.

[69] Russell, *The eighteen seventies*, p. 286.

[70] G.W. E. Russell *The household of faith. Portraits and essays* (London: Hodder and Stoughton, 1902) pp. 208-10.

[71] E. Maitland *Anna Kingsford. Her life, letters, diary and work* (2 vols., London: G. Redway, 1896) ii, pp. 236-7, letter dated 27 Aug 1886.

[72] Russell, *Household of faith*, p. 210.

[73] Herbert H. Jeaffreson (ed.) *The letters of Andrew Jukes* (London: Longmans, 1903): 'There was no quarreling and the mutual admiration was perfectly sincere', quoting from *The Pilot*, 26 Oct 1901.

[74] *MTM*, p. 107; H. Tuttle and J. M. Peebles *The yearbook of spiritualism for 1871* (Boston: Adams and Co., 1871); L.P. Smith *A religious rebel. The letters of 'H.W.S.'* (London: Nisbet, 1949) p. 67.

[75] BP, BR 45/9, seance dated *c*.Oct 1869.

[76] See *Light*, 20 Oct 1888, p. 519 for obituary note of Lord Mount Temple, 'so well known to many of our readers'. One of his few letters to *The Times*, 4 Jan 1875, p. 8, was an appeal for money in aid of the 'New Forest Shakers', followers

of Mary Ann Girling. On the sect (*c*.1872-5) which was defended by other spiritualists, see D. Hardy *Alternative communities in nineteenth century England*
(London: Longman, 1979) pp. 145-50; and P. Hoare *England's lost Eden:
adventures in a Vicotrian utopia* (London: Fourth Estate, 2005), which also has
chapters on the Mount Temples.

[77] *MTM*, p. 108. Letters from Oliphant to the Cowpers were first published in
H.W. Schneider and G. Lawton *A prophet and a pilgrim* (New York: Columbia
University Press, 1942). In Bradley, *Letters of John Ruskin to Lord and Lady
Mount Temple*, there is a reference in a letter of 1868 to Oliphant's 'society in the
west'. The Mount Temples bought a painting of St Anthony to send to him, about
1870, see Clifford, *Broadlands as it was*, p. 4. Georgina's friend Emelia Gurney
visited Harris in 1872: Gurney, *Letters*, pp. 112, 119, 121-2. See B. Strachey *Remarkable relations. The story of the Pearsall Smith family* (London:
Gollancz, 1980) p. 104 for Hannah Smith's comment that Georgina 'had been led
to think that the "objectionable part of their practices" was abandoned'.

[78] Lady Palmerston to Lady Jocelyn, Dec 1848, in M. Ogilvy (Countess of Airlie)
Lady Palmerston and her times (2 vols., London: Hodder and Stoughton, 1922)
ii, p. 125.

[79] Clifford, *Broadlands as it was*, p. 9.

[80] Gurney, *Letters*, p. 139 (to Julia Wedgwood, 1 Dec 1875); Russell, *Portraits
of the seventies*, p. 280.

[81] M. Girouard *The return to Camelot. Chivalry and the English gentleman* (New
Haven and London: Yale University Press, 1981) p. 199.

[82] *MTM*, p. 73; Clifford, *Broadlands as it was*, p. 22; Bradley, *Letters of John
Ruskin to Lord and Lady Mount Temple*, p. 360.

[83] Clifford, *Broadlands as it was*, p. 9.

[84] *MTM*, p. 68. See BL Add. Ms. 45,799, fols. 149-155b for correspondence after
Palmerston's death between Georgina and Florence Nightingale: letter from
Georgina (dated in another hand, 31 Oct 1865) speaking about the 'great gulph
[sic] it has made in which our poor little lives are swallowed up' and agreeing that
Palmerston believed in 'the *true* Religion of Trust in God & His Righteous laws'.

[85] K.D. Reynolds *Aristocratic women and political society in Victorian Britain*
(Oxford: Oxford University Press, 1998) pp. 73-80 (p. 71); see *MTM*, p. 48

[86] Gurney, *Letters*, p. 159 (Gurney to Andrew Jukes, 5 Mar 1875).

[87] Bradley, *The letters of John Ruskin to Lord and Lady Mount Temple*, p. 11.
Bradley admitted the 'hint of the sanctimonious' is based on a reading that is
fragmentary (p. 8).

[88] Tollemache, *Some reminiscences*, p. 10.

[89] *MTM*, p. 117.

[90] Smith, *A religious rebel*, p. 132.

[91] The key published source for the family is E.D.H. Tollemache *The Tollemaches*

of Helmingham and Ham (Ipswich: W.S. Cowell, 1949) chs. 18-20.

[92] Ilchester, *Lady Holland and her son*, p. 221, letter dated 17 Dec 1844.

[93] Tollemache, *Some reminiscences*, p. 7.

[94] *MTM*, p. 46.

[95] *Ibid*., pp. 49-50.

[96] Russell, *Portraits of the seventies*, p. 283. For Georgina's hatred of cruelty and dislike of ill-natured gossip, see Tollemache, *Some reminiscences*, p. 10.

[97] Gurney, *Letters*, p. 128 (to Julia Wedgwood, 13 Oct 1873).

[98] *MTM*, p. 59: a childhood friend, Lady Maria Forester, contacted Florence Nightingale about nursing and William Cowper (at the Admiralty) thought that sailors could be similarly nursed. Nurses were led by a daughter of Thomas Chalmers. The Cowper-Temples are ignored in the reference to Therapia in Lord Stanmore *Sidney Herbert. Lord Herbert of Lea. A Memoir* (2 vols., London: John Murray, 1906) i, p. 332.

[99] *Transactions of the National Association for the Promotion of Social Science, 1860* (London, 1860); tracts preserved in the British Library; *MTM*, p. 62. See Octavia Hill *Homes of the London poor* (London: Macmillan, 1875), ch.7 on L.S.A. outings. The *English Woman's Journal* became the L.S.A.'s organ.

[100] *Wilde* (dir. Brian Gilbert, 1997).

[101] E.F. Benson *As We Were* (1930; London: Longmans, 1941) pp. 98-103, esp. p. 101.

[102] See M. Holland and R. Hart-Davis (eds.) *The complete letters of Oscar Wilde* (London: Fourth Estate, 2000), pp. 537, 555; and J. Gregory, 'Lady Mount Temple and her friendship with Constance Wilde', published on-line in *Oscholars. An international journal of Oscar Wilde Studies* 3: 12 (Dec 2006).

[103] Gurney, *Letters*, p. 128 (9 Apr 1876).

[104] H. Cust (ed.) *Echoes of a larger life. A selection from the early correspondence of Victoria Lady Welby* (London: J. Cape, 1929) pp. 76-7, 126.

[105] Emelia Gurney to Lady Mount Temple, BP, BR 57/37/2.

[106] Clifford, *Broadlands as it was*, p. 9; and photograph in Russell, *Portraits of the seventies*, p. 2764.

[107] On Shields, see Gurney, *Letters*, pp. 270-84; on MacDonald, see G. MacDonald *George MacDonald and his wife* (London: G. Allen and Unwin, 1924) pp. 472, 544-5, and G. E. Sadler (ed.) *An expression of character. The letters of George MacDonald* (Grand Rapids, Michigan: W.B. Eerdmans Pub. Co, 1994) pp. 138, 260. Whitman presented Georgina with a copy of *Specimen days and collect* in 1886, she sent him a waistcoat.

[108] E. Hodder *Life and works of the seventh Earl of Shaftesbury* (3 vols., London: Cassell, 1887) iii, p. 191.

[109] Tollemache, *Some reminiscences*, p. 8.

[110] Jackson, *The life that is life indeed*, p. 43.

[111] E. Hodder, *Shaftesbury* has little on the Mount Temples; but ii, p. 79 refers to a meeting on behalf of seamstresses in 1844 in which Cowper was one of the two chief supporters. Georgina recalled (*MTM*, p. 48) Shaftesbury's kindness and her worship of his 'noble, self-sacrificing character'; yet he disapproved of her heretical influence on her husband. Their speeches before the Social Science Association in Liverpool in 1858 were jointly published.

[112] 'The old and the new philanthropist', *The Spectator*, reprinted in *Littell's Living Age* 167 (7 Nov 1885) pp. 321-84 (p. 382).

[113] *Manchester Guardian*, 1901, reprinted in Russell, *Portraits of the seventies*, p. 280.

[114] The epithet 'blesseds' appears in a letter to Hannah Whitall Smith from Broadlands, 8 Sep [1886?], Whitall Smith Papers, B.L. Fisher Library, Wilmore, Kentucky. The verdict on Broadlands is the philanthropist Mrs Craven's, quoted in Jackson, *The life that is life indeed*, p. 26. The daughter of the Comte de la Ferronays, she married Augustus Craven, attaché to Sir William Temple, British Minister at Naples (and Lord Palmerston's brother). See M.C. Bishop *Mrs Augustus Craven* (2 vols., London: R. Bentley and Son, 1894) i, p. 61; ii, p. 105, for references to the Mount Temples and Broadlands. Craven wrote a French life of Palmerston.

INDEX